'The book offers the first detailed study of the interactions between the international financial institutions and the global labour movement through a little-known but formal dialogue process. Given the wider questioning of World Bank and IMF economic policy in general – and labour and social policy in particular – the study offers fascinating insight into the organisational, ideological and power imbalances that reinforce the status quo. The author uses mixed research methods including structured interviews with key actors to present a nuanced examination of the potential of this ongoing process to improve the quality of global economic governance'.

Sandra Polaski, *former Deputy Director-General for Policy, International Labour Organization*

'There is much on transnational social dialogue, but this book focuses on international financial institutions and the much broader policy role of international labour organisations. It looks closely at the way these relations develop and the range of challenges that emerge in a detailed manner. It successfully fills a gap in debates on this level of political engagement'.

Professor Miguel Martinez Lucio, *University of Manchester*

'This is a very topical, valuable and insightful analysis of the Global Unions, the ILO and the International Financial Institutions. It is highly recommended to all who are interested in global governance and employment relations'.

Greg J. Bamber, *Professor, Monash University, Australia; Co-Editor, International & Comparative Employment Relations: Global Crises & Institutional Responses (SAGE)*

EMPLOYMENT RELATIONS AND GLOBAL GOVERNANCE

Globalisation has created many opportunities for economic development, but it is also associated with rising income inequality and poverty. International crises such as the international financial and economic crisis of 2008, and more recently the global health pandemic, have led to a rise in unemployment and income losses for workers and a surge in the violation of workers' rights.

At global level, intergovernmental organisations including the World Bank and the IMF are influential actors and policy makers which promote the UN Sustainable Development Goals. However, the International Financial Institutions (IFIs) have been criticised for their internal political power imbalances and macroeconomic policy prescriptions based on neo-liberal principles. The Global Unions and their affiliates as well as the International Labour Organization (ILO) regularly comment on the negative impact of the IFI's policies in regard to labour flexibilisation and the privatisation of public and social services.

In 2002, a formalised dialogue was established between the Global Unions and the IFIs, which addresses labour, social, and environmental issues. This dialogue takes place at three levels: the country level, the sector level, and the headquarters level. The ILO maintains its own dialogue with the IFIs, but it also participates at the headquarters-level dialogue between the Global Unions and the IFIs.

Employment Relations and Global Governance focuses on the headquarters-level dialogue which can be considered as a strategic instrument that helps the Global Unions and their affiliates to exercise influence over the policies of the IFIs, especially those policies which concern workers. The book describes and analyses the development of the dialogue since its establishment with a particular focus on factors which promote and hinder the dialogue.

The book provides important insights into the real-world functioning of the institutions of economic global governance and its broader impact on the world of work. It is likely to be key reading for academics, researchers, and students studying global employment relations, political economy, and international organisations. It will also be of interest to international and national trade unions, nongovernmental organisations, and policy makers.

Yvonne Rueckert is Senior Lecturer in the Faculty of Business and Law at the University of Portsmouth, UK. She has held several research and teaching posts in Germany and Spain and was awarded a PhD scholarship from the prestigious German research foundation the Friedrich Ebert Stiftung.

Routledge Research in Employment Relations

Series editors

Rick Delbridge and Edmund Heery

Cardiff Business School, UK.

Aspects of the employment relationship are central to numerous courses at both undergraduate and postgraduate level.

Drawing from insights from industrial relations, human resource management and industrial sociology, this series provides an alternative source of research-based materials and texts, reviewing key developments in employment research.

Books published in this series are works of high academic merit, drawn from a wide range of academic studies in the social sciences.

Contemporary Work and the Future of Employment in Developed Countries

Edited by Peter Holland and Chris Brewster

Work and Labor Relations in the Construction Industry

Edited by Dale Belman, Janet Druker and Geoffrey White

Employment, Trade Unionism and Class

The Labour Market in Southern Europe since the Crisis
Gregoris Ioannou

Contemporary Employers' Organizations

Adaptation and Resilience
Edited by Leon Gooberman and Marco Hauptmeier

Employment Relations as Networks

Methods and Theory
Edited by Bernd Brandl, Bengt Larsson, Alex Lehr, Oscar Molina

Employment Relations and Global Governance

The Dialogue Between the Global Unions and the IFIs
Yvonne Rueckert

For more information about this series, please visit: https://www.routledge.com/Routledge-Studies-in-Intervention-and-Statebuilding/book-series/RSIS

Employment Relations and Global Governance

The Dialogue Between the Global Unions and the IFIs

Yvonne Rueckert

Routledge
Taylor & Francis Group

NEW YORK AND LONDON

First published 2024
by Routledge
605 Third Avenue, New York, NY 10158

and by Routledge
4 Park Square, Milton Park, Abingdon, Oxon, OX14 4RN

Routledge is an imprint of the Taylor & Francis Group, an informa business

© 2024 Taylor & Francis

ISBN: 978-1-138-20880-3 (hbk)
ISBN: 978-1-032-53175-5 (pbk)
ISBN: 978-1-315-45841-0 (ebk)

DOI: 10.4324/9781315458410

Typeset in Bembo
by Apex CoVantage, LLC

Contents

Acknowledgements

The book is based on my PhD thesis which was supervised by Professor Christoph Scherrer and Professor Holm-Detlev Koehler and supported by a scholarship from the Friedrich Ebert Foundation. After successfully completing my PhD in 2015, I undertook further research and started working on the book. I want to thank everyone who agreed to take part in the interviews over the years; without their time and support, this project would not have been possible. In particular, I would like to thank the former directors of the ITUC/Global Unions office in Washington D.C., Peter Bakvis and Leo Baunach. Both have been incredibly helpful in providing me with support and contacts in Washington D.C. and for providing me with an observer status at the high-level and technical meetings between the Global Unions and the IFIs in 2009 and 2017. I would also like to thank all the representatives from the ITUC and its affiliates, the Global Union Federations, the TUAC, the German IG Metall and the DGB, the AFL-CIO, the ILO, the World Bank, the IFC, and the IMF. Furthermore, I would like to thank all those who helped me with the proofreading of the book including Professor Tony Royle, Dr Peter Scott, Dr Iona Byford, and Ruth Watkins. Last but not least, I want to thank my family and friends for their ongoing support and encouragement during the long journey of finalising the book.

Acronyms

ACFTU	All-China Federation of Trade Unions
ACT/EMP	Bureau for Employers' Activities
ACTRAV	Bureau for Workers' Activities
ACTU	Australian Council of Trade Unions
ADB	Asian Development Bank
AEU	Australian Education Union
AfDB	African Development Bank
AFL-CIO	America Federation of Labour and Congress of Industrial Organisations
AM	Accountability Mechanism (World Bank)
AMC	Asset Management Company
ATI	Africa Training Institute
ATUC	Arab Trade Union Confederation
BBA	Bilateral Borrowing Agreement
BEE	Business Enabling Environment
BWI	Building and Woodworkers' International
CAFOD	Catholic Agency for Overseas Development
CAO	Compliance Advisor Ombudsman
CCSA	Cross-Cutting Solutions Area
CD	Capacity Development
CEACR	Committee of Experts on the Application of Conventions and Recommendations
CEART	Committee of Experts on the Application of the Recommendations concerning Teaching Personnel
CGG	Commission on Global Governance
CGU	Council of Global Unions
CI	Communications International
CICA	Confederation of International Contractors' Association
CLS	Core Labour Standards
CPIA	Country Policy and Institutional Assessments
CSO	Civil Society Organisation

CSPF	Civil Society Policy Forum
CST	Civil Society Team
DAC	Development Assistance Committee (OECD)
DB	Doing Business
DDG	Deputy Director General
DGB	German Trade Union Confederation
DPF	Development Policy Financing
DPG	Deutsche Postgewerkschaft (German Postal Union)
EA	External Affairs
EB	Executive Bureau
EBC	Ethics and Business Conduct (World Bank)
EBRD	European Bank for Reconstruction and Development
EC	European Commission
ECB	European Central Bank
ECSC	European Coal and Steel Community
ED	Executive Director
EDRC	Economic and Development Review Committee
EI	Education International
ELS	Directorate for Employment, Labour and Social Affairs
ELSAC	Employment, Labour and Social Affairs Committee
EPC	Economic Policy Committee
ERI	Earth Rights International
ESCP	Environmental and Social Commitment Plan
ESF	Environmental and Social Framework
ESG	Environmental, Social and Governance (ESG) Advice and Solutions department
ESMS	Environmental and Social Assessment and Management System
ESRS	Environmental and Social Review Summary
ESS	Environmental and Social Standards
ETUC	European Trade Union Confederation
ETUI	European Trade Union Institute
EU	European Union
EWC	European Works Council
EWI	Employing Workers Indicators
FIDIC	International Federation of Consulting Engineers
FIET	International Federation of Employees, Technicians and Managers
GC	General Council
GFA	Global Framework Agreement
GG	Global Governance
GGC	Global Governance Complex
GPG	Global Public Good

GS	General Secretary
GUF	Global Union Federation
HDN	Human Development Network
HQ	Head Quarters
IAEA	International Arts and Entertainment Alliance
IBRD	International Bank for Reconstruction and Development
ICB	International Competitive Bidding
ICEM	International Federation of Chemical, Energy, Mine and General Workers' Unions
ICFTU	International Confederation of Free Trade Unions
ICLS	International Conference of Labour Statisticians
ICSID	International Centre for the Settlement of Investment Disputes
IDA	International Development Association
IEG	Independent Evaluation Group (World Bank)
IEO	Independent Evaluation Office (IMF)
IFA	International Framework Agreement
IFC	International Finance Corporation
IFIs	International Financial Institutions
IFJ	International Federation of Journalists
IGF	International Graphical Federation
IGO	International Governmental Organisation
IL	Investment Lending
ILC	International Labour Conference
ILO	International Labour Organization
IMF (GUF)	International Metal Workers' Federation
IMF	International Monetary Fund
IMFC	International Monetary and Financial Committee
INGO	International Nongovernmental Organisation
IP	Inspection Panel
IPF	Investment Project Financing
ITF	International Transport Federation
ITGLWF	International Textile, Garment and Leather Workers' Federation
ITS	International Trade Secretariat
ITUC	International Trade Union Confederation
IUF	International Union of Food, Agricultural, Hotel, Restaurant, Catering, Tobacco and Allied Workers' Association
LAC	Latin America and the Caribbean
LIC	Low Income Country
MDB	Multilateral Development Bank

MDTF	Multi-Donor Trust Fund
MEI (trade union)	Media and Entertainment International
MEI	Multilateral Economic Institution
MFD	Maximising Finance for Development
MIGA	Multilateral Investment Guarantee Agency
MNC	Multinational Corporation
NAB	New Arrangements to Borrow
NCP	National Contact Point
NGO	Nongovernmental Organisation
OECD	Organisation for Economic Co-Operation and Development
OLC	Open Learning Campus
OPCS	Operations Policies and Country Services
P4R	Programme-for-Results
PERC	Pan European Regional Council
PPP	Public–Private Partnership
PPSD	Project Procurement Strategy for Development
PRSP	Poverty Reduction Strategy Paper
PS	Performance Standards
PSI	Public Services International
SAP	Structural Adjustment Programme
SAPRI	Structural Adjustment Participatory Review Initiative
SARTTAC	South Asia Regional Training & Technical Assistance Centre
SBD	Standard Bidding Document
SBDW	Standard Bidding Documents for Procurement of Works
SDGs	Sustainable Development Goals
SEJLS	Supporting Effective Jobs Lending at Scale
SFI	Sabah Forest Industries
SFIEU	Sabah-Forest Industry Employees Unions
SME	Small- and medium-sized enterprises
SPD	Standard Procurement Document
SPIAC-B	Social Protection Inter-Agency Cooperation Board
STIEU	Sabah Timber Industries Employees Union
TNC	Transnational Company
TUAC	Trade Union Advisory Committee to the OECD
TUC	Trade Union Congress
TUCA	Trade Union Confederation of the Americas
UN	United Nations
UNDP	United Nations Development Programme
UNI (GUF)	Union Network International Global Union
USA	United States of America
WB	World Bank (IBRD/IDA)

WBG	World Bank Group
WCL	World Confederation of Labour
WDR	World Development Report
WEO	World Economic Outlook
WFTU	World Federation of Trade Unions
WRC	Worker Rights Consortium
WTO	World Trade Organization

1 Introduction

Background

Globalisation is a 'powerful engine' and a complex process which creates opportunities and challenges at different levels and which has a considerable impact on employment and the distribution of incomes (Bacchetta and Jansen, 2011; Ritzer and Dean, 2019). Wealth and income inequalities have increased significantly within most countries since the 1970s and workers' bargaining power and rights have weakened (Burgmann, 2016). In the last decade, global crises such as the financial crisis in 2008 and more recently the Covid-19 pandemic, as well as geopolitical tensions, have further deepened income inequality and increased the violation of workers' rights. The crises have also revealed the continuing influence of the International Financial Institutions (IFIs) on governments and within the global governance system. During the Covid-19 pandemic, the International Monetary Fund (IMF) provided emergency financing to many countries making about a quarter of its total lending capacity (US$ 250 billion) available to member countries, and the World Bank (WB) committed more than US$ 70 billion in assistance in 2022, the highest level of commitment ever. However, despite these vast sums of money, economic challenges with regard to growth, redistribution, and structural inequality remain. Ortiz and Cummins (2021) warn of a post-pandemic austerity shock, which in connection with the food and energy price inflation could, according to Oxfam (2022b), push an additional 263 million more people into extreme poverty in 2022, resulting in a total of 860 million people living below the current $1.90 a day poverty line.[1] Against this background, the following question has not lost its importance: 'can we imagine a twenty-first century in which capitalism will be transcended in a more peaceful and more lasting way, or must we simply await the next crisis or the next war . . .'? Piketty (2017) raises the question of suitable political institutions and suggests a progressive global tax on capital in order to promote collective interests over private interests and to regain control over the dynamics of accumulation.

Globalisation and the implementation of a neoliberal economic agenda in many countries have weakened the capacity of trade unions to regulate work and employment at national level. However, trade unions remain important social,

DOI: 10.4324/9781315458410-1

political, and economic actors at national, regional, and global levels despite the existing challenges. At the global level, international trade union organisations are a countervailing power to globalisation by representing the voice of workers worldwide and fostering exchange and coordination between trade union organisations at different levels (Hennebert and Bourque, 2011; Turner, 2004). Like many other international organisations, the international trade union movement supports the UN Agenda 2030 and the Sustainable Development Goals (SDGs), which include amongst others to end poverty in all its forms (Goal 1), access to inclusive and equitable education and learning opportunities (Goal 4), the promotion of decent work (Goal 8), and the reduction of inequality (Goal 10). Furthermore, the agenda stipulates access to affordable and sustainable energy for all people (Goal 7), which is becoming a challenge not only in developing countries but also in industrialised countries. In order to achieve the SDGs and to regulate different domains of global politics, effective global governance and international community building are fundamental. Over time the increased complexity and interdependencies of actors across policy areas led to a formation of clusters of collective actors which govern specific policy issues (Eilstrup-Sangiovanni and Westerwinter, 2021). The clusters are often based on asymmetric power relations, in particular when international organisations are involved as they exercise a high level of authority over state and nonstate actors (Zürn, 2018). The authority exercised by organisations like the IFIs produces contestation and resistance, expressed, for example, in criticism and opposition of certain policies and the demand of a reform of organisational decision-making structures by nongovernmental organisations (Deitelhoff and Daase, 2021). In this context, relatively little attention has been attributed to the regulatory function of international trade union organisations and their role in trying to move towards a more socially orientated global governance system (Koch-Baumgarten, 2006). In response to the increasing globalisation of the world economy, the expansion of multinational firms since the 1980s, and the influence of intergovernmental organisations, international trade union organisations, also called the Global Unions,[2] have increasingly played an important role within global governance:

> The work of these organisations [*Global Unions*] is important in coordinating union responses to longstanding distributive and procedural justice issues that have been exacerbated by globalisation. Real possibilities exist for international trade unionism to build its position within these discussions.
>
> (Croucher and Cotton, 2009: 4)

Trade unions voice their concerns with regard to the ruling order and they demand, amongst other things, a reform of the existing multilateral system in order to allow labours' interests to be efficiently taken into account. The call for 'transformation' has become even more urgent during the latest crises, which have a strong impact on national economic outputs, world trade, and labour markets.

Since the turn of the millennium, much of the existing research on the Global Unions has focused on transnational trade union strategies and their instruments within the field of labour relations. This has included, for example, research on international trade union campaigns (Fox-Hodess, 2017; McCallum, 2013; Bronfenbrenner, 2007), trade union coalition building (Holgate, 2015; Barton and Fairbrother, 2009), International Framework Agreements (IFAs) (Lévesque et al., 2018; Bourque, 2008; Hammer, 2005), transnational trade union networks (Müller et al., 2004), and transnational worker representation structures (European Works Councils and World Works Councils) (Köhler and González Begega, 2010; Waddington, 2010; Müller et al., 2006). Other research has focused on the implications of the shift of the International Labour Organization (ILO) towards Core Labour Standards (CLS) in its 1998 Declaration of Fundamental Rights and Principles at Work[3]; attempts to include social clauses in multilateral trade agreements (Royle, 2010; Standing, 2008; Greven and Scherrer, 2005; Alston, 2004), as well as the functional roles and central fields of action of the global trade union organisations (Croucher and Cotton, 2009; Platzer and Müller, 2009; Stelzl, 2006).

Yet however, few people are aware that the Global Unions and the International Financial Institutions,[4] which are made up of the World Bank Group (WBG)[5] and the International Monetary Fund (IMF), have been engaged in a formally structured policy dialogue for two decades. The dialogue was formalised in 2002 by a joint agreement (protocol of engagement) (World Bank, 2002). There had been exchanges between the IFIs and the Global Unions on a nonregular basis before 2002, but these exchanges had no formal structure and were often prompted by potentially negative impacts of structural adjustment programmes initiated by the IFIs. After 2008, the Global Unions took the international financial crisis and the debate around the re-organisation of the international financial system and the development of new forms of governance and participation at the international level,[6] as an opportunity to further develop the existing dialogue with the IFIs and to form new alliances (Oswald, 2009). In this context, the Global Unions (2009: 22) demanded that,

> labour must be involved in discussions for designing a new global financial architecture. . . . Coming out of this crisis we need a new development model where the state is able to balance the extremes of markets with social environment and public policy objectives. Governments must set the limits of the financial economy by directing investment to long term goals of creating decent work, building equality in society and ensuring a fair distribution of the fruits of growth. Achieving that goal will require far more union action at the international level – the global union task is just beginning.

A decade after the beginning of the economic and financial crisis, the ITUC Frontline Poll 2018 revealed that almost 60 per cent of people in work worldwide are struggling to make ends meet, a situation which worsened further with the economic impacts of the global health crisis. In this context, the ITUC General Secretary Sharan Burrow pointed out, 'Multilateralism is in crisis and democracy is at risk'. Therefore, it is necessary to 'change the rules of the global economy to rebuild trust' (ITUC, 2018a). The call to reform the multilateral system and the existing multilateral order is not new. In 2015, the chair of the OECD Development Assistance Committee (DAC) pointed out that the existing system must be used 'more effectively', and that the multilateral system must be reformed in order to 'reflect the rise of the South' (OECD, 2015). The IFIs play an important role in this context as these organisations represent a 'cornerstone of the liberal world economy' and 'exercise a considerable influence on the daily lives of the world's population' (O'Brien et al., 2000: 11). Since the 1980s, the IFIs have increasingly adopted a neo-liberal economic policy regarding their debtor countries with neo-liberalism arguably being a central plank of the process of economic globalisation (Stieglitz, 2002). These policies, which amongst others include market orthodoxy, privatisation and deregulation, have arguably contributed to the rapid diffusion of the international financial crisis (Stieglitz, 2010). In many cases, these policies also led to an increase in social and income inequality (Reinsberg et al., 2019), which is of particular concern for the Global Unions. International crises have strengthened and expanded the influence of the IFIs over the global economy. In response to the international financial crisis, multilateral agencies such as the IFIs increased and replenished their capital amongst the shareholdings of nation states (OECD, 2011a). For example, in 2013, the WBG received 22 per cent of the total multilateral funding of US$ 59 billion (OECD, 2015: 23).

In April 2010, the Development Committee[7] of the World Bank and the IMF stated in their communiqué that the support of the WBG and the IMF was essential in resolving the crisis:

> The crisis response underscored the importance of international cooperation and effective multilateral institutions. With global mandates and memberships, the WBG and the IMF must play key roles in a modernized multilateralism.
>
> (Development Committee, 2010: 1)

The global health crisis in 2020 reversed progress made on the achievement of the SDGs and ending extreme poverty. In autumn 2021, the Development Committee praised the WBG for its 'largest crisis response in history' (Development Committee, 2021: 1). However, despite the financial support provided by the IFIs, from the perspective of the Global Unions multilateralism remained weak during the crisis and IFI policies still lack a comprehensive approach to economic and social recovery based on collective bargaining, strong trade unions and decent jobs (Global Unions, 2022). It appears that in the last decade the IFIs and other international organisations such as the OECD and the United Nations have been unable to realise a coherent and effective growth policy and have done little to promote income equality in real terms at the global level (Ocampo et al., 2017).

Nevertheless, the importance of the IFIs as global governance actors has increased rather than diminished, and the IFIs play a key role in delivering the post-2015 development agenda, which is based on the UN Agenda 2030. Alongside the ILO, which is a key governance actor with regard to labour-related issues, international organisations such as the WBG and the IMF have become increasingly important in this field (Ebert and Novitz, 2020). This explains the importance of the dialogue with the IFIs for the Global Unions and their affiliates. The Global Unions were questioning the policy of the IFIs since the introduction of the structural adjustment programmes in the 1980s. Structural adjustments describe required reforms of macroeconomic and fiscal policies and aim to ensure that recipient countries can service their debts. Fiscal consolidation measures often impact social spending negatively and result, amongst other things, in a reduction of spending on public services. Other measures including privatisation and deregulation often come with high social costs. For example, there is evidence that labour market deregulation increases labour market segmentation at national level and does not bring economic benefits (Myant and Piasna, 2017). The policy advice and recommended labour market policies and reforms by the IFIs have been criticised by the trade unions and other external stakeholders many times. Criticisms refer to the suitability and the long-term sustainability of recommended reforms and changes to labour markets in terms of reducing social inequality and promoting economic growth worldwide.

The policy dialogue between the IFIs and the Global Unions has so far received little scholarly attention despite its importance as a strategic tool for cooperation between these fundamentally different organisations. Reasons could be the relatively small amount of research work carried out on transnational trade union organisations and global trade unionism (Hyman and Gumbrell-McCormick, 2020), and the remaining focus on intergovernmentalism in global governance research (Scholte, 2021). According to Koch-Baumgarten (2011: 57):

> Neither the trade union influence on bilateral regime building of nation states, decision-making processes within international organisations nor its integration within network structures has yet been systematically examined.

Furthermore, the lack of attention may be due to the limited availability of information and the difficulty of accessing information on intergovernmental organisations. In this context, the dialogue with the IFIs has so far had a *'shadow'* existence, even though it has arguably become a more important element of global trade union policy during the last decade.

The book argues that the dialogue with the IFIs can be seen as an instrument of transnational trade union policy which serves to integrate a social dimension within the globalisation of financial and labour markets. It can be seen as a strategic instrument for the Global Unions to exercise influence over the policy of the IFIs and to shape the rules and institutions of global governance towards a more worker-friendly regime. Due to its specific characteristics, the dialogue between the Global Unions and the IFIs differs substantially from social dialogue (as defined by the European Union and the ILO), as well as lobbying in terms of its interlocutors, structure, and process. The dialogue takes place between intergovernmental organisations (IGOs) – in this case the IFIs – and nongovernmental international organisations (the Global Unions) on a formal and informal level. The ILO is also involved in the dialogue, but it holds a particular position because of its tripartite structure and as it is the only UN organisation where trade unions have direct access. Since the beginning of the dialogue the international trade union movement has tried to focus and direct the consciousness of the IFIs towards the CLS, decent working conditions, the importance of collective bargaining and workers' rights. In other words, the Global Unions have tried to persuade the IFIs to take action in relation to the CLS and working conditions and to promote collective bargaining in order to fight increasing income inequality.

The dialogue takes place on three levels. The highest organisational level is the headquarters (HQ) level which is the focus of the study. The HQ-level dialogue between the Global Unions and the IFIs can be defined as a form of international policy dialogue which takes place between organisations which are active at the global policy level. The organisations involved do not act as social partners and they do not negotiate specific agreements. Rather, this form of dialogue serves to continuously exchange views on predefined topics which are of interest to all parties involved, to develop a better understanding of each other's approaches and to identify possible areas for more in-depth cooperation. The high-level meetings take place every two years and are attended by organisational representatives of the World Bank, the IMF, the Global Unions and its affiliates, and some ILO representatives. Additionally, there are thematic meetings every year which focus on a particular topic such as labour markets and social protection in 2022. Interim meetings take place on a more irregular basis and serve to follow up the implementation of the commitments from the high-level and technical meetings.

The second level of the dialogue is at the sector level and is based on the operation of 'focal-points' between the international sector-level trade unions (GUFs) and relevant WB departments (World Bank, 2004). The third level is the country level, which includes exchanges between the trade unions and the IMF mission teams and the trade unions and national World Bank offices. Since the IFIs are active in more than one hundred countries and the ITUC and the GUFs have their affiliates all over the world, the trade unions have put a lot of effort into decentralising the dialogue and creating opportunities for their national affiliates to be able to take part in the dialogue process.

Up to now, the results of the dialogue have been mixed, but there has been progress in certain areas including the promotion of the ILO Core Labour Standards in World Bank policies, the research cooperation with the IMF, and a general increase of awareness of the IFIs with regard to labour market issues, including the importance of inclusive jobs as well as universal social protection. Two major achievements for the Global Unions are, however, the 'seat at the table' and that they were able to maintain the continuity of the dialogue process since 2002.

A key objective of the book is to shed light on factors that are promoting and hindering achievements within the dialogue process. In this context, the analysis pays particular attention to organisational characteristics, the influence of individual actors as organisational representatives, as well as developments in the external environment to the organisations. The book focuses on demonstrating how the actors participating within the dialogue coordinate their actions to gain meaningful outcomes. The study is led by two research questions:

How do perceptions and attitudes of individual actors which represent the international organisations as well as the characteristics of the organisations, impact on the communication within the dialogue and its outcomes?
What role do the dialogue and information exchange play regarding organisational learning?

The book aims to describe and analyse the dialogue process and considers contextual conditions and structural mechanisms of the dialogue such as communication structures and mutual perceptions of individual actors. An important question which arises in this context is to what extent the dialogue has become an institution which is independent from individual actors, thus ensuring its existence and efficiency over the medium and long terms. In order to frame the analysis of organisational characteristics, including the organisational structure, identity, knowledge management and power, and their influence on individual representatives' organisation theories will be applied. These theories will be interlinked with the global governance concept with the objective to strengthen its analytical perspective which considers, amongst others, power relations between global governance actors.

Methodology

The data derive from a qualitative research project based on semi-structured expert interviews, nonparticipant observation, and a content analysis of documentary materials. This kind of data triangulation allows the researcher to adopt 'different perspectives on an issue under study' (Flick, 2018a: 192) and it helps to systematically extend the possibilities of knowledge production. The combination of interviews and observations allows to gather subjective knowledge and experiences as well as to focus on practices and interactions at a specific point of time (high-level meetings). In addition, a document analysis including the minutes of the headquarters-level dialogue, documents relating to the spring and annual meetings of the IFIs, and statements and working papers published by the IFIs and the Global Unions was conducted.

The study is based on a total of 56 semi-structured expert interviews which were conducted between 2008 and 2019 with representatives from the trade unions (32), the ILO (11), and the IFIs (13). A large number of interviews (33) were conducted between 2008 and 2011 as part of the author's PhD study. Expert interviews represent a specific form of semi-structured interviews and focus on the collection of technical and processual knowledge of an expert in a certain professional field of action (Döringer, 2021; Flick, 2018a). The problem-centred expert interview supports a social constructivist perspective and represents a 'promising approach for investigating and analysing the increased complexity and informality of decision-making processes' (Döringer, 2021: 276). The interviewed trade union officials included the directors of the ITUC/Global Unions Washington D.C. office, the ITUC general secretary, representatives from the ITUC regional organisations such as ITUC-Africa and ITUC-TUCA, general secretaries and other staff involved in the dialogue at the GUFs, the general secretary from TUAC, the general secretary of the ETUC, and representatives from the international departments of the German IG Metall and the DGB and the US American AFL-CIO. At the ILO, several interviews were conducted with staff, including the former director of the Multilateral Cooperation Department, the former deputy-directors for policy at the ILO, and staff of the ILO Washington D.C. office. At the IFIs, interviews were conducted with staff from the civil society team, the procurement department and the jobs group (WB), environmental and social development specialists (IFC), and the IEO and public affairs (IMF). The data collection over several years meant that by now some interviewees have left their jobs or changed their jobs. In some cases, organisational representatives had already left the organisation when they were interviewed the first time. All interviews were guided by an interview schedule which included several topic areas: 'characteristics of the organisation involved in the dialogue', 'aims of the dialogue', 'individual perceptions on the dialogue', 'topics and results of the dialogue', and 'progress and challenges of the dialogue process'. The problem-centred approach to interviewing offered the possibility to reveal complex processes of action and evaluation patterns around the dialogue. The individual opinions and views expressed by the interviewees provide insights into the dialogue process; however, it is important to note that they do not represent the whole spectrum of individual views which potentially exists within the involved organisations.

The interviews lasted one hour on average and most of the interviews were conducted face to face at the headquarters of the organisations in Geneva, Brussels, London, Washington D.C., and Berlin. In addition, some interviews were carried out during the high-level meetings in 2009 and in 2017, and some of the later interviews were also conducted via telephone. Contacts with the interviewees were made directly with the help from the ITUC/Global Unions office in Washington D.C. and some of the contacts came from respondents who had already been interviewed (snowballing). The author is multilingual and was able to conduct the interviews in English, Spanish, and German. The majority of the interviews were recorded and transcribed, and on some occasions, written notes were made by the researcher. The data were organised with the help of a QDA-Software (MAX-QDA) and analysed by using the thematic analysis approach, which is a method for 'identifying, analysing, and interpreting patterns of meaning ("themes") within qualitative data' (Clarke and Braun, 2017: 297). The analysis of the data aimed to reveal ideas and views of participants in relation to the analytical interests of the researcher; in other words, the data were analysed with the overall research questions in mind. After reading through the transcripts several times, initial codes were retrieved from the data. In this context, the analysis focused on the views of individual participants in order to identify commonalities and differences across the organisations which are involved in the dialogue. Single codes were combined, when possible, into overarching themes whereby some codes were linked to different themes at the same time. For example, the overarching theme 'impact of the organisational structure' is based on the general codes 'bureaucracy and democracy', the 'allocation and distribution of competencies', 'internal complexity and contradictions', and 'degree of technocracy'.

In addition to the interviews, the author was invited to observe the high-level meetings in Washington D.C. in 2009 and 2017, which lasted three days each. The author acted as a formally invited nonparticipant observer which facilitated the 'analysis of the production of social reality from an external perspective' (Flick, 2018a: 328). Conversations during the meetings were followed without any reference to a pre-prepared schema; this allowed the author to act flexibly and openly within the observation situation. The high-level meetings follow the Chatham House rule as some of the discussed issues are of a sensitive nature. The observations provided some useful insights into the selection of topics and the way in which topics were discussed and how interactions between the different actors in the dialogue process are structured.

Data collection using qualitative methods and the analysis of such data are to a considerable extent subjectively shaped processes. Therefore, qualitative research often faces questions about 'quality' and the application of 'quality criteria'; however, these questions are more complex and not so easy to answer than they are with regard to quantitative research designs. In contrast to quantitative research, which focuses largely on standardisation and generalisation, the leitmotifs of qualitative research are 'diversity, flexibility and concreteness' and the researcher is an important part of any research situation (Flick, 2018b: 80). However, there is agreement that the quality of qualitative research can be increased by, for example, methodological planning of the research study and a careful consideration of the question of indication of selected qualitative research methods (Flick, 2018a). Triangulation also promotes the quality of qualitative research although quality criteria are likely to vary for each applied method (Flick, 2018b). Regarding research interviews, for example, Brinkmann and Kvale (2018: 92) define as quality criteria the extent of 'rich, specific and relevant answers from the interviewee', the verification and clarification of interviewee's statements in the course of the interview and interviewer qualifications. According to Flick (2018b: 92), quality in qualitative research is only possible to achieve if the researcher allows room for 'diversity'. The researcher has applied this as a leading principle by trying to consider all individual and collective perspectives and views equally when studying the policy dialogue between the international organisations.

The structure of the book

The book is divided into six chapters. Chapter 2 sets out the theoretical framework for the study and draws on the concept of global governance and organisation theories. The chapter defines some key terms and concepts such as 'organisation' and 'corporate actor' and 'human and workers' rights', which are important for the broader understanding of the topic. It also summarises some of the key points in relation to the debate about global governance and the theorisation of global governance. The second part of the chapter introduces organisation theories which are used to describe and analyse organisational characteristics of the organisations involved in the dialogue in the following chapters. The focus is on the organisational structure, identity and culture, knowledge and power, and organisational change and learning.

Chapter 3 describes and examines organisational characteristics of the Global Unions. The three sub-chapters about the ITUC, the GUFs, and the TUAC follow a similar structure and pay particular attention to the organisational structures, values, identity, and organisational learning. Chapter 4 focuses on the organisational characteristics of the World Bank (IBRD and IDA), the International Finance Corporation (IFC), and the IMF, which influence attitudes and perceptions of individual organisational representatives and organisational change, and which are, therefore, important for the dialogue. In this context, important policy areas such as procurement and safeguard policies (World Bank and IFC) and loan conditionality (IMF) as well as publications (Doing Business, World Development Report) are considered.

Chapter 5 examines the involvement of the ILO in the dialogue process. Although the ILO was not involved in signing the dialogue protocol in 2002, it is an important actor due to its capacity as global standard setter in the field of work and employment and because it is the only UN organisation to which the trade unions have direct access. The chapter summarises some historical milestones of the ILO and focuses on the development of its own high-level cooperation with the IFIs, which takes place independently from the policy dialogue between the Global Union and the IFIs.

Chapter 6 examines the development of the dialogue since its formalisation in 2002. The chapter provides a definition of the policy dialogue and presents and examines the expectations of organisational representatives regarding the dialogue. The chapter provides an overview of the dialogue outcomes in relation to four topics, including the promotion of the ILO core labour standards, labour markets and social protection, privatisation, and loan conditionality. The second part of the chapter focuses on factors which promote and hinder the dialogue and the dialogue's future prospects and challenges.

Chapter 7 summarises some of the key arguments in relation to the examined policy dialogue and its importance with regard to tackling global economic and social challenges, the creation of a 'new social contract' and a social global order.

Notes

1 In autumn 2022, the WB has updated the global poverty line to US$2.15 a day.
2 The Global Unions comprise the nine sector-organised Global Union Federations (GUFs), the International Trade Union Confederation (ITUC), and the Trade Union Advisory Committee (TUAC) to the OECD.
3 The CLS were originally made up of eight 'fundamental' or core conventions including the freedom of association, nondiscrimination, the abolition of child labour, and the right to collective bargaining subsumed under four thematic areas or 'principles' (Alston, 2004). In June 2022, the International Labour Conference decided to add a fifth area, which is occupational health and safety.
4 The IFIs, which are also known as the Bretton-Woods-Organisations, are 'owned' and 'directed' by governments of member nations. Their objectives are to promote cooperation, support growth and economic development, and secure financial stability.
5 The WBG includes the World Bank, the International Bank for Reconstruction and Development (IBRD), the International Development Agency (IDA), and the International Finance Corporation (IFC). The World Bank is a multilateral development bank (MDB), and there are other MDBs such as the Asian Development Bank and the African Development Banks. All these banks have a widespread geographical focus, and their core business includes the offering of loans and policy advice to client governments.
6 In this book, the term 'international' is used to describe the work of trade unions beyond the level of the state and is used in the same sense as 'transnational'. The term can be understood as participation and action relating to the solution of global problems beyond bilateral relationships.
7 The Development Committee (Joint Ministerial Committee of the Boards of Governors of the Bank and the Fund on the Transfer of Real Resources to Developing Countries) was founded in 1974; its objective is to act as a forum for bilateral consensus building between nation states with regard to development issues. The Committee has an advisory function regarding development issues on the Board of Governors of the World Bank and the IMF.

2 Theoretical framework – global governance and organisation theories

Organisations as 'actors'

The term *organisation* and the term *corporate actor* are fundamental to understanding the interlocutors who interact with one another within the dialogue. The Global Unions, in particular the ITUC and the GUFs, as well as the WBG (in particular the WB and the IFC), the IMF, and the ILO are central to the analysis of the dialogue. The ILO is not directly involved in the Global Unions – IFI dialogue but it is an important actor because trade unionists perceive the ILO as a strategic partner. The Bureau for Workers' Activities (ACTRAV) is the connecting link between the trade unions and the ILO. Furthermore, the ILO has developed its own 'dialogue' with the IFIs since it explored areas for further cooperation with the IMF in the 2010 Oslo conference and chairs the Social Protection Inter-Agency Cooperation Board (SPIAC-B) with the World Bank.

In a general sense, organisations can be defined as 'purposeful social systems which are characterised by a functional division of labour' (Eldridge and Crombie, 2013: 37). It can be argued that organisations are able to act purposefully with regard to the objectives which they establish and the means which they employ in order to achieve those objectives (Ibid., 2013). Both the setting of objectives and the choice of means are not static and can change over time.

All organisations which participate in the dialogue at the HQ level are international organisations. They can be classified according to political science terminology into international governmental (IGO) and international nongovernmental organisations (INGOs). One distinguishing feature between international governmental and international nongovernmental organisations is the institutional design. IGOs have a membership dominated by states represented through government agencies (e.g. the finance ministry) and they are founded either through an intergovernmental agreement or through a decision of an existing IGO. Furthermore, to some degree, states defer decision-making authority to international organisations which function as 'quasi-actors, often at the bidding of their most powerful member states' (Rittberger et al., 2012: 5). In contrast, INGOs consist of nongovernmental actors which do not delegate authority to the organisation. The ILO is a special type of international governmental organisation because of

DOI: 10.4324/9781315458410-2

its tripartite structure. In its central decision-making bodies, there are not only government representatives but also representatives of national employees' and national employers' associations.

In accordance with these definitions, the Global Unions represent INGOs and the IFIs belong to the group of the IGOs. All international organisations are bureaucracies which create binding agreements in the form of rules that affect people within and outside the organisation:

> Rules are explicit or implicit norms, regulations, and expectations that define and order the social world and the behaviour of actors in it. Bureaucracies are both composed of and producers of rules.
>
> (Barnett and Finnemore, 2004: 18)

International organisations can function as corporate actors which are capable of independent action (Rittberger et al., 2012). With regard to the dialogue, it is important to understand the participating organisations as actively engaged actors if only because doing so makes it 'possible to bring to account at the theoretical level, that organisations not only adapt to their environments but that they intervene actively' (Felsch, 2010: 17). Organisations can be considered as both *corporate* and *social* actors which dispose of a certain degree of sovereignty, which enables them to act independently of the wishes of their members to some extent. According to Coleman (1990), corporate actors are collective formations and can be perceived as units of action, for example, with regard to the decision-making of individual actors regarding the handling of resources. Organisations can be considered as social actors because society grants them their status and directs expectations towards them and, organisations are able to act in an intentional manner because they are 'capable of deliberation, self-reflection, and goal-directed action' (King et al., 2010: 292).

Within the neo-institutional discourse, the sovereignty attributed to individual and collective actors is interlinked with *responsibility* and *accountability*. The instigation for actors to assume responsibility for their actions is, on the one hand, driven by the external environment and on the other hand, generated by the actors themselves through self-attribution. The members of the global union organisations (national trade unions and national trade union centres) and the IFIs (governments) are sovereign collective actors which to a certain extent determine the objectives, activities, and resources of the international organisations. However, the international trade union movement has a much longer history and was founded on completely different grounds than the IFIs. In particular, due to its membership, the political sovereignty of the IFIs is arguably more limited than in comparison with the international trade union organisations.

> IGOs are actors on the world stage, working according to both their own bureaucratic logic and the whims of those who are hired by states to run them.
>
> (Oestreich, 2007: 183)

Despite the fact that some governments have a critical influence on the political direction of the World Bank and the IMF, this study is not based on the state-centred approach[1] of international governmental organisations. In fact, it is assumed that these organisations have a certain degree of independence which allows them to develop their own priorities and ideas and to conciliate conflicts between their stakeholders. Oestreich (2007) provides a detailed analysis of the extent to which international organisations are capable of playing an independent role within international politics and to promote public goods.[2] Although Oestreich (2007) is partly focused on state-centred research, his focus is on the self-contained developed preferences, aims, and strategies of organisations themselves. In this context, he demonstrates that international organisations can act as 'norm entrepreneurs' and that this capacity is not only related to a simple bureaucratic self-interest (Ibid., 2007: 3).

The author of the book ascribes the status of a corporate social *actor* to all international organisations participating within the dialogue, which includes at least a partial autonomy of action for these organisations. The term *actor* will be used not only regarding collectives but also with regard to individuals. According to Mayntz (2009: 110), international organisations such as the sub-organisations of the United Nations (UN) are hybrids, which consist of 'a global actor which is able to act autonomously and a negotiating system comprising government representatives'. In addition to government representatives, individual actors can also be staff members, delegates, and policy makers, such as the Executive Directors of the IFIs for example. These individuals are influenced by their social environment, able to form their own opinion and to reflect on their social and economic backgrounds and experiences according to their own values and standards. In this context, they may try to initiate organisational change within the scope of their professional role. They may partly act in an intentional way, and in principle, they are able to assume responsibility for their own actions, even though the organisational structure, and the responsibilities and authority related with certain job roles, provides some individuals with more power resources than others. Mintzberg (1983: 22), a management theorist, refers to people who aim to control organisational decisions as 'influencers'. In the context of the dialogue, the individual actors which represent an organisation steer the direct objective-oriented communication and its course; a capacity which an organisation as a whole does not possess. The analysis of the dialogue will, therefore, consider the extent to which the results of such communication are reflected within the collective memory of an international organisation, which means in its values, knowledge and behavioural norms, and which preconditions are necessary for that to occur.

Institutions and institutionalisation

Institutions influence and affect behaviours, beliefs, and opportunities of individuals and organisations (Lawrence, 2008). In organisation studies, the terms institution and institutionalisation have become prominent largely due to writers such as Zucker (1977), Meyer and Rowan (1977), and DiMaggio and Powell (1983). Institutions represent a link between organisations and society and a framework of orientation for the member agents of an organisation. They involve 'normative obligations', which must be considered by individual actors (Meyer and Rowan, 1977: 341). As Foreman and Whetten (2002: 622) put it:

> (. . .) an institution is a set of widely shared and persistent beliefs about what constitutes proper practice for specific purposes.

In this sense, institutions can be understood as constraints to options that individual and corporate actors are likely to exercise, even though these constraints can become modified in the course of time (Barley and Tolbert, 1997). According to Scott (2001), institutions can constitute first, a formal constraint (e.g. in the form of laws and rules), second, a pressure felt by individual actors (e.g. in form of norms and values), and third, a cognitive impact which is manifested in mutual beliefs and meaning systems which are not questioned. Institutions which have a cognitive impact can be considered as 'scripts', which means that they can lead to the result that actions proceed 'routinely, as a matter of course and quasi-automatic' (Senge, 2006: 39). Institutions in form of rules and conventions help individuals and organisations to decide which problem to attend and which solution to consider (Thornton and Ocasio, 2008). Beliefs, values, principles, rules, practices, and sanctions vary depending on the social context in which they are created and embedded, in other words, the way a particular social world works is determined by its institutional logic. Institutional logics provide a meta-theory on institutions which is based on its power to shape 'heterogeneity, stability and change in individuals and organisations' (Thornton and Ocasio, 2008: 103).

Institutionalisation is a dynamic and ongoing process (Barley and Tolbert, 1997), during which individual actors 'transmit what is socially defined as real' and 'at any time in the process the meaning of an act can be defined as more or less taken-for-granted part of this social reality' (Zucker, 1977: 728). This means that, for example, certain facts or obligations 'take on a rule like status in social thought and action' (Meyer and Rowan, 1977: 341). The quality of the examined dialogue can be inferred from the extent of institutionalisation and the effectiveness of newly institutionalised rules and norms, even though it is important to notice that practices and behavioural patterns are not equally institutionalised. This depends, amongst other things, on the time an institution has been in place, on its acceptance by organisational members (Barley and Tolbert, 1997), and on the power and willingness of institutional 'entrepreneurs' to create new and modify old institutions (Thornton and Ocasio, 2008). In this context, the introduction of new standards and guidelines in the IFIs which concern workers as well as labour market issues in general, and the institutionalisation of new procedures such as providing external stakeholders like the trade unions with a formal advisory function, are important aspirations for trade unions.

Human rights and workers' rights

Human and workers' rights play an important role within the dialogue. Human rights include societal, cultural, economic, political, and social rights which are based on the principles of universality and inalienability. This means that every individual actor should be able to call on these rights without discrimination, and that they are not a privilege which is allocated by an authoritative entity (Twomey, 2007). An important reference which has shaped the social understanding of human rights is the 1948 Universal Declaration of Human Rights.[3] Articles 23 and 24 refer explicitly to worker rights:

> 23 (1) Everyone has the right to work, to free choice of employment, to just and favourable conditions of work and to protection against unemployment.
> 23 (4) Everyone has the right to form and to join trade unions for the protection of his interests.

However, the ideas underpinning the creation of international labour standards date back to the late 19th century, and the first major institutional change in this respect was with the establishment of the ILO in 1919 (Hepple, 2005). The ILO is a specialised UN organisation and has produced a broad range of labour standards (conventions) at the global level. With the adoption of the ILO Declaration of Fundamental Principles and Rights at Work in 1998, the ILO started to promote eight core conventions or Core Labour Standards (CLS) which constitute 'universally recognized human rights' (Sengenberger, 2005: 7). The conventions are summed up within four main areas, which are described as 'Freedom of association and the effective recognition of the right to collective bargaining'; 'Elimination of all forms of forced or compulsory labour'; 'Abolition of Child Labour' and 'Elimination of discrimination in respect of employment and occupation' (ILO, 2002). In June 2022, the ILO added a fifth category 'Occupational Safety and Health' to the 1998 Declaration.

The close relationship between the UN Declaration of Human Rights and the conventions and recommendations of the ILO becomes, amongst others, apparent in the shared 'essence of their inspiration and objectives' (Valticos, 1998: 136). This suggests that all ILO conventions and recommendations contribute to the promotion and protection of human rights and, for example, the ILO conventions on freedom of association, the abolition of forced labour and the elimination of discrimination have had a great impact on human rights in the sphere of civil and political rights. Although human rights and labour rights are conceived as individual rights, they both have a collective dimension, which means that individual rights are 'in fact meaningful only when exercised in a collective manner' (Ibid.,

1998: 137). However, even though human rights and international labour standards have entered universal consciousness, it is difficult to assess their real impact, which lies in their implementation and practice. The ILO was also criticised for the 1998 Declaration and its emphasis on selected conventions at the expense of other conventions. Critics argue that the 1998 Declaration reflects the ILO's marginalisation in the global system of economic governance, and the dominance of neo-liberal economic policy promoted by the Washington consensus and US foreign policy from the 1980s onwards (Alston, 2004; Standing, 2008).

Both human rights and international workers' rights can be considered as Global Public Goods (GPGs). GPGs represent public goods across national borders (Long and Woolley, 2009). The concept has been promoted by the UN Development Programme (UNDP, 1999) and is nowadays a key concept in international development. The benefits of such goods cover more than one country, they include preferably all population groups, and they have a cross-generational impact. GPGs comprise natural global commons, human-made global commons, and policy outcomes (Carbone, 2007). Thus, human rights according to the 1948 Declaration and the ILO core conventions, belong to the second group because they are universal principles which are independent of citizenship or nationality (UNDP, 1999). In addition to the ILO and the UN, organisations which produce and promote GPGs are, amongst others, the World Bank and the IMF as they make decisions as regards their priority and their funding. GPGs are available to everyone (nonexcludable) at the level they are provided (local, national, and global), and their benefits to others do not diminish if an individual or a group of people makes use of them (Chin, 2021).

According to the definition of the World Bank, GPGs 'benefit every country, irrespective of which one provides them' (Barrett, 2014: 39). The WB recognises its role with regard to the provision of GPGs in order to reduce poverty and that it 'should play a strategic role in looking for connections among the different global public goods and its own development agenda' (Ibid., 2014: 69). This definition of the World Bank is rather broad, and despite defining general desirable policy outcomes in terms of development and poverty reduction, it lacks to mention the importance and implementation of human and workers' rights. The demand for GPGs is growing but there are few incentives to create these kinds of goods as they do not generate profit. Furthermore, at global level, international organisations 'often lack the legal authority to enforce regulation and taxation or the institutional capacity to coordinate the needs of all citizens in the world and across generations' (Chin, 2021: 63). For example, in the case of the World Bank, the principle of political neutrality towards borrowing governments is part of the Articles of Agreement. The World Bank and the IMF are aware of human and labour rights, but they do not underpin their mission and organisational objectives as it is the case for the Global Unions. Rather, the IFIs use these rights as a guideline or moral compass if the expected output of their programmes implies potential ethical and social consequences. A new architecture for development cooperation would require a strong commitment of the WB and the IMF to 'social and economic justice and increased international cooperation' (BetterAid, 2011: 6). In this context, the dialogue between the IFIs and the Global Unions can contribute to a change of perception and the use of labour rights by the IFIs, which is closer to the position of the Global Unions.

Global governance

Stieglitz (2002: 9) defines globalisation as

> the closer integration of the countries and peoples of the world which has been brought about by the enormous reduction of costs of transportation and communication, and the breaking down of artificial barriers to the flow of goods, services, capital, knowledge, and (to a lesser extent) people across borders.

New communication technologies and forms of information processing within the globalisation process have changed and restructured economic and political activities at all levels (Held, 2007), requiring the creation of transnational regulatory arrangements and involving multitudinous political and economic challenges such as global finance, food, and the climate crisis. Although the globalisation perspective considers the sovereign nation state as important (Albert, 2005; Meyer et al., 2006), these challenges cannot be overcome at the national level alone. The paradigm of free market politics, which is supported by many national governments, the expansion of international trade of commodities and services, and the battle for foreign direct investment, has led to increased competitive pressure between nation states and transnational companies. The expansion of world trade also implies a division of labour between societies which 'produces a relationship of domination and mutual dependency which is self-reproducing' (Waters, 1995: 70). Many employers from developed countries exploit structural differences between geographical regions, and by this, they further promote competition between states and a race to the bottom in terms of workers' rights and labour conditions which creates considerable challenges for trade unions (Hepple, 2005; Sengenberger, 2005).

The ILO is an important standard setter at the international level and its objective is to regulate labour conditions internationally through conventions and recommendations. However, two of the eight ILO core conventions, No. 87 (Freedom of Association) and No. 98 (Right to Collective Bargaining), are increasingly under threat due to the lack of ratification, bogus ratification (Hepple, 2005) or a lack of implementation on the part of the ILO members. As yet the USA, for example, has ratified only two of the eight ILO core conventions including No. 182 Worst Forms of Child Labour and No. 105 Abolition of Forced Labour (ITUC, 2010a). Many other countries have also only partly ratified the core conventions, for instance, neither India nor China has so far ratified the conventions on freedom of association and collective bargaining. When governments or transnational companies contravene basic worker rights, it makes the work of the GUFs much more difficult (Croucher and Cotton, 2009). The ITUC Global Rights Index from 2021 revealed a further dismantling of workers' rights during the Covid-19 pandemic, with 87 per cent of the surveyed countries having violated the right to strike and 79 per cent of countries having violated the right to collective bargaining (ITUC, 2021a). Against this background, it is essential to develop global democratic structures and 'mechanisms of political cooperation' (Held, 2007: 40) which can build a framework for the interaction of international organisations, nation states, and civil society organisations (Becker et al., 2007).

The term 'global governance' implies different meanings, but generally it can be described as 'the overarching system that regulates human affairs on a worldwide basis' (O'Brien and Williams, 2016: 299). An earlier definition by Finkelstein defines global governance as 'governing, without sovereign authority, relationships that transcend national frontiers' (Finkelstein, 1995: 369). The concept of Global Governance (GG)[4] is relatively new in comparison with, for example, sociological organisation theories. Since the beginning of the 1990s, it has become more and more important within the socio-scientific debate and has been further developed by organisations and academics. Overviews of trend-setting contributions to the development of the concept as well as further developments of the concept are, for example, provided by Weiss (2013) and Coen and Pegram (2018).

Over time, the understanding of the term *governance* has gradually adapted with the changing political reality. Until the mid-1980s, it was used synonymously with 'political steering'; later the term included two different meanings which were, however, both focused on the nation state. On the one hand, the term was geared towards the nonhierarchical shaped interaction between different actors that is the cooperation between governmental and nongovernmental actors in public–private networks. On the other hand, the term was seen as representing the coordination of individual action and the generation of a social order. At the beginning of the 1990s, the Commission on Global Governance (CGG) named the national actors as main actors within GG. Even though the incorporation of national actors (governments) within the global system led to a 'reconfiguration' of their political power, national actors are still key to the development and compliance of global standards and norms (Scherrer and Brand, 2011; Held, 2006; Karns and Mingst, 2004; Messner, 2005).

The processes of European integration and globalisation have raised questions about the characteristics of governance theory. In comparison to the European level, the theoretical context at the global level is far more complex due to the much greater variety of forms of governance (Mayntz, 2009). For example, during the last decades, IGOs, multinational companies, and civil society have become more important at the global level, with the latter including grassroots movements, INGOs, and trade unions. One characteristic of global governance is 'the decreased salience of states and the increased involvement of nonstate actors in norm- and rule-setting processes and compliance monitoring' (Brühl and Rittberger, 2001: 2). Rittberger et al. (2012: 274) describe global governance as a model of world order which is based on 'horizontal, networked policy coordination and cooperation between states, international organisations and non-state actors'. Cooperation between these actors rests on norms and rules which are promoted within the programmes and activities of international organisations.

> International organisations thus constitute an organisational backbone and network hub for the policy coordination among various state and non-state actors. However, not only do they provide forums for international cooperation, but, through their programme, operational and information activities, they actively contribute to global governance.
>
> (Ibid., 2012: 274)

More recently, Zürn (2018) analysed in his book the development of global governance and persistent struggles over legitimacy applying an institutionalist international relations perspective. His analysis contributes to the development of a theory of global governance, focusing on the concept of authority and the 'exercise of authority across national borders' and increasing contestation (Ibid., 2018: 3–4). Although his theory is considered as ambitious and a milestone work (Keohane, 2021; Scholte, 2021), it falls short in certain areas. Scholte (2021) considers as such areas, for example, the limited number of global governance actors which have been considered and the state-centred focus of the theory, as well as a lack of integration of normative and positive analysis. For that reason, it can be argued that the concept remains 'slippery' to some extent (Weiss and Wilkinson, 2014: 207). A stronger analytical focus could be developed around the exercise of power and power relations amongst corporate actors within the system of global governance, and on 'how interests are articulated and pursued' and 'the kind of ideas and discourses from which power and interests draw substance as well as which will help establish, maintain, and perpetuate the system' (Ibid., 2014: 207; Scherrer and Brand, 2011).

All attempts to theorise global governance emphasise the connection between the process of globalisation and the issue of regulation. The latter means the 'intentional designing of regulatory structures as a precondition for problem solving' (Haus, 2010: 469). Furthermore, all GG conceptualisations have in common a focus on global problems whose solution would arguably require a stronger international cooperation. Global problems are associated with different types of problems, which include 'global goods' and 'global problems of interdependence' (Messner, 2005: 34–35). The latter refers to interdependencies between different policy fields, or rather the implications of political actions which cannot be taken into consideration by individual corporate actors in a comprehensive way because they do not have the ability to do so. For example, the IFIs only have limited capacity to evaluate the social implications of their development programmes and support programmes at an earlier stage because of the limited available expert knowledge in certain areas. Such expert knowledge comprises, for example, knowledge of trade unions around 'social policy, the world of employment and its organisational and institutional context . . . all over the world' (Koch-Baumgarten, 2011: 64). This knowledge could, at least partly, support the IFIs regarding the estimation of the social implications of their programmes. At the same time, a knowledge transfer of this kind could help to strengthen political coherence between these international actors at the global level. Trade union officials argue that in order to reach a maximal efficiency regarding the transfer and the processing of knowledge, it would make sense to integrate trade union representatives in the process of project planning. It is in this context that the trade unions aim for 'a seat at the table in order to have the voice of working people in the heart of those discussions' (Interview ITUC03, 2009).

With the help of the global governance concept, existing forms of international cooperation and new steering processes can be analysed. The basis for international cooperation includes 'a minimum of trust, reliability, capacity to compromise and respect for the legitimate interests of others' (Nuscheler, 2002: 81). This is particularly important as in recent decades institutional complexity of GG has increased. Nowadays institutions and actors which govern a particular global policy issue overlap and form 'global governance complexes' (GGC) which vary in terms of scale, diversity, and density (Eilstrup-Sangiovanni and Westerwinter, 2021: 234). The relations between the actors of a GGC are potentially shaped by hierarchy, by conflict, or by cooperation.

So far, the existing international cooperation within global governance has been characterised by a democratic deficit (in addition to governance and control problems) through which only a limited spectrum of interests is effectively represented. This can be related to existing power asymmetries at the global level, for example the ILO has less enforcement power than the IFIs (Meardi and Marginson, 2014). In this context, the question arises as to what extent the international trade union organisations are able to act as a democratic, social balancing entity (Koch-Baumgarten, 2011). Civil society organisations do not have a (direct) regulatory influence due to their limited access to the decision-making bodies of IGOs; however, they have been able to extend their area of influence since the end of the 1980s. Since that time, many international organisations began to open up to civil society actors and to provide them with the option, albeit often channelled through specific departments, to express their views and concerns to the organisations. In this context, the World Bank Group and the IMF established, respectively, external relation departments which screen and coordinate the exchange with civil society organisations. Despite their opening up to civil society groups, the IFIs are not globally inclusive institutions which equip nongovernmental actors with participation rights. Rather, the norms and rules of international organisations constrain their 'civil society agenda' (Tussie and Riggirozzi, 2001: 175). According to the assessment of Boorman (2007: 19), the IMF is 'very close to being an all-inclusive organisation'; however, this seems to characterise more the self-perception of the organisation than reality. Neither the World Bank Group nor the IMF exploits all the opportunities to obtain 'useful and precise information for problem identification and diagnosis as well as for adequate policy implementation and the monitoring of norm compliance' (Rittberger, 2008: 14). Yet it is important to note that in recent decades organisations like the IMF have 'gradually adopted a democratic legitimation narrative' highlighting, for example, the democratic dimension of decision-making processes and organisational accountability (Dingwerth et al., 2020: 715–716)

The concept of global governance for the purpose of this study is oriented towards a new 'culture of cooperation' which is based on a multilateral understanding of politics adjusted to democratic principles (Huber, 2008: 57). In this context, it is about the initiation of cooperation and coherent action between corporate actors towards a specified global problem, where each actor has different resources available and represents different interests. Furthermore, global governance is not considered as equal to established forms of governance such as at the national level where socially binding programmes are decided and implemented. The mechanisms of regulation at the global level comprise 'flexible standards, targets, guidelines, or benchmarks rather than precise requirements' (Abbott and Snidal, 2010: 530). Dingwerth and Pattberg (2006) distinguish between three general uses of the global governance concept: first as an analytical concept, second as a political programme which includes the normative perspective, and third as academic discourse. Scherrer and Brand (2011) add a further perspective, which is the use of the global governance concept as a descriptive category. In this context, global governance describes new developments in international relations and stresses the importance of other spatial levels in addition to the national level. Whilst the normative perspective of global governance focuses on the establishment of order that is an intentional form of regulation, the analytical perspective focuses on possible forms of interaction and its mode of operation (Brand, 2007). The analytical perspective considers actual or perceived reality of world politics and the factors which determine new forms of political regulation. The focus is on the efficiency of mechanisms of interaction at the global level and its impact. Thus, global governance as an analytical concept attempts to explain a structure-process-impact relationship (Mayntz, 2008; Brand and Scherrer, 2005). However, it is difficult to consider both perspectives separately as the analytical perspective also integrates normative elements. These normative elements concern, for example, requirements for shaping global governance, as well as the different perceptions of global problems by individual and corporate actors and the need to take on responsibility (Woods, 2003).

The study aims to apply an analytical perspective of global governance which considers the existing power relations between corporate actors and addresses the issue of 'power political calculation' (Mayntz, 2004: 74). Such a calculation can, amongst others, manifest itself as a lack of intended direction in the form of 'non-decision-making' and the avoidance of problems, as well as the selection of political reform objectives which primarily serve to protect the own position (Ibid., 2004: 75). It is assumed that learning and knowledge transfer amongst corporate actors can help to achieve a more 'favourable international distribution of power' and to promote more effective global governance (Zürn, 1998: 201). The governance arrangement concept suggested by Koenig-Archibugi (2003) can contribute to the characterisation of the starting conditions for the interaction of corporate actors. Both the IMF and the World Bank are 'governance-givers', that is they define sets of rules and policies at the global level and have therefore, in contrast to the Global Unions, a strong public profile at their disposal (Koenig-Archibugi, 2003: 50). The dialogue cannot change the advantage enjoyed by the IFIs which is related to their organisational nature. However, arguably it can help the Global Unions to achieve a more favourable position within the system of global governance, which in turn may allow them to take a more active role as interest representing organisations.

In the following, the cooperation and exchange between the IFIs, the Global Unions, and the ILO within the dialogue is considered as a constellation or type of GGC which contributes to political regulation at the global level. Due to the broad range of challenges which international organisations face with regard to global governance, the latter can be understood as a determining factor which puts limits on organisational capabilities. This means that:

> each international institution is no longer able to deal effectively with its primary mandate without strategic guidance and well-defined relationships with other institutions that address related issues outside its primary mandate, mission, and capacity.
>
> (Bradford and Linn, 2007: 130)

Labour issues are outside the primary mandate and mission of the IFIs. For that reason, the IFIs can profit from amplifying their own expertise in this field through the dialogue with the trade unions and the ILO. The amplification of expertise and the consideration of arguments brought forward within the dialogue depend on the willingness of the organisations to cooperate and to learn. Due to the high degree of voluntariness involved in global governance, corporate actors have an even higher self-responsibility as regards the development of a global social dimension. The exercise of this responsibility, which includes exchange and cooperation with other international corporate actors, is determined by organisational characteristics, which will be considered in the following sections.

Organisation theories

Organisation theories can help to explain and analyse organisational characteristics and contribute to the analytical perspective of global governance. The analysis

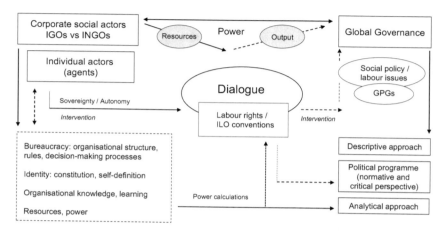

Figure 2.1 Organisational Theories and Global Governance

Source: Own illustration

of these characteristics is important because of two reasons. First, organisational particularities can illuminate possible obstacles and common grounds as regards joint interaction. Second, they can help to specify and further develop the analytical dimension of the global governance concept by explaining the mode of operation of new forms of regulation and cooperation, such as manifested in the examined policy dialogue.

The link between the global governance concept and organisation theories relating to the dialogue aims to provide a better understanding of how the participating corporate actors react to and deal with global problems, how they respond to stimuli anchored in their environment, and why they respond in the way they do.

> International relations theorists are not the only ones who are important for understanding international cooperation and global governance. Organisation theorists, especially from sociology, provide insights relevant to studying international organisations as organisations.
>
> (Karns and Mingst, 2004: 56)

According to the selection of approaches within organisational sociology, different priorities can be set concerning the analysis of organisations. Sociological theories have the advantage that they 'expect and explain a much broader range of impacts that organisations can have and specifically highlight their role in constructing actors, interests, and social purpose' (Barnett and Finnemore,

1999: 702). Organisations can be considered as open systems which engage with their environment, and their structures reflect broader societal developments and conditions. This is also true of international organisations whose structures partly reflect global economic, political, and social (power) relations. The environment consists of different institutions and actors, which are continuously generating new stimuli for organisational action. On the one hand, the environment provides resources and opportunities to an organisation, and on the other hand, it contains constraints and demands which can be perceived as threats (Scott and Davis, 2007: 19). Regarding the latter, international organisations respond, for example, with the earlier mentioned democratic legitimation narratives. Generally, organisations assimilate the input from their environment in the form of information and convert such inputs according to the resources they have available and their organisational characteristics (Scott, 1998). The following sections consider some of these characteristics, including the organisational structure, identity and culture, knowledge and power, and organisational learning.

Organisational structure

The structure of an organisation determines the character of the corporate actor and influences the actions of individual actors. Structural elements are job positions, policies, programmes, and procedures. These elements of the formal structure are a manifestation of powerful institutional rules which 'function as highly rationalised myths that are binding on particular organisations' (Meyer and Rowan, 1977: 343). That suggests that, first, they are rationalised and impersonal prescriptions for individual actors which specify appropriate means for achieving organisational objectives. Second is that they are highly institutionalised elements which limit the autonomy for decision-making of individual actors. Examples for such myths are technical procedures which are considered as taken-for-granted means by organisational members, and which are introduced independently from their possible and real efficiency.

The formal structure becomes partly visible in the bureaucratic apparatus, which through its administrative hierarchy and its rules and routines guarantees a fluency of workflows for individual actors (Friedberg, 1994; Blau and Schoenherr, 1971). Bureaucratisation is partly influenced by the proliferation of rationalised myth in society (Meyer and Rowan, 1977). Scott and Davis (2007: 55) describe the functions of the formal structure and its elements as follows:

> Specialized roles and rules, information channels, training programs, standard operating procedures – all may be viewed as mechanisms both for restricting the range of decisions each participant makes and for assisting the participant in making appropriate decisions within that range.

The formal structure is directly connected to elements which characterise the informal structure. The latter is 'necessary to the operation of formal organisations as a means of communication, of cohesion and of protecting the integrity of the individual' (Williamson, 1995: 39). The informal level plays an important role within the dialogue because most formal decisions between corporate actors are preceded by informal agreements at the individual level. The capacities, abilities, and attitudes of individual actors affect the development of strategies which are necessary for the attainment of organisational goals and decisions regarding the establishment of cooperation with external actors. In the broadest sense, individuals form informal structures through their personal contacts by which they exert influence on the development and the continuance of the formal structures.

The formal structure of organisations simplifies decision-making processes for organisational members because it reduces complexity by standardising processes, distributing responsibility amongst different individuals, and regulating and constraining information flows (Blau and Schoenherr, 1971). Decision-making is largely attributed to individual actors. Important contributions in this respect have been made by Barnard (1968), as well as the scientists of the Carnegie Institute of Technology March and Simon (1961, 1976) and Cyert and March (1992). In comparison to decision-making of individual actors, there has been less research on decision-making of corporate actors. However, it is argued that corporate actors which are able to act in a sovereign way to a certain extent are also able to make decisions on their own. The decision-making of an organisation as a corporate actor is often directed by its self-view, which becomes manifest in its identity and objectives (King et al., 2010).

In most human decision-making processes, the key question surrounds the discovery and selection of satisfactory alternatives and not optimal alternatives. This means that decision-makers stop searching when 'they identify an alternative that satisfies their various performance criteria' (Gavetti et al., 2007: 526). The search and selection processes for suitable solutions are supported by organisational programmes, which set off an elaborate programme of activities or responses if a certain stimulus appears in the environment (March and Simon, 1976; March and Simon, 1961). Programmes may be developed if there is a need for a high level of coordination. Due to the fact that organisational programmes determine individual behaviour by simplifying the selection process of a reaction towards a specific problem, they can lead to the routinisation of activities.

In a very broad sense, the concept of routines refers to simple decision rules that require low levels of information processing (rules of thumb), but also to complex, automatic behaviours that involve high levels of repetitive information processing.

(Dosi et al., 2008: 1166)

The development of new programmes or the modification of programmes by higher level officials does not correspond to such a routinisation (March and Simon, 1976). This, for example, could lead to the creation of a new organisational unit responsible for development and implementation (Tosi, 2009). In the case of the IMF, the former Managing Director Dominique Strauss-Kahn tried to institutionalise a new mindset in the organisation. It could be argued that during his time in office Strauss-Kahn took some first steps to loosen the IMF's neoliberal discourse by introducing a governance reform and a reform of conditions attached to loans (Falk and Unmüßig, 2011).

Organisations try to protect their formal structure by minimising the evaluation and control of activities from the outside, and by coordinating structural units in an informal way. However, in some cases, the incorporation of externally legitimated institutions, such as laws, norms, or societal expectations, can protect an organisation from having its conduct questioned and help to maintain organisational stability and to promote its own success (Meyer and Rowan, 1977). The integration of externally legitimated elements, regardless of whether they increase organisational efficiency or not, is referred to as isomorphism. DiMaggio and Powell (1983) distinguish three isomorphic processes, including coercive, mimetic, and normative isomorphism,[5] all of which can lead to homogeneity amongst organisations belonging to the same organisational field. The organisational field is a central element of neo-institutionalism, and its definition has changed and evolved during the last decades. Originally, institutional theorists conceptualised the field as a 'recognised area of institutional life referring to commonalities between organisations, such as common meaning systems and more frequent and fateful interaction' (Wooten and Hoffman, 2017: 56). Since the late 1990s, a re-configuration of the field conception has taken place, shifting the focus from 'static' fields to notions of change within fields. In this context, the definition of the field started changing by 'forming around the issues that became important to the interests and objectives of a specific collective of organisations' (Ibid., 2017: 59). According to this definition, the Global Unions, the ILO, and the IFIs could be considered as belonging to the same field as they all have an interest in promoting economic growth, inclusive jobs, equality, and achieving the UN 2023 Agenda.

With regard to the dialogue, coercive isomorphism could be of concern. According to DiMaggio and Powell (1983: 150), coercive isomorphism is the result of formal and informal pressure exerted on an organisation by organisations of the same organisational field, or by cultural expectations of society. Such pressures are perceived as 'force, persuasion, or as invitations to join in collusion'. However, expectations of society or other external institutions' norms and beliefs must not necessarily be concordant with the organisational structure. One strategy which organisations may apply in order to deal with internal and external requirements at the same time is described as 'decoupling', which means that 'elements of structure are decoupled from activities and from each other' (Meyer and Rowan, 1977: 357). In other words, an organisation decouples what it professes to do from how it operates. This disconnection between (announced) formal procedures from everyday practices can provide members of an organisation with more flexibility.

One example is the creation of specific departments and professional roles by the World Bank and the IMF, whose main tasks consist of coordinating and administrating the contact with civil society actors. The Civil Society Team (CST) of the World Bank, which replaced the Bank's former NGO unit in 2004, organises the engagement with civil society, for example, through the Civil Society Policy Forum (CSPF).[6] The CST is considered as a 'central resource for advice, technical assistance, and strategy development for Bank staff and senior management' (World Bank, 2005: 4). However, taking into consideration the decentralised organisational structure of the World Bank, the influence of the CST within the whole organisation seemed to be limited in the past suggesting a decoupling from other organisational units and activities. According to the information of a former director of the ITUC/Global Unions office in Washington, the CST has made some real efforts to meet trade union concerns and 'to push Bank people to deal seriously with trade unions' in the past; however, the department has never had a lot of influence in the organisation (Interview ITUC02, 2008).

Organisational identity and culture

Organisational identity and organisational culture are two different concepts, which both play an important role in characterising organisations. The concept of organisational identity is often linked to individual actors (Brickson, 2005), which have a personal and a social identity. The first is related to the way in which individuals see themselves and the second, in how they want to be seen by their social environment. As such, individual actors present images which they think are appropriate to a given situation and the expectations of others in relation to their environment and social group.

> A social identity does not simply spring fully formed from the demands of the situation but requires effort and practice from the individual and appropriate feedback from others. . . . Social identity, where it is different to the former, consists of the negotiated position between our personal identity and the meanings and images demanded of us in our current social context.
>
> (Thompson and McHugh, 2009: 390)

The concept of social identity can help to explain why individual actors behave in certain circumstances in a specific way. Furthermore, individual actors construct, to some extent, organisational identity through their involvement in organisations.

In this context, organisational rules and procedures are mechanisms for controlling individual behaviour and performance but they cannot secure identity. In fact, individual actors develop different tactics to cope with organisational restrictions and 'they may in time transform themselves into an image that functions in a way that is useful to the organisation they work for' (Ibid., 2009: 394). From the perspective of individual actors, organisational identity is what is central, distinctive, and enduring about an organisation (Whetten and Mackey, 2002 citing Albert and Whetten, 1985). This perception of identity reflects shared perceptions and beliefs amongst members concerning the identity of an organisation. Therefore, identity is an 'important source of heterogeneity' because every organisation is perceived in a different way by its members (King, Felin and Whetten, 2010: 299).

Organisational identity can not only relate to individual actors but also be ascribed to organisations as social actors. In this context, identity is defined as 'institutionalized claims available to members' and expresses their self-definition (Whetten and Mackey, 2002: 395).

> Identity is thus conceived of as those things that enable social actors . . . to be unique actors or entities.
>
> (Whetten and Mackey, 2002: 396)

Both individual identity and organisational identity require continuity. With regard to organisations, that means that organisational identity works like a constitution which gives security to individual members concerning their rights and responsibilities as well as 'for planning, explaining, and justifying collective action' (Ibid., 2002: 397). Thus, individuals and organisations tend to defend their identities and, therefore, reduce their opportunities to achieve learning that could promote an identity change (Brown and Starkey, 2000). The willingness to reflect on organisational identity is based on a perceived pressure to do so. This pressure can be created by the environment and/or other corporate actors which are active in this environment or, which is less likely, be due to an objective self-assessment of an organisation. The latter is less likely as institutionalised values and rules very often limit the range of vision of individual actors within an organisation.

In comparison to organisational culture, organisational identity 'is more purely cognitive in definition' (Brickson, 2005: 580). The connection between organisational identity and culture can be examined from different perspectives. On the one hand, organisational identity might be considered as a 'self-referencing aspect of organisational culture' (Whetten, 2006: 227). On the other hand, culture can be treated as a distinguishing property of identity. This means that 'members are most likely to invoke specific cultural elements of their organisation as distinguishing features when they are experienced as central and enduring organisational attributes' (Ibid., 2006: 228). The focus of the following sections is based on the latter proposition.

Organisational culture can be considered as something that an organisation '*is*' or a variable which means that it is considered as something an organisation '*has*' and which can be manipulated (Meek, 1993: 202). Here culture will be considered as something the organisation '*is*', which means that culture cannot be created or destroyed by powerful individual actors as, for example, managing directors or presidents. However, organisational culture is related to the social interaction of individual actors and the process of social reproduction. It influences their behaviour with regard to the use of language, rules, and knowledge, but it does not just become passively absorbed. Rather it becomes produced and reproduced and the latter can lead to the transformation of culture (Ibid., 1993). In the following, the author defines organisational culture according to Schein (1993):

> Organisational culture is the pattern of basic assumptions that a given group has invented, discovered, or developed in learning to cope with its problems of external adaptation and internal integration, and that have worked well enough to be considered valid, and, therefore, to be taught to new members as the correct way to perceive, think, and feel in relation to those problems.
>
> (Schein, 1993: 237)

According to Schein (1993: 243), 'cultural elements are learned solutions to problems', and all cultural elements derive from consensus. With regard to the adaptation to the environment, consensus comprises core missions, goals, strategies to achieve these goals, and criteria for evaluation. In relation to internal problems, consensus must be found on criteria for inclusion of members, the allocation of influence and power, peer relationships, as well as incentives and punishments (Schein, 1989). If the objective would be to describe the whole culture of an organisation, all these issues would have to be considered. However, within this study, only aspects of culture which are relevant to the understanding of the dialogue between the corporate actors will be applied.

Schein (1993) distinguishes three different levels of culture which interact with each other. The first level comprises visible artefacts like behaviour patterns or documents open to the public including charters, constitutions, or guidance for employees. The problem with these data is that they do not give information on why a group behaves in the way it does. The second level of culture comprises organisational values which 'represent accurately only the manifest or espoused values of a culture' (Schein, 1993: 238). These values are contained in organisational documents and can be accessed by content analysis; however, they do not reveal the underlying reasons for the behaviour of individuals. For that reason, Schein refers to the underlying assumptions which 'are typically unconscious but which actually determine how group members perceive, think and feel' (Ibid., 1993: 239). Underlying assumptions are based on values which, at the beginning, guide individuals' behaviour to solve a problem, and if the problem solving is successful those values are transformed in underlying assumptions. Underlying assumptions can also be influenced by the occupational backgrounds of individual members (Morgan, 1997).

Organisational knowledge and power

The knowledge of an organisation forms part of its culture and it is an important organisational power resource. It enables an organisation to act autonomously, which can be perceived by other actors as a claim to power. Knowledge can be defined as 'a justified belief that increases an entity's capacity for effective action' (Alavi and Leidner, 2001: 109). Organisational knowledge is the product of learning and includes the interpretation of information received by individual actors and know-how (Huber, 1991).

Organisational knowledge is, on the one hand, stored in the minds of organisational members, and on the other hand, is incorporated into routines and other organisational practices as, for example, norms and rules (Dosi et al., 2008). The knowledge development process includes several steps. It starts with the creation of knowledge, which is followed by the use of knowledge, its transfer and sharing, as well as its storage and retrieval for further use (Lindner and Wald, 2011). For the creation of new knowledge in an organisation, it is necessary that organisational leaders establish a favourable social context which supports the knowledge development process. For example, the creation of networks, the application of suitable technological developments (such as internet communities), and strong social relationships support the knowledge creation process (Argote et al., 2003). Due to the long-term continuity of international organisations, organisational departments and units 'act as knowledge silos' which have available specific mechanisms for knowledge capturing, storing, dissemination, and organisational learning (Lindner and Wald, 2011: 877).

The corporate actors participating in the examined dialogue share their knowledge with each other. The uptake of this knowledge is preceded by processes of individual perception and its classification. In order that knowledge can be recognised, it must be available in an explicit form (explicit knowledge) as, for example, digital recordings or transcriptions. Apart from explicit knowledge, implicit (tacit) knowledge plays an important role for individuals and groups. The latter is connected to elements of individual 'perception, skills, experience and history' and 'underscores that knowledge is never free from human values and ideas' (Nonaka et al., 2006: 1182). In contrast to explicit knowledge which 'is uttered and captured in drawings and writing' (Nonaka and von Krogh, 2009: 635) and which is accessible through consciousness, implicit knowledge is unarticulated and connected to experiences and the intuition of individual actors (Lindner and Wald, 2011). Therefore, tacit knowledge becomes explicit knowledge when individuals are able to communicate their cognitive maps through words and actions and to articulate ideas and concepts (Crossan et al., 1999).

> By interacting and sharing tacit and explicit knowledge with others, the individual enhances the capacity to define a situation or problem and apply his or her knowledge so as to act and specifically solve the problem.
>
> (Nonaka et al., 2006: 1182)

Knowledge management includes all practices or processes of an organisation to create, store, use and share knowledge. These main processes can be subdivided into sub-processes, including the creation of internal knowledge, the acquisition of external knowledge, the storage of knowledge in documents and routines, as well as the updating and sharing of knowledge (Alavi and Leidner, 2001). The development and implementation of knowledge management processes require a long-term perspective. In this context, stable organisations such as the IFIs, the ILO, and the trade unions have the advantage that they can revert to organisational routines and organisational memory, and that they are able to learn on that basis. In other words, experiences from successfully implemented projects and activities can be transferred to other projects and later into organisational programmes, which means that knowledge management can help to develop new routines. Furthermore, the fundamental composition and durability of organisational units helps to integrate individual and organisational knowledge independently of the number of staff involved.

Organisational knowledge is an important power resource which helps organisations to create their own social reality through classification, regulation and dissemination mechanisms (Barnett and Finnemore, 2004). In the context of the examined dialogue, the acquisition and the transfer of knowledge between organisations and within organisations are important. Knowledge transfer refers, for example, to passing on specific expert knowledge on the part of the Global Unions to the IFIs and vice versa. Apart from organisational knowledge, other resources such as formal authority, the control of resources the organisation depends on for actions (finance, skills, personnel), internal decision-making processes and the ability to cope with uncertainty which exists within and outside an organisation, determine the power of corporate social actors (Morgan, 1997). These resources influence 'who gets what, when, and how' (Morgan, 1997: 170), and they determine the possibilities of an organisation to resist pressure or to refuse cooperation without suffering from reputational damage.

Crucial characteristics of power resources are the costs involved in using them. Mobilisation costs describe the relative ease with which resources can be mobilised, and application costs concern the costs when a power resource is applied, as for example, the costs of monitoring activities (Korpi, 1985). Furthermore, the organisational capability to determine membership criteria and the control of the behaviour of individual members is an important source of power for organisations:

> This source of power is important as it provides a comparative, distinguishing characteristic of the organisation. . . . From an organisational actor perspective, the organisation exercises power in deliberately admitting and dismissing members of the organisation and in 'controlling' behaviour through rules, rewards, and sanctions.
>
> (King et al., 2010: 293)

The international trade union organisations exercise power through the activity of members and use power in an offensive, open, and concentrated way (Offe, 1985: 193). In contrast, at the inter-organisational level, the IFIs exercise power through leadership and use power in a more defensive, hidden, and dispersed way. For example, the boards of the World Bank and the IMF have considerable power within and outside their organisations and they 'can be a very persuasive force in framing problems as well as formulating solutions' (Oestreich, 2007: 10). Furthermore, the IFIs make use of their knowledge in terms of 'technical' imperatives, whereas the international trade union organisations communicate in terms of 'demands and explicit normative claims' (Offe, 1985: 193). Due to the dispersed way in which IFIs use their power, it could be argued that these organisations are 'vehicles for power politics' (Hafner-Burton and Montgomery, 2006: 4). For the international trade unions, it is much more difficult to force institutional change with regard to other actors because of their limited power resources in material terms. However, they can resort to social and cooperative relations, which also represent a kind of power, even though this kind of power is more concentrated on the national level than at the international level. The disadvantage in comparison to the IFIs is, however, that the Global Unions have quite high mobilisation costs because collective action by a large number of actors is more costly to organise than if a department of the IFIs (which is led by a small number of staff) sets up financial support in a particular country.

Organisational change and learning

The ability to change and to learn is likewise important for all the organisations involved in the examined dialogue because it allows them to be responsive to global political and economic challenges, and to maintain their legitimacy. Organisational change is closely linked to the processing of knowledge and organisational learning (Child and Heavens, 2001).

There are two different organisational strands which describe organisational change. The first of these suggests that change occurs mainly through adaptation to prior changes, for example in the environment, and it fits with institutional theory. DiMaggio and Powell (1983) suggest that uncertainty triggers organisational change because organisations try to imitate other organisations and this can lead to a change in 'formal structure, organisational culture, and goals, programme, or mission' (DiMaggio and Powell, 1983: 149). According to institutional theory, the preservation of legitimacy is one of the driving forces for this process. The second strand describing organisational change refers to selective mechanisms of organisational change and suggests that some organisations might fail during the adaptation process (Barnett and Carroll, 1995).

Organisational change can be related to internal and external factors. Internal factors are, for example, the age, size, and the culture of an organisation. The larger and older an organisation is, the less likely it is that organisational change will occur because such organisations have well-developed bureaucratic structures, procedures, and roles. In general, large organisations:

> tend to become complacent about their competences. They fail to perceive the need for change until confronted with necessity in the form of a crisis.
>
> (Farquhar et al., 1989: 34)

If the organisational culture supports trustful relationships between individual actors, organisational change and learning are more likely to be promoted in a positive way. However, the occupational culture, in particular traditionally defined job roles, can also contribute to rigidity and resistance to change (Lucas and Kline, 2008). External factors include the development of technology, competitive pressures, social expectations, and environmental constraints and opportunities (Barnett and Carroll, 1995).

The outcomes of change processes can affect the organisational identity and culture, the organisational structure (e.g. hierarchy), as well as organisational functions and modes of action (e.g. practices, procedures, and routines) (Schneider et al., 1996).

> Changes in function can be traced in the programs of international organizations. There may be changes in the scale of operations. . . . There may also be changes in the authority of an organization, either because members become more responsive to its decisions or because the organization begins to make enactments of a new kind that place more demands upon members. . . . Finally, there may be changes in the relative importance of an international organization within the issue-area or areas with which it is concerned.
>
> (Cox and Jacobson, 1997: 78)

However, there is no measure for organisational change, which can vary in its scale and scope (organisation-wide or not), its characteristics (perceived as necessary to all or only some units), its timeframe, and its importance for the organisation – for example, if change is critical for the survival of the organisation or not (Andersson and Pan Fagerlin, 2011). For the achievement of an organisation-wide change, incentives for individual actors to support change play an important role.

Both organisational change and learning determine the dynamic of an organisation. The more flexible an organisation is with regard to the initiation and implementation of learning processes, the more dynamic it is. Organisational learning is always connected with a certain level of change, whilst barriers to organisational learning can constrain organisational change. Such barriers include the focus of individual actors regarding their job positions, organisational and departmental boundaries, which hinder the flow of information amongst individuals and control systems, which may lead to the result that individual actors keep specific knowledge to themselves. However, an increasingly dynamic environment challenges organisations and puts them under pressure to change, learn and adapt and arguably 'to take actions that are ethically acceptable and sustainable, and which balance the interests of a range of different stakeholders' (Rowley and Gibbs, 2008: 357). Organisational learning has been examined by different academic disciplines focusing on different phenomena such as information processing, product innovation, or bounded rationality (Crossan et al., 1999). There are cognitive theories which focus on the contents of individual minds (March and Olsen, 1975) and which conceptualise learning as cognitive processes. Organisational theories, such as the situated learning theory (Contu and Willmott, 2003), focus on the process and outcomes of learning and the embeddedness of learning practices in power relations.

Overall, organisational learning is a dynamic process and a social phenomenon which is related to processes of individual learning, but which can not only be reduced to such individual processes (Dosi et al., 2008; Huber, 1991). On the contrary, it is different from the learning of individual actors. The turnover of individual members of an organisation does not necessarily mean that an organisation loses the knowledge associated with these individuals as some learning is embedded in the organisational structure, strategy, and routines. In a very broad sense, learning can be defined as a change in the organisations' knowledge, which manifests itself in changes in cognition or behaviour and which could be embedded in different repositories such as routines and individual actors (Argote and Miron-Spektor, 2011: 1124). Transformative organisational learning leads to the modification of the identity and the cultural core of an organisation (Brown and Starkey, 2000). In addition, organisational learning does not require all departments and units to acquire the same knowledge; however, it is broader when more units 'obtain this knowledge and recognize it as potentially useful' and when the same units 'develop a uniform comprehension of the various interpretations' (Huber, 1991: 90).

The starting point for organisational learning is the individual actor and his cognitive capacities. The interpretation of information is highly subjective, often unconscious, and related to personal experiences, beliefs, knowledge, and attitudes. Attitudes and opinions are based on established individual beliefs, and perceptions refer to the processes of gathering, organising, and interpreting social information. The limited cognitive ability of individual actors can, to some extent, limit the perception of information, for example leading to selective processing of information or stereotyping (Heijden, 1992). Selective perception describes the process of categorising and interpreting information in a way that favours one specific interpretation over another. As a result, individual actors tend to selectively perceive information in ways that are congruent with their own goals, values, attitudes, and beliefs, and tend to scrutinise information which is not in accordance with their beliefs (Sullivan, 2009). Stereotyping describes assumption making and judgements by individual actors about other actors based on generalisations about the groups to which they belong (Wilson and Rees, 2007). Both selective perception and stereotyping can be an obstacle to the dialogue process and make communication more difficult.

In order to develop innovative ideas and views, individual actors need to be willing to acknowledge their own mistakes and those of others, to reflect on them, to consider different ideas and to test unproven approaches (Bunderson and Reagans, 2011). In long-established organisations, spontaneous learning of individual actors becomes less likely because prior learning which is embedded in organisational institutions, guides interpretations, and actions. Furthermore, relations amongst actors in long-established organisations are more formalised:

> Intuiting and interpreting occur at the individual level, interpreting and integrating occur at the group level, and integrating and institutionalizing occur at the organizational level.
>
> (Crossan et al., 1999: 524–525)

If individual actors work together with other actors, they may interpret, in other words explain through words and/or action, an idea to oneself and to others. The interpretation process, which in contrast to intuiting reflects the conscious part of individual learning, can result in the development of a common language. The latter passes into an 'integrating' process when a group of individuals develops a shared understanding and acts in a coordinated way through mutual adjustment (Crossan et al., 1999). The headquarter-level dialogue between the Global Unions, the ILO, and the IFIs can be understood as a crucial instrument for developing such a new and shared understanding, as well as coordinated action at the global level.

Notes

1 Amongst international relation theories, realism and the more recent concept of liberal intergovernmentalism focus on the nation state as a main actor of international politics.
2 The term 'public good' originally derives from economics where it describes goods which are nonrival and nonexcludable, such as national financial stability or defence (Long and Woolley, 2009).

3 Source: UN (2022) https://www.un.org/en/about-us/universal-declaration-of-human-rights

4 A sub-concept of global governance which focuses on global labour regulations is the concept of 'Global Labour Governance' which assumes that global labour problems require governance (Meardi and Marginson, 2014). However, the conceptualisation of the concept in terms of its analytical dimensions covering different actor constellations is relatively weak.

5 Beckert (2010) added the mechanism 'competition' and suggested that isomorphism does produce not only homogeneity but also heterogeneity.

6 Source: World Bank (2022) https://www.worldbank.org/en/about/partners/civil-society

3 The Global Unions – the ITUC, GUFs, and the TUAC

The Global Unions – A short overview

The Global Unions include the International Trade Union Confederation (ITUC), the nine Global Union Federations (GUFs), and the Trade Union Advisory Committee (TUAC) to the OECD. The Global Unions and their national affiliates work on issues which influence the 'well-being of people and society as a whole', including 'political and social democracy, civil and democratic rights, poverty elimination, equality, and the rule of law' (Gallin, 2000: 1). Both the ITUC and the GUFs face the challenge of organising and promoting the rights of millions of workers around the world. In this context, they act as connectors between the global North, where relatively well-resourced trade unions are concentrated, and the global south, where trade unions often struggle in terms of their resources and recognition by employers (Fox-Hodess, 2022). The diversity of member organisations, which for example becomes reflected in their organisational priorities, cultures, and political backgrounds, creates both advantages and challenges for the Global Unions.

Whilst the ITUC is an international umbrella organisation which brings together national trade union centres from all over the world, the GUFs are international sector-/industry-based bodies affiliating national unions of which many are themselves organised within sectors (Croucher and Cotton, 2009; Abbott, 2011). The international labour movement has a long history which is not within the scope of this book; for a more recent overview on labour internationalism, see, for example, Hyman (2005) or Gumbrell-McCormick (2013a). However, there have been important structural changes over the years, including the creation of the ITUC in 2006 and the merger of some of the GUFs (formerly known as International Trade Secretariats [ITS]). These structural changes intended to 'create more unity, not just in structure but also unity of voice' (Interview UNI, 2019). Both the ITUC and the GUFs are independent from each other regarding their programmes, rules, priorities, and structures (Fairbrother and Hammer, 2005). However, they have in common that they are 'at the junction of complex social and political interactions' and that they try

DOI: 10.4324/9781315458410-3

to ensure the 'representation of a "voice of labour" worldwide' (Hennebert and Bourque, 2011: 158).

In 2006, the ITUC, the GUFs, and the TUAC created the basis for a more structured cooperation and coordination by ratifying a consensus agreement on the establishment of the Council of Global Unions (CGU). The CGU, which had its first meeting in 2007, is not an organisation in itself but a 'mechanism for cooperation bringing people together for sharing information' (Interview ITUC01, 2008). Education International (EI) was one of the driving forces with regard to the foundation of the Council (Interview EI, 2008), and since 2012, all GUFs are members of the CGU, although this has not always been the case. The International Metalworkers Federation (IMF-GUF), for example, which now forms part of IndustriALL, did not join at the beginning because of the fear of adding an 'additional bureaucratic burden' to its own organisation (Interview IMF-GUF, 2008). With the help of the CGU, the Global Unions aim to 'promote growth in union membership and to advance the common interest of trade union members worldwide' (Global Unions, 2006: 1). The Council meets once a year and its tasks generally relate to 'organizing and trade union recognition' (Global Unions, 2009: 4), and it provides its members with the opportunity to discuss different topics without compromising their autonomy. The topics include the

> world of work, the main campaigns they [*the members*] have to run, the political position they have to take with regard to the G20 and the L20 . . ., this is not impacting on the autonomy of each organisation because each organisation has also its own programme, can run its own programme.
>
> (Interview ITUC05, 2015)

Generally, the Council's tasks are of operational and cooperative nature, such as the consideration of joint political and strategic initiatives and activities which serve to defend the interests of working people. Furthermore, the CGU supports information sharing amongst the Global Unions with regard to global economic and social developments, and it facilitates and supports the operation of the ITUC/Global Unions office in Washington in its dealings and relations with the IFIs (Global Unions, 2006). The General Secretary of the ITUC is the secretary of the CGU and forms part of the coordinating committee of the Council. The work of the CGU is supported by different working groups, including the 'Communications Task Force' which tries to find common ground amongst the different positions of the GUFs so that a joint platform can be developed around strategically important policy issues.

The Global Union organisations have a very large membership and clearly defined mandates which make them important social and political actors at the international policy level. The ITUC, for example, has 331 affiliated member organisations and represents the interests of 207 million workers from all over the world (ITUC, 2018b). Their broad membership base and democratic structures provide the global trade union organisations with a source of power and legitimacy which clearly distinguishes them from nongovernmental organisations.

> Unions remain by far the largest membership organizations in the world and have extensive international coverage, dwarfing non-governmental organizations (NGOs) and they are also engaged with the impact of globalization.
>
> (Croucher and Cotton, 2009: 4)

Trade unions and NGOs have in common that both are created purposefully and that they are civil society actors which focus on the improvement of society (Gallin, 2000; Poole, 1981); their actions are value driven and not profit driven (Brunt and McCourt, 2012). The number of NGOs in the field of human and workers' rights has noticeably increased in the last decades (Egels-Zandén and Hyllman, 2011), and there have been many examples of successful cooperation between trade unions and NGOs. One example of such cooperation is NGOs helping to organise workers in difficult environments such as in companies where trade unions find it challenging to achieve access (Hale, 2004; Compa, 2004). Trade union representatives value the work of NGOs, but at the same time they highlight that NGOs are advocacy organisations that support specific groups and issues which distinguishes them from trade unions:

> The NGOs do very good work. Most of them are just brilliant organisations, but they are advocacy organisations, not representational organisations.
>
> (Interview ITUC03, 2009)

In relation to the examined policy dialogue, it is important to differentiate between trade unions and other civil society actors such as NGOs, and to highlight the particular characteristics of the trade unions as opposed to these other societal actors. In other words, a clear distinction needs to be made between the dialogue which the IFIs have with civil society actors more generally and the policy dialogue between the IFIs and the Global Unions.

Trade unions and NGOs can be differentiated in terms of their members, structures, objectives and strategies, acquisition of resources, values, cultures, and forms of collective action. In comparison to NGOs, trade unions provide an 'organised structure to groups of working people' which is based on the principles of democracy and equality (Harrod and O'Brien, 2002: 3). The power of individual actors, such as trade union officials and governing bodies, is constrained by the organisational constitution. Meanwhile trade unions can be held accountable by their members; NGOs do not have political accountability (Braun and Gearhart, 2004). Regarding their organisational strategies, trade unions focus on different actors such as international organisations, governments, and employers when they represent their members. NGOs often are focused on a small group of actors or single actor and try to 'create or leverage political opportunity structures (POS) to influence public policy' (Johnson and Prakash, 2007: 224). A further difference between NGOs and trade unions is the approach in which they acquire resources. Whilst trade unions depend on the contributions of their members, NGOs are often strongly tied to the financial support of donors and governments which have 'considerable influence on strategic choices, programmatic practices and the political orientation', and NGOs are also accountable to them (Nelson, 2006: 709).

The Global Unions have a clear and unique set of characteristics in that they are the 'only universal and democratically organised movement at world level, with an unequalled capacity for resistance' and they are 'the only movement through which millions of workers achieve power through organization' (Gallin, 2002: 250). However, the World Bank (WB) and the IMF barely distinguish between trade unions and other civil society actors. In 2019, the WB stated on its website that it 'works with civil society, which includes: the wide array of non-governmental and not for profit organizations that have a presence in public life' (World Bank website, 2019).[1] Although the IMF has a more specific definition of civil society organisations, there is very limited differentiation between trade unions and NGOs. In a factsheet from 2017, civil society organisations are said to be comprised of 'business forums, faith-based associations, labour unions, local community groups, nongovernmental organizations (NGOs), philanthropic foundations, and think tanks' which are considered as 'experts in economic and social issues and many focus on issues that are at the core of the work of the IMF and other international organizations' (IMF, 2017: 1). At individual level, however, some organisational representatives recognise the specific role and characteristics of trade unions to some extent. For example, a former staff member of the World Bank considered trade unions as 'key constituency' and 'very important' actors because of their large memberships and because 'they are also more organic than other constituencies' (Interview WB01, 2008). An IMF representative also acknowledged that the legitimacy of trade unions is beyond question, and he considered the dialogue with trade unions as 'essential' (Interview IMF01, 2008).

National trade unions usually act in political areas clearly defined by national governments and they have evolved in accordance with the national and local political environment in which they were created; in some cases, for example seeing themselves as reformist, radical, or religiously influenced. In comparison, the Global Unions which represent meta-organisations do not act in such a bounded political field although their daily work is strongly influenced by their affiliates, which have different views and priorities regarding political issues. This heterogeneity is also reflected in the perceived importance of the dialogue with the IFIs and in the different approaches and attitudes which prevail regarding the dialogue amongst the GUFs (Interview IG Metall, 2008). It is important to emphasise that the Global Unions do not necessarily think and act in a homogenous way, even though on the surface mergers amongst international trade union organisations have arguably led towards a greater unity within the trade union movement worldwide (Hennebert and Bourque, 2011: 157). For that reason, joint trade union statements, such as the statements released concerning the spring and the annual meetings of the IFIs, do not necessarily reflect the opinion of each GUF and their members.

The International Trade Union Confederation

The ITUC was founded in 2006 through the merger of the International Confederation of Free Trade Unions (ICFTU), the World Confederation of Labour (WCL), and some influential left-wing union confederations (such as the French CGT). Until then the ICFTU, which was established in 1949 after several trade unions seceded from the WFTU (World Federation of Trade Unions),[2] was the largest and most influential confederation and the main focal point for developing contacts with governments and other international agencies (O'Brien, 2000; Gordon, 2000). The merger in 2006 gave the newly formed ITUC, a much broader international coverage and influence, and put an end to the international division between social-democratic and Christian unionism (Abbott, 2011). The overall effect on the WFTU has been to reduce its influence with its main affiliates now being based in India, Latin America, and the Arab countries (Cotton and Gumbrell-McCormick, 2012). The foundation of the ITUC has been considered as a 'top-down enterprise' by some researchers which, however, 'removes major obstacles to the cooperation of unions at the national and international levels and creates new opportunities for the trade union movement at all levels' (Gumbrell-McCormick, 2006).

The ITUC considers it as a 'permanent responsibility' to act as 'countervailing force in the global economy' (ITUC, 2010b: 7), and in this context, the organisation mainly does political work at the global level and represents its affiliates in relation to other major global organisations such as the World Bank and the IMF. In particular, the ITUC 'Economic and Social Policy' department 'seeks to increase intergovernmental cooperation to ensure that the social dimension of globalisation, including decent work and fundamental workers' rights, is at the centre of decision-making within the world's major global and regional institutions' (ITUC, 2021 website[3]). The political work at the global level involves following approaches and concepts relating to social and employment protection which are promoted by the World Bank, structural development programmes at the IMF, and multilateral initiatives such as the Social Protection Inter-Agency Cooperation Board (SPIAC-B). The latter was founded in 2012 with the objective to coordinate the work of different international organisations in the area of social protection. The members of SPIAC-B are, amongst others, the WB, the IMF, the OECD, and the ILO, as well as bilateral organisations and five NGOs; the ITUC is invited to the meetings as an observer.

Structure

Trade union organisations have a 'clearly defined administrative structure' (Poole, 1981: 152) and the ITUC is no exception in this regard. However, in contrast to national trade union organisations, both the ITUC and the GUFs represent 'meta-organisations'; in other words, their affiliates are organisations themselves which all 'claim their own democratic mandate and possess their own capacity to act collectively' (Hyman and Gumbrell-McCormick, 2020: 261). In the case of the ITUC, the affiliates are national trade union centres from all over the world, such as the American AFL-CIO and the German DGB, which vary in terms of their size, resources, and priorities. According to the ITUC's organisational constitution, which determines organisational rules and conditions for membership, the ITUC is 'open to affiliation by democratic, independent, and representative trade union centres' (ITUC, 2010b: 6). Thereby, the organisation aims to ensure that its affiliates have, despite being heterogeneous, the same basic values and political orientation in common. At the same time, the ITUC respects 'their autonomy and the diversity of their sources of inspiration, and their organisational forms' (Ibid., 2010b: 6). According to Hyman and Gumbrell-McCormick (2020) and Ahrne and Brunsson (2005), the members of meta-organisations have often more resources and action capacity as the meta-organisation itself leading to competitive struggles about identity and authority.

In addition to the rights and obligations of its affiliates, the ITUC determines through its constitution the composition and the way of working of its formal governing bodies as well as its relationships with the GUFs, the CGU, and the TUAC. The three governing bodies of the ITUC are the Congress, the General Council (GC), and the Executive Bureau (EB). The highest decision-making body of the Confederation is the Congress, which meets every four years and is composed of delegates from trade union centres which have the right to speak and to vote. The tasks of the Congress consist of determining the policies and the programme of the ITUC and involve, for example, dealing with general trade union policy questions (ITUC, 2010b). The decisions of the Congress are made by an absolute majority of delegates, and in the case of amendments to the constitution, a two-thirds majority of delegates is required. External stakeholders such as governments, politicians, employers, and religious groups are explicitly excluded from having any influence over the decision-making processes within the ITUC (ITUC, 2010b).

The Congress is headed by the President, two Deputy Presidents, the Vice-Presidents, and the General Secretary (GS). The organisational role of the President, who has a voting right in all governing bodies, rotates amongst the regions of the ITUC at each Congress. The two Deputy Presidents serve as chairpersons of the Executive Bureau and the Solidarity Fund Management Board.

The General Secretary of the Confederation is elected by the Congress and is also the Secretary-General of the Congress. The General Secretary is the representative and spokesperson of the ITUC, leads the secretariat, and is a member of

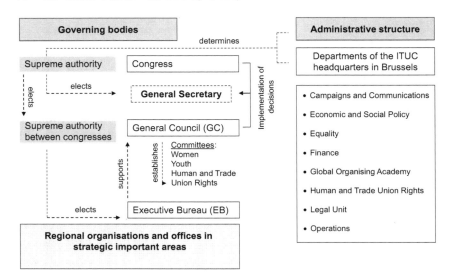

Figure 3.1 Formal Structure of the ITUC

Source: Own illustration, based on the ITUC Constitution (2018c) and website

the GC and the EB with the right to vote. The General Secretary is responsible for implementing the policies set out in the 'Programme of the ITUC' which was adopted at the founding congress in 2006 (ITUC, 2006). Furthermore, Article XII of the Constitution (Right to Address the Congress) stipulates that the GS, who is accountable to the Congress and the GC, has 'at all times . . . the right to speak on any subject', and that responsibilities include the implementation of decisions from the Congress and the General Council as well as administration tasks. The GS can also make decisions about financial matters such as the raising of funds for clearly defined purposes or the application for financing from public and private sources. He or she is supported by the Deputy General Secretaries, which are the General Secretaries of the regional organisations of the ITUC. The Deputy General Secretaries are elected by the General Council and support the Secretary-General in leading the secretariat (Croucher and Cotton, 2009: 43). They are not allowed to vote at the General Council and the Executive Bureau.

In between Congress meetings, the General Council is the supreme authority and responsible for the activities of the Confederation and the implementation of the decisions and recommendations of the Congress. The GC's 70 members are elected by the Congress with the European trade union centres having the biggest share with 26 members (ITUC, 2010b, 2018c). By contrast, Africa is represented with 11 members, America with 18 and the Asia-Pacific region with 15. The agenda for the GC meetings is prepared by the GS, but any member of the Confederation has the right to put forward suggestions. In addition, the GC carries out administrative tasks such as the preparation of the Congress, which includes the preparation of the agenda, the invitation of members and the review of proposals for agenda items. The GC is supported by the Executive Bureau which meets at least twice every year and deals with all questions of urgency which arise between the meetings of the GC, or which are delegated to it by the GC.

The ITUC also has regional organisations which form 'organic parts' and are determined by the Congress (ITUC, 2018c: 24). These organisations have a certain level of autonomy, but they are responsible for 'promoting the priorities and policies of the Confederation' and they are accountable for their actions to the ITUC (ITUC, 2018c: 24). Currently there are five regional organisations: the Trade Union Confederation of the Americas (TUCA), ITUC Africa, ITUC Asia-Pacific, ITUC PERC (Pan European Regional Council), and the Arab Trade Union Confederation (ATUC). The Middle East has a limited presence, and there is no formal recognition of the All-China Federation of Trade Unions (ACFTU) and the Chinese regional federations and national industrial unions (Croucher and Cotton, 2009). However, the ITUC and most of the GUFs engage in a dialogue with the ACFTU and aim to promote a 'constructive' relationship (Lambert and Webster, 2017; Zajak, 2017). Generally, dominant political systems within the regions and the heterogeneity of member organisations cause power imbalances between and within the regional organisations. The ITUC resembles closely the structure of its predecessor the ICFTU, but it has raised the status of regional secretaries to that of 'deputy general secretary' and the presidents of the regional organisations to 'global vice presidents' (Gumbrell-McCormick, 2013a). In addition to its regional organisations, the ITUC is represented through offices in big cities in strategically important areas: Washington D.C. (ITUC/Global Unions Washington Office), Sarajevo (ITUC South-East European Office), Moscow (ITUC Office for the New Independent States), Geneva (ITUC Geneva Office), and London (Permanent Representative to the International Maritime Organisation).

The headquarters of the ITUC is in Brussels where about 70 officials are employed within different departments exercising representative and administrative functions. These representatives are important connectors between the ITUC and its members because they receive members' views and opinions, develop strategies, and represent member organisations at the global level. For example, the 'Human and Trade Union Rights' department follows the development of workers' rights worldwide, and staff work together with regional coordinators (appointed in each regional organisation) and 'focal points' in order to obtain relevant information. 'Focal points' comprise staff in ITUC member organisations at national level who lead either the legal department or the human and trade union rights department in their organisation. The main tasks of the ITUC department are to analyse information such as reports and messages from ITUC affiliates, and to write to governments and employers in order to raise complaints and to get problems resolved (Interview ITUC05, 2015).

Organisational values and identity

The mission of the ITUC consists in giving effective representation to working people; this and the fact that the organisation is the 'global voice of the world's working people' determine its identity (ITUC, 2019 website[4]). However, the foundation of the ITUC is based on the merger of two organisations including two different identities (religious values of the WCL vs. secularism of the ICFTU), which created a challenge in terms of potential conflicts regarding organisational objectives and approaches (Hyman and Gumbrell-McCormick, 2020; Gumbrell-McCormick, 2013b). Over the years, the ITUC has established its recognition and profile as an important global actor holding a critical perspective and outspoken criticism on issues such as the globalisation process, MNCs, the mainstream neo-liberal economic model, and climate change. In order to achieve its mission, the ITUC follows some central values which are the pillars of its identity and culture, and which are connected to political and economic objectives. Trade union values are 'principles and standards' which 'underpin the structure and strategy of unions' and 'motivate and explain activity' (Burchielli, 2006: 140). The values of the ITUC are described within its constitution; they include the commitment to practical solidarity, the promotion and protection of democracy, the promotion of equality in terms of social and economic development for workers, and the condemnation of all forms of discrimination (ITUC, 2018c). The identity and culture of the ITUC is based on solidarity amongst its affiliates and officials; however, the wide range of national identities of trade union centres and their ideologies make it sometimes difficult to obtain solidarity within specific projects (Stirling, 2010). In fact, the funding of activities of southern trade unions by northern trade unions tends to reinforce organisational differences. Nowadays, 'Southern labour movements increasingly question the use of the ITUC in the representation of their concerns', which makes the building of a joint identity more fragile (Bieler, 2012: 371).

The organisational values guide not only collective behaviour but also the behaviour of individual actors such as ITUC officials. Some trade unionists consider 'class consciousness', which relates to collective struggle and solidarity in the broader sense, as an important characteristic of organisational leaders (Interview BWI, 2009). In comparison to the World Bank and the IMF, the ITUC has no specific code of conduct for staff, but it is assumed that individuals representing trade unions or working for the ITUC act in concert with the universally recognised values and principles relevant to trade unions. This means that they should behave in a solidaristic way with other staff and trade union representatives, and that they should not take advantage of a situation or information.

Organisational knowledge and knowledge management

The ITUC's organisational knowledge is strongly related to the values and the paradigm it follows, which are oriented towards global welfare, human and workers' rights, and a more equal distribution of economic wealth. One of the main tasks of the ITUC in this regard is the intervention with intergovernmental organisations (such as the World Bank and the IMF) 'on issues relating to the recognition of union rights and the respect of international labour standards' (Hennebert and Bourque, 2011: 154). These kinds of regular interventions enable the ITUC to develop expert knowledge regarding the bureaucratic functioning of intergovernmental organisations, their views on political and economic issues, and their activities and development programmes.

Staff of the ITUC tend to come from the developed countries, most of whom have good language skills and higher levels of education, and there is nowadays a tendency for officials to work their way up through the internal hierarchy starting at research positions (Cotton and Gumbrell-McCormick, 2012; Hyman and Gumbrell-McCormick, 2020). In addition, many staff can draw on years of experience of trade union work, such as being involved in collective bargaining or in the organisation of trade union campaigns. A former president of the ITUC, Michael Sommer, worked for example for the post office, gathered experiences at the German Postal Union (DPG), and was strongly involved in the founding process of the German multi-service trade union Ver.di. The ITUC General Secretary Sharan Burrow worked as a teacher and was active in the Australian Education Union (AEU). Since many individual actors working for the ITUC contribute their personal experiences from the national level, international trade unionism can be considered as 'an extension of national experience' (Hyman, 2005: 138). However, in comparison to national trade unionism, and as outlined earlier, international trade unionism is a 'distinctive social phenomenon' which requires a different approach to national level trade unionism (Ibid., 2005: 138).

In comparison to intergovernmental organisations such as the IFIs, which employ several thousand staff in their headquarters, the ITUC employs a relatively small number of staff in its secretariat, which has to deal with a broad range of tasks. In particular, administrative tasks create their own challenges and tend to undermine the capacity of union officials to develop agendas and appropriate strategies for their implementation (Lévesque and Murray, 2002). Depending on the departmental focus, staff follow, for example, discussions and outputs of intergovernmental organisations, such as the economic forecasts of the IMF, and analyse and summarise the information for ITUC affiliates. Furthermore, they provide information about the course and outcomes of campaigns and other collective activities to affiliates and the public on the ITUC website. In 2013, the ITUC launched the publication 'Economic Briefing', which regularly presents outlooks on global economic developments. The briefings address all unionists at the national level, and the Global Unions, and present part of the available explicit knowledge of the ITUC. Since 2014 the ITUC publishes the annual 'Global Rights Index', which is based on a comprehensive data base of workers' rights violations and exposes countries and organisations with poor working conditions. The index aims to serve as a monitoring tool for policy makers and socially responsible investors (ITUC, 2014). In addition, the ITUC supports the website 'Equal Times'[5] which provides information prepared by local journalists on global issues and campaigns about work, politics, and economics. In comparison to the IFIs, the ITUC has a lower turnover of staff and as such, the organisation can also draw on the tacit knowledge of staff for longer periods of time. However, there is as yet no explicit organisational strategy to make more use of available tacit knowledge or to organise it in a more strategic way so that it is available within the ITUC at all times.

What power does the ITUC have?

The power of the ITUC is clearly defined by its representation of trade union centres around the world and the weight of its membership. The strong foothold through national trade unions centres provides the ITUC with representativity and visibility at global level, although in comparison to other international actors, the ITUC's financial resources are limited. The ITUC depends on the payment of membership fees and every year the GC determines the affiliation fees of which Germany, the USA, Canada, Japan, and the Nordic countries provide about 80 per cent (Croucher and Cotton, 2009). The ITUC constitution stipulates that the minimum membership fee per affiliated organisation is €100 annually. In 2018, the actual income of the ITUC based on affiliation fees accounted for more than €12 million (ITUC, 2019a). Affiliation fees must be paid by national unions in relation to the number of affiliates; furthermore, these fees are defined in relation to the national income of each country. In 2009, trade unions from the richest countries paid almost €200 per thousand members and unions from the poorest countries about €3 per thousand members (Cotton and Gumbrell-McCormick, 2012). The weighting of membership fees has resulted in the problem that 'any fall in paying membership in the wealthiest countries has a disproportionate impact on the resources of the Global Unions' (Ibid., 2012: 714).

When the ITUC increases fees, it is a common practice that members report lower membership figures to avoid higher payments to the ITUC (Croucher and Cotton, 2009). This is partly due to the problem of a declining union membership which ITUC affiliates face at the national level, but also because national trade unions tend to have a stronger focus on intra-regional relationships than on international work (Cotton and Gumbrell-McCormick, 2012). For that reason, the ITUC nowadays requires their affiliates to submit their 'paying membership' numbers only and not the 'declaring membership' numbers for the calculation of the affiliation fees (Interview ITUC05, 2015). Crises such as the international financial crisis in 2008 created some additional challenges for some of the ITUC members to pay their fees on time. The 'paying membership' of the affiliates determines their number of delegates by which they are represented at the

Congress. Some affiliates are also stronger donors than others, allowing them to exercise their influence through funds, such as the Solidarity Fund and the Development Aid Fund to which members can contribute on a voluntary basis. The first receives its contributions mainly from Germany and Japan and the second from the Dutch government, the ILO, and Dutch and Swedish trade unions (Cotton and Gumbrell-McCormick, 2012). These funds are 'increasingly dependent on the ability to show concrete outputs and benefits for the donor countries' (Cotton and Gumbrell-McCormick, 2012: 715).

Due to the limited financial resources, the main power sources of the ITUC are its legitimacy, which it gains through election processes, and the power to mobilise and to unite the 'democratic and independent forces of world trade unionism' (ITUC, 2010b: 5). Collective power determines the sanction power of the organisation and is based on solidarity amongst workers and trade unions worldwide. This solidarity can be challenged by the different cultural and political backgrounds of ITUC affiliates, which can lead to different views concerning the priority of issues and activities. For many national trade unions and trade union centres, economic issues relating to national industries and collective bargaining have priority over international issues. The ITUC, however, is more focused on political-diplomatic issues such as the development of policy statements to the annual and spring meetings of the IFIs which the ITUC drafts on behalf of the Global Unions.

Regarding the individual level, the democratic structure of the ITUC and its strong organisational values arguably limit the exploitation of organisational roles by individual actors. However, there are power imbalances due to the concentration of knowledge and expertise within the ITUC headquarters in Brussels, where senior officers, for example, control and distribute information and have significant power with regard to agenda setting (Croucher and Cotton, 2009). The concentration of knowledge and funds at the headquarters results in a situation where 'regional organizations have tended to act as recipients of policies or resources, rather than initiators' (Cotton and Gumbrell-McCormick, 2012: 714).

Organisational change and learning

Since its foundation at the beginning of the 20th century, the international trade union movement has experienced several structural changes with implications for its identity and mission. More than two decades ago, the trade unions acknowledged that 'globalization is a new paradigm which demands new strategies, tactics and organizational modalities' (Munck, 2010: 219). The merger of the ICFTU and the WCL in 2006 led to an increase in collective power in terms of membership, but only to a limited increase in financial resources as many members were from poor regions. In addition, the size and the variety of its members make it more difficult for the ITUC to change and to quickly develop adequate answers to new problems and situations. One of the challenges for the ITUC is to anticipate problems and 'to frame coherent policies; and to implement these effectively' (Hyman, 2007: 198). However, in order to resolve anticipated problems such as the loss of jobs during the financial crisis in 2008 which the ITUC predicted early, the global trade union organisations depend on the cooperation with other stakeholders, including governments and intergovernmental organisations.

Learning within the ITUC is driven by individual actors, but less so within the most important decision-making body which is the Congress. Regarding the latter, representatives of trade union centres often exhibit a very diplomatic form of behaviour and contentious issues are rarely raised publicly (Croucher and Cotton, 2009). Research and cooperation with other trade union bodies, such as the European Trade Union Confederation (ETUC) and the European Trade Union Institute (ETUI), also play a role, although the ETUI's research focuses on EU member states and cannot provide the ITUC with research for other continents (Interview ETUC, 2017).

The ITUC does not promote an explicit learning culture like the WB, but its democratic structure provides a favourable context for learning. ITUC officials have diverse backgrounds and experiences which allow them to think in reflexive and imaginative ways and to develop new strategies and activities (Hyman, 2007). Officials working at the ITUC secretariat reflect their own experiences and get input from member organisations which provide them with insights as regards political and economic developments at the national level. However, in this context, the routinisation of procedures which helps ITUC officials to cope with administrative tasks and to resolve problems (Howard, 2007) can be a hindrance to innovative thinking.

In comparison to other organisations, at the ITUC, change and learning are less influenced by leadership. The President and the General Secretary of the ITUC do not influence the general political orientation of the organisation or its way to adapt to changing processes, rather they have representative and administrative roles which are connected to the commonly agreed and accepted organisational values.

The Global Union Federations

The GUFs represent national trade unions from the private and public sectors at the international level. Each GUF represents a different sector and has different issues of priority, which are to a large extent determined by their members (Interview IMF-GUF [*now IndustriALL*], 2008). In the broadest sense, each GUF is a kind of 'docking station' for different sector trade unions (Traub-Merz and Eckl, 2007: 5). All GUFs noted a growth of membership since the 1990s when the political division into East and West came to an end. Through their geographical expansion, the GUFs became for the first time real global players and these structural changes helped to 'strengthen the representativeness of federations and enhance their legitimacy as the global voice of the interests of individual trade unions' (Müller et al., 2010: 5).

Many GUFs deal with multinational companies and try to 'achieve material gains for their members' (Abbott, 2011: 162). Over time the number of GUFs has decreased as some of them have merged to form larger organisations. Two of the biggest mergers led to the establishment of UNI in 2000 and IndustriALL in June 2012. The main goal of such mergers consists in gaining more weight in influencing employer organisations and governments and having more strength and building power across the supply chain at the global level. UNI was created

Table 3.1 Global Union Federations

GUF	Workers represented	Sectors
BWI (Geneva)	Around 12 million in 130 countries	Building, building materials, wood, forestry, allied industries
EI (Brussels)	Around 30 million in 172 countries	Teacher, education employees
IAEA		Arts and entertainment sector
IFJ (Brussels)	600,000 in more than 140 countries	Journalists
IndustriALL Global Union (merger of IMF, ICEM, ITGLWF) (Geneva)	Over 50 million in 140 countries	Extraction of oil and gas, mining, generation and distribution of electric power, metal production, shipbuilding, automotive, electronics, chemicals, rubber, pulp and paper, building material, textiles, garments, leather and footwear, environmental services
ITF (London)	18.5 million in 147 countries	Transport industry: seafarers, dockers, civil aviation, railways, road transport
IUF (Geneva)	Over ten million in 127 countries	Agriculture and plantations, preparation and manufacture of food and beverages, hotels, restaurants and catering services, tobacco processing
PSI (Geneva)	20 million in 163 countries	Personnel employed in local, national and regional governments: social services, health care, municipal and community services, central government and public utilities
UNI (Nyon)	20 million in more than 150 countries	Cleaning and security, commerce, finance, gaming, hair and beauty, media, entertainment and arts, post and logistics, sports, social insurance, temporary and agency workers, tourism industries

Source: Global Union Federation websites, 2019

through the merger of four international organisations: the International Federation of Employees, Technicians and Managers (FIET), the Media and Entertainment International (MEI), the International Graphical Federation (IGF), and the Communications International (CI). Nowadays UNI represents more than 20 million service sector workers around the world.

> So UNI was kind of the first on the mega scale of restructuring with the creation of UNI Global Union, . . . this acted as a catalyst, it gave pause for people to reflect on what direction they were going in, and when affiliates of international organisations saw that there was this effort away from unnecessary duplication and so forth they quite liked the look of it, and as a result these changes kind of unfolded during the course of the years.
>
> (Interview UNI, 2019)

IndustriALL brings together the International Federation of Chemical, Energy, Mine and General Workers' Unions (ICEM), the International Metal Workers' Federation (IMF) and the International Textile, Garment and Leather Workers' Federation (ITGLWF) and represents more than 50 million workers. Currently there are nine GUFs in total. They include the International Transport Federation (ITF), the Building and Wood Workers' International (BWI), the IndustriALL Global Union (IndustriALL), the International Union of Food, Agricultural, Hotel, Restaurant, Catering, Tobacco and Allied Workers' Association (IUF), the Union Network International (UNI), the International Federation of Journalists (IFJ), and the International Arts and Entertainment Alliance (IAEA). Most of these organisations focus on the private sector except for Education International (EI) and the Public Services International (PSI) which deal with the public sector. The following table provides an overview of the sectors which the different organisations represent and their membership numbers.

Organisational structure

The headquarters offices of most of the GUFs are in Geneva or in Brussels, only the ITF has its headquarters in London. The headquarters offices employ different numbers of staff and are organised by the topics that each GUF is focused on. All GUFs have 'well-developed governance systems and all maintain strict formal decision-making procedures based on their rules or "statutes"' (Croucher and Cotton, 2009: 41). Every GUF has its own constitution and standing orders which determine the governing bodies, the rights and obligations of members, and procedures for election processes. The governing bodies of each GUF differ regarding their names, but generally organisational structures are very similar amongst these organisations.

The highest and key decision-making authority in each of the GUFs is the Congress, which meets every four or five years and determines organisational priorities, long-term aims, strategies, and organisational rules. It has the authority to amend the constitution and oversees the election of trade union officials including the President, the General Secretary, the Vice Presidents, and the members of different committees. Meanwhile the President chairs the meetings of the Congress and is the principal representative of the organisation, the General Secretary is the principal spokesperson and has an executive role, leading the headquarters office (secretariat) supported by members of staff. The responsibilities include administration and management tasks such as handling of staff issues and the preparation of meetings. The administration of finances and the managing authority exercised by the General Secretary are overseen by an auditor committee which is elected by the Congress.

Furthermore, the Congress makes decisions on motions and resolutions and determines the annual affiliation fees, which are calculated in relation to membership figures. Every member which pays the affiliation fee has participation rights and is entitled to send delegates to the Congress, whereby depending on each GUF, the number of delegates is determined by the constitution or by the affiliated organisations themselves. For example, trade unions affiliated to the ITF can send up to 23 delegates, and organisations affiliated to the EI can send a maximum of 50 delegates depending on their organisational size (ITF, 2018; EI,

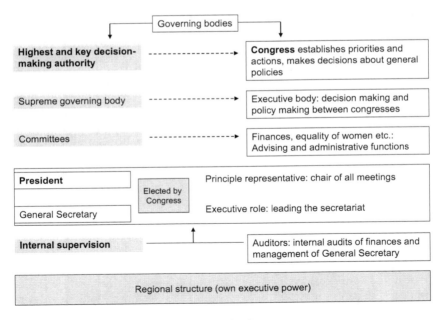

Figure 3.2 Formal Structure of a GUF (generalised)

Source: Own illustration based on the constitutions of different GUFs

2019). In the case of the BWI and IndustriALL, affiliated trade unions determine the number of their representatives. The relatively high number of participants at congresses and the infrequency of meetings arguably result in a situation where the Congress is not a forum for effective strategy development (Croucher and Cotton, 2009).

Some GUFs have a governing body which is responsible for decision-making and policies in the periods between congresses. The BWI, for example, names this governing body the 'World Council' (BWI, 2017), and it is responsible for the general policy in the period between congresses. It is chaired by the BWI President, meets once a year, and it elects the regional Vice Presidents and the members of the 'World Board'. The latter is the executive body of the BWI, which is responsible for the implementation of decisions from the Congress and the World Council, administration and affiliation issues, the annual budget, and the planning of yearly activities. Other GUFs, such as EI and IndustriALL, do not have such an additional decision-making body apart from the Congress but only an executive body. In addition to its governing bodies, each GUF appoints different committees which, for example, are responsible for finances, the equality of women, and advice regarding constitutional matters.

The executive bodies of the GUFs are supported by regional offices, which develop policies on their own and have an advisory role to the respective GUF's executive body as regards policies and activities undertaken in the region. These strategies of regionalisation and decentralisation of the GUFs 'reflect the differentiation and pluralisation of members' interests and needs which have gone hand in hand with geographical expansion' (Müller et al., 2010: 6). The regional structures are developed in conformity with the respective constitution of the GUF concerned and in most GUFs the regions are Africa, North America and the Caribbean, the Middle East, Asia and the Pacific, Europe, and Latin America. In addition, IndustriALL divides Africa into North Africa and Sub-Saharan Africa, and the ITF includes the Arab World. Each region has its own governing bodies including executive bodies and committees which are provided with executive power.

Organisational identity

The identity of each GUF is shaped by its membership, the mission to defend the rights of workers, and the sector within which they are active. As one of the GUF representatives stated, 'we are what our affiliates want us to be' (Interview IMF-GUF, 2008). However, the members of the GUFs differ in their organisational and formal decision-making structures, and cross-national differences influence the perceptions as regards internal union democracy and the distribution of power:

> In most unions, organizational structures exist at workplace level, but patterns
> of authority between such structures and the national, regional or local union

are complex and shifting; an added complexity in most European countries is the relationship between workplace union representation and works councils.
(Gumbrell-McCormick and Hyman, 2019: 101)

Generally, the GUFs are very diverse in terms of their governance arrangements and their ideological and political orientation (Ford and Gillan, 2015). Furthermore, all GUFs vary in terms of the issues they give priority in relation to their sector, although with regard to general policies, collaboration between the different international trade union organisations and the umbrella federation, the ITUC, is considered as indispensable.

Like at the ITUC, the organisational culture of all the GUFs is shaped by the values of democracy, solidarity, and equality. These collective organisational values also guide individual behaviour although there is no explicit organisational code of conduct for staff. Many trade union officials have a practical grounding and relationship to these values as they have a lot of sector work experience and 'enormous understanding of particular industry-sectors' (Croucher and Cotton, 2009: 44). In more general terms, democracy refers to internal democratic procedures, the strengthening of democratic trade unions worldwide and the promotion of democracy through trade unions. In relation to internal democracy, the question arises to what extent and how international trade union organisations, which represent 'meta-organizations', can be democratic as their membership is very heterogeneous in terms of geography, resources and traditional industrial relation systems, as well as their perceptions on tactics and strategies to exert influence (Hyman and Gumbrell-McCormick, 2020). In this context, Hyman and Gumbrell-McCormick stress the importance of transparency, accountability and 'opportunities for effective participation' (Ibid., 2020: 268). Furthermore, the GUFs promote participation through the creation of global and regional solidarity networks, and they foster solidarity amongst their members, for example, regarding the implementation of Global Framework Agreements (GFA). GFAs are a form of a voluntary agreement between an MNC and one or more Global Unions and arguably offer a possibility to regulate the behaviour of MNCs (Gumbrell-McCormick, 2008). Although these agreements are not comparable to 'detailed collective agreements', they are 'enabling frameworks built around commitments by the corporations concerned to implement and respect the core labour standards of the International Labour Organization (ILO)' (TUAC, 2005: 18). Meanwhile such agreements require the active participation of GUF members, they also foster ongoing connections between the GUFs and therewith across sectors. An example is the renewal of the GFA signed by the BWI, IndustriAll, and PSI with ENGIE, a French multinational, which was first signed in 2010 and renewed in January 2022.

Organisational knowledge and learning

The GUFs 'represent workers in their market role and seek to improve their bargaining power as sellers of labour-power' (Munck, 2010: 227). In this respect, the organisations have increasingly orientated themselves around the activities of multinational companies and their global supply chains. They provide support with regard to defending existing trade union rights and promoting solidarity amongst national affiliates, sharing information, organising meetings and cross-border union campaigns, and lobbying national governments. The GUFs try to adapt to the challenges which they encounter in the respective sectors, although in the view of one trade union representative a less 'conservative' approach and a stronger anticipation of future developments in industrial sectors could help to develop strategies in a more anticipatory and proactive way (Interview IFJ, 2008). The GUFs have a broad expertise as regards legal and economic issues, which is developed by their respective secretariat, and which arises from practical experiences regarding company networks, GFAs and campaigning. In particular, in relation to multinational companies the GUFs must regularly 'improve their knowledge of the internal dynamics of large corporations' (TUAC, 2005: 14). This specific knowledge can provide the GUFs with an initiator role in respect of trade union policy at the global level (Cotton and Gumbrell-McCormick, 2012).

In order that the GUFs can do their work effectively, they rely on the contribution of specific knowledge by their affiliates and from the regions. The staff of the secretariats analyses and reflects on the data and information they receive from member organisations and other organisations, as well as on the success of organisational activities. This is not an easy task considering the limited number of staff within the secretariats in comparison to the velocity of economic and political changes at the global level and increasing administration tasks. Even though the number of staff varies in relation to the size of a GUF, most GUFs face the problem that they are understaffed. The small number of staff in comparison to the number of tasks means that staff of the GUFs tend to draw on 'traditional routines and practices' (Müller et al., 2010: 7), which can make organisational changes and the testing of new ideas and approaches more difficult.

The core activities of the GUFs include the implementation of training and education programmes and the provision of information services for their members (Müller et al., 2010). The provision of these education and information services requires that staff of the GUFs are always well informed and that they follow the latest economic and political developments within the industrial sectors and at the global level. For example, the ITF regularly commissions research reports and 'aims to step up its monitoring and gathering of data on job losses and union strategies to combat them, including the setup of an ITF "hotline" and a website with down-loadable resources' (Global Unions, 2009: 35). However, in comparison to the IFIs, the trade unions are 'dwarfed' in terms of their research capacity and in particular 'economic research', which is because of their limited financial resources (Interview AFL-CIO, 2017). The research and publication sections of the GUFs are much smaller than they are at the IFIs, which is largely due to their limited resources. Explicit knowledge is mainly disseminated to affiliates and the interested public via internet through websites, social networks (Facebook) and blogs, as well as through microblogging (Twitter). In their function as 'infor-mation service providers' (Müller et al., 2010: 9), each GUF provides informa-tion on their website which relates to the latest events within sectors, including amongst other things, the violation of workers' rights and violence against trade union leaders. There is also information available about more general issues such as children rights, gender equality, and migration, as well as information on cam-paigns and solidarity appeals organised by the GUF or the regions. One of the challenges of the GUFs is to make tacit knowledge of trade union officials and workers within their own organisations accessible. Generally, democratic proce-dures and participation rights within the GUFs, supported by the use of com-munication technology, are a good basis for their members to participate actively in policy discussions and to express their concerns and ideas in relation to specific issues. Within meetings, storytelling is 'an integral part of information-sharing and comparing of experiences' (Cooper, 2006: 40). In this respect, the GUFs offer a favourable context for individual and organisational learning as informa-tion exchange enables mutual learning and the 'imitation of proven practices' between the GUFs (Müller et al., 2010: 10).

Power and influence

One of the main power resources of the GUFs is their representativeness and 'their legitimacy as the global voice of the interests of individual trade unions', which they achieve through a growing membership and geographical spread (Müller et al., 2010: 5). At the global level, the GUFs have a 'monopoly position' in the sectors they represent (Ibid., 2010: 5), and as the former General Secretary of UNI reflected:

> We punch above our weight, there's no question, when you look at the extent of the work that we do, the depth of our engagement, the issues that we're dealing with, it's a miracle every day frankly. We're the pitchfork guys, the pitchfork movement, in a very challenging era, politically, economically and socially, and we've done an enormous amount to prepare ourselves for the future, to bring about structural change.
>
> (Interview UNI, 2019)

However, in terms of financial resources and personnel, the power of the GUFs has always been limited. The gradual decline of trade union membership at the national level and challenges in organising workers has further aggravated the financial situation of the GUFs. These trends have 'been reflected in a reduc-tion of payments to the Global Unions, and often an increased incidence of late payment of affiliation fees' (Cotton and Gumbrell-McCormick, 2012: 7). Some member organisations, however, have the capacity to make higher contributions to their respective GUF, and as a result, they have potentially more influence with regard to the agenda setting and intra-organisational decision-making. The fact that the European region has historically had far greater resources than elsewhere can also create problems for the GUFs as there is often a tendency for European trade unions to focus on regional issues at the expense of the international work of the GUFs (Cotton and Gumbrell-McCormick, 2012). These power imbalances at the collective level are reflected at the individual level to some extent where leading roles are frequently taken on by trade union officials from developed countries (Cotton and Gumbrell-McCormick, 2012).

The disposition of national trade unions to support international work is influenced by their own national conditions and organisational interests (Ghigliani, 2005). Some national trade unions, for example, struggle with an unfavourable political environment which requires them to put a lot of resources into their work at the national level (Müller et al., 2010: 5). One strategy to tackle resource problems and to concentrate collective power has been for some GUFs to form mergers and to expand its presence at regional level. For example, UNI has an extensive global reach which is supported by strong regional organisations, and the headquarters-office in Brussels has grown in size over the years. In addition, UNI established a strong connection with workers in the different sectors which the organisation represents:

> What UNI did was to establish what we called 'sector global unions', and that gives you a kind of industrial discipline, and an institutional discipline, and it gives you power because you're talking to the unions who are active in the industries where you're present. . . . So I think the power comes from the membership and the membership has to be able to see and anchor in the organisation where they are.
>
> (Interview UNI, 2019)

The sector-related work helps UNI to support membership growth within sectors, to engage with members as well as the development and application of instruments such as GFAs. UNI developed, for example, the 'Breaking Through' organising strategy which is supported by an organising fund. In addition to internal power foundations, there are external influences which enable GUFs to gain further ground in terms of impact. One of them is the growing sensitivity of governments and consumers with regard to unethical behaviour of businesses which helps to promote the power leverage of the GUFs.

The Trade Union Advisory Committee to the OECD

The TUAC is an important interface for trade unions dealing with the OECD and it works closely together with the ITUC, the GUFs, the ETUC, and the ILO. It ensures the input of these organisations into the sectoral work of the OECD, coordinates the input of the trade unions to G8 economic summits and employment conferences, and it informs its affiliates about what the OECD is working on or planning to do. The TUAC considers itself as 'sort of continuing point of pressure', in particular as there are issues on which trade unions do not agree with the OECD (Interview TUAC01, 2009).

Organisational structure

The TUAC was originally set up in 1948 as part of the Marshall Plan structure providing a consultative mechanism for governments. After the establishment of the Organisation for Economic Co-Operation and Development (OECD) in 1961, the TUAC continued its work of representing trade union views from the industrialised countries. During the Cold War, it represented anti-communist and Christian unions, the then so-called 'free trade unions', and nowadays it represents most of the national trade union confederations (58 in total) from OECD countries.

The TUAC Plenary is the general assembly and the formal governing body of the TUAC. It meets twice a year in Paris and the meetings are attended by the representatives of the TUAC affiliates and representatives of the Global Unions. The participants discuss and approve policy statements as well as the TUAC's future work and priorities. The input for the Plenary is prepared by working groups, which also prepare trade union positions for consultation with the OECD. The Plenary elects the TUAC officers, the General Secretary, the President, and the three Vice Presidents, whereby the seats of the Vice Presidents are traditionally allocated to Japan (RENGO), the Nordic trade unions, and to the Christian trade unions. The permanent secretary in Paris has a small number of staff (officers) including the General Secretary. The majority of the officers are policy advisors, and they focus on a broad range of issues including economic policy, employment, labour market policy, trade and investment, taxation and pension funds. The General Secretary of the TUAC has taken part in the dialogue and the high-level meetings with the IFIs since the early 1990s. This is because many issues which are covered by the TUAC in discussions at the OECD are also relevant in the context of the dialogue between the IFIs and the Global Unions, such as international finance and the promotion of inclusive growth (Interview TUAC01, 2009). The TUAC is exclusively funded by its members who pay fees in proportion to their respective membership.

Organisational objectives and achievements

The TUAC has two objectives, which can also be described as a 'two-way-function' (Interview TUAC02, 2019). On the one hand, it has an 'advocacy function' representing the interests of workers and the labour movement to the OECD, and on the other hand, it has a 'research function' and feeds information back to the labour movement and its members. The OECD is a complex organisation with about 200 committees and working groups and the TUAC participates regularly in around 60 committees and working parties (sub-committees) on topics which are particularly relevant for trade unions. One of the committees which is of strategic importance is the 'Employment, Labour and Social Affairs Committee' (ELSAC). The committee develops OECD recommendations about labour market reforms, and it defines the OECD position as regards labour market institutions, collective bargaining and the minimum wage (Interview TUAC02, 2019).

ELSAC oversees the work of the 'Directorate for Employment, Labour and Social Affairs' (ELS) which 'leads the OECD's work on employment, social policies, international migration and health' (OECD, 2017). ELSAC has meetings twice a year during which senior officials from all OECD countries, as well as observers from other countries, share their experiences and views. One of the ELSAC working parties prepares the 'OECD Employment Outlook', which is a key publication for the trade unions and the TUAC follows the preparation and drafting of this annual report closely (Interview TUAC02, 2019).

Furthermore, the 'Economic Policy Committee' (EPC) of the OECD is important for the TUAC. The EPC works closely with the OECD Economics Department, and it collects and publishes macroeconomic forecast data and monitors economic policies of OECD member states and publishes the 'OECD Economic Outlook'. Both publications, the 'OECD Economic Outlook' and the 'OECD Employment Outlook', often disseminate different messages; this is partly because of the limited information exchange between the different working parties which are responsible for drafting these reports. The Employment Outlook report is often more in favour of trade unions and collective bargaining than the Economic Outlook report (Interview TUAC02, 2019). These differences, which can be considered as the result of an existing 'silo mentality' at the OECD, present a 'risk but also as an opportunity' for trade unions:

> (. . .) what we are asking for is very simple, it's to move away from the individualisation of risks and reversing the trend towards a more collective organisation, collective protection of employment, bargaining, pensions, health and so on.
>
> (Interview TUAC02, 2019)

In the last decade, the TUAC has had a notable impact on some OECD publications and reports. For example, since the 2008 international crisis, the TUAC and its members have brought the inequality debate to the centre stage of the OECD, and the importance of the topic has become reflected in several OECD reports, such as 'Growing Unequal? Income Distribution and Poverty in OECD Countries' (2008), 'Divided we stand: Why inequalities keep rising' (2011), and 'Under pressure: The squeezed middle class' (2019). From the TUAC's point of view, these are positive developments:

> (. . .) this descriptive exercise that's new, that's very good. Obviously, when it comes to the policy recommendations and policy findings then what the

OECD comes up with, we're still not there.(. . .), it's always the thinking about individual empowerment not collective empowerment, you can see the ideological foundation of that. In the last two or three years at least, our impact has been to support this descriptive exercise at least, realise, at least acknowledge, that nobody has a tool right now, is far away from coming up with a definitive solution to address the cancer, which is attacking, undermining our society, which is 'inequalities'.

(Interview TUAC02, 2019)

The TUAC and its members also contributed to the drafting of the new 'OECD Due Diligence Guidance for Responsible Business Conduct' (2018) which requires MNCs to apply due diligence principles in the supply chain and to identify and address risks relating to human and labour rights. The guidance can be considered as a 'fundamental shift' for the OECD as it acknowledges that MNCs have responsibilities beyond their countries of origins and with regard to the supply chains. Furthermore, in 2019 the OECD adopted the 'Recommendation of the Council on Artificial Intelligence (AI)'. The contribution of the TUAC consisted in raising awareness regarding the impact of artificial intelligence on the employment relationship and to ensure the inclusion of a paragraph on the fair transition for workers:

> Governments should take steps, including through social dialogue, to ensure a fair transition for workers as AI is deployed, such as through training programmes along the working life, support for those affected by displacement, and access to new opportunities in the labour market.

(OECD, 2019a: 9)

OECD policy recommendations on labour markets fall into the category of general recommendations. General recommendations can involve OECD member governments and bind member states, or they are prepared under the sole responsibility of the OECD secretariat without any legal implications. An example of the latter is the revised 'OECD Jobs Strategy' (OECD, 2018) which provides a 'policy blueprint' on how labour markets should be organised (Interview TUAC02, 2019). In relation to the jobs strategy, the TUAC achieved a more positive view on sector-level collective bargaining within the OECD and challenged the dominant favourable perception of company level bargaining. However, the revised Jobs Strategy does not include a formal monitoring mechanism for the implementation of the recommendations. The Jobs Strategy provides a framework document which is closely connected with the annual 'Employment Outlook', and although both documents are not legally binding for OECD members, they have in common a normative impact because of the OECD's authoritative nature and legitimacy.

The OECD also exercises some direct influence at country level through the mandatory economic performance reviews. These reviews, which are conducted by the OECD 'Economic and Development Review Committee' (EDRC), are comparable to the IMF Article IV consultations. The EDRC surveys the economy of the OECD member countries and nonmember countries and develops recommendations based on the findings. In recent years, the reviews have been extended to Brazil, China, India, Indonesia, Russia, and South Africa.[6] Labour markets, social security, and public spending are amongst the assessed policy areas, and the TUAC argues that labour markets should be assessed in line with the OECD jobs strategy (Interview TUAC02, 2019).

The TUAC works closely with its affiliates and partners (the ITUC, the GUFs, the ETUC, and ETUI) and all draft papers and positions are jointly agreed. For example, the TUAC took part in the stocktaking exercise on the 'OECD Guidelines for MNCs' in 2021–2022 and provided different inputs. In this context, the TUAC conducted two consultations with national and global trade union organisations on the thematic chapters of the guidelines and the National Contact Point (NCP) procedures (OECD, 2022). Generally, the TUAC involves the ETUC and the ETUI and on many occasions a staff member from the ETUI joins TUAC round tables for example. From the perspective of the ETUC, there is a significant cooperation with the TUAC, in particular with regard to research and analyses in relation to macroeconomic policies such as public investment and wage increases:

> We still have a significant gap between productivity developments and real wages developments in all the European countries, and so this is a very good basis for us to argue for a wage increase, a general wage increase, in the European countries. Everything in this regard comes from the TUAC and the OECD. So, we really have some helpful pieces of research and other figures coming from them that are really useful for us to back our policy.
>
> (Interview ETUC, 2017)

About some topics, such as competition, tax, and corporate governance, the TUAC takes the lead in defining a general trade union position. Topics which are considered as very political and contentious to some extent, such as trade investment, the focus is on consolidating the work done by different trade union organisations. Furthermore, the TUAC considers it as its task to ensure that 'whatever the OECD does that it respects the ILO definitions' (Interview TUAC02, 2019). There is no institutional link between the OECD and the ILO and both organisations apply a different approach regarding employment, which manifests in an economic approach (OECD) versus a rights/social justice approach (ILO). However, joint work between both organisations can help to promote and consolidate a rights-based approach to labour markets.

Notes

1 Source: World Bank (2019) http://www.worldbank.org/en/about/partners/civil-society#2
2 The first international trade union 'umbrella' organisation was the 'International Trade Secretariat of National Trade Union Centre' (ITSNTUC) which was founded in 1913.

Later it was renamed as the 'International Federation of Trade Unions' (IFTU). The IFTU was the forerunner of the 'World Federation of Trade Unions' (WFTU). The 'World Confederation of Labour' (WCL) was established in 1920 under the name of the 'International Federation of Christian Trade Unions' (IFCTU) and presented an alternative to the secular IFTU (Gottfurcht, 1962; Carew et al., 2000).

3 Source: ITUC (2021) https://www.ituc-csi.org/about-us?lang=en
4 Source: ITUC (2019) https://www.ituc-csi.org/about-us?lang=en
5 Source: Equal Times (2021) http://www.equaltimes.org/about-us
6 Source: OECD (2021) https://www.oecd.org/economy/surveys/

4 The IFIs – The World Bank Group and the IMF

The World Bank Group (WBG) and the IMF belong to the group of intergovernmental organisations which have become central actors in international politics acting as 'agents of global change' (Carbone, 2007: 180). Both organisations have played an important role in governing the international economy and promoting development since the post-World War II period (Chorev and Babb, 2009). They were founded with the objective of providing stability to the global economic and financial system and global public goods (GPGs) for people across the world (Wouters and Odermatt, 2014). A further objective was to offer governments the possibility to participate in activities 'that required some separation from domestic politics in order to generate legitimacy and trust' (Martinez-Diaz, 2008: 7).

Governments are both founders and members of the WBG and the IMF. Although governments can be divided into money lenders and money borrowers, all member governments are shareholders of these organisations (Phillips, 2009). The level of monetary contribution which member governments are able to provide to the WBG and the IMF determines their political weight within these organisations and their influence on decision-making. Given the dependence of the IFIs on member government financial contributions, one might assume that governments would be able to limit the sovereignty of the IFIs as corporate social actors. However, the IFIs do have some autonomy and they are not fully controlled by shareholders, which also means that they do not necessarily do what their creators originally intended them to do (Barnett and Finnemore, 1999). In this respect the IFIs can be considered as sovereign corporate social actors. They have their own culture and agenda (Barnett and Finnemore, 1999), authority and competence (Oestreich, 2007; Barnett and Finnemore, 2004) and they 'exercise power as they constitute and construct the social world' (Barnett and Finnemore, 1999: 700).

The IFIs have a normative influence within the system of global governance and on their member governments, which is mainly centred on the 'coercive diffusion of neoliberal economic policies' (Torfason and Ingram, 2010: 357). The IMF, for example, provides information about certain norms such as 'austerity' and has the 'hands-on expertise required to establish structures of conformity with those norms' (Ibid., 2010: 357). After the outbreak of the international financial crisis in 2008, many European governments needed external financial support to rescue their banking and financial services industries. Those countries requiring help have not been able to avoid the policy advice of the 'Troika', that is the European Commission (EC), the IMF, and the European Central Bank (ECB). The advice has usually included the administration and implementation of austerity measures at the national level. The international financial and economic crisis, and the support provided by the Troika in some European countries in the years following the crisis, reflected a loss of influence of national governments in terms of shaping their own national policies and institutions. The impact on labour market institutions in particular tended to promote the weakening of employment protection and labour rights, which in turn has had and still has a negative effect on national and international trade union organisations.

The following subchapters describe and analyse some of the organisational characteristics of the World Bank, the IFC, and the IMF which are important in relation to the dialogue with the Global Unions. Although both the World Bank and the IFC belong to the World Bank Group, they have different objectives, target groups, structures and identities, which means that an explicit differentiation of these organisations is necessary.

The World Bank

The WB is at the heart of the WBG and is made up of two organisations: the International Bank for Reconstruction and Development (IBRD), which was originally created to help re-build Europe after World War II, and the International Development Association (IDA). The IDA was founded in 1960 as a result of the demands of a growing group of underdeveloped countries and was later incorporated into the structure of the IBRD (Darrow, 2003). Currently the IBRD has 189 member countries and the IDA 173 member countries. The IBRD is generally referred to as the World Bank and is a central focus for the study because of its direct relations with the Global Unions. In contrast to the WB, which lends to governments, the International Finance Corporation (IFC), which has 184 member countries, works directly with the private sector (World Bank, 2011a).

The Multilateral Investment Guarantee Agency (MIGA) and the International Centre for the Settlement of Investment Disputes (ICSID) complement the work of the World Bank. MIGA promotes foreign direct investment in developing countries and the ICSID is an autonomous international arbitration institution which deals with international investment disputes. However, neither of these two organisations plays a role in the dialogue with the Global Unions.

The members of the WBG and the IMF, which are also referred to as the 'shareholders', are national governments. In order to become a member of the World Bank a country has to apply for membership to the IMF. When a country applies to the IMF, it has to provide data about its economy which will be compared with other member countries which are of similar size. Depending on the amount of a country's financial subscription to the IMF, a quota is assigned to that country which determines its voting power within the IMF and the number of shares it has in the WB (IMF, 2019, website[1]). A member country's quota reflects its relative position in the world economy. Currently the largest donor governments of the World Bank which have the greatest shares of voting power are the USA, Japan, China, Germany, France, and the United Kingdom. Despite the 2016 voting reforms at the IMF, which provided China with a more favourable position, the G7 countries continue to dominate policies in the IFIs. In particular, the veto power of the USA over many major decisions and the under-representation of smaller and poor countries raises questions about democratic decision-making and legitimacy of the WBG (Bretton Woods Project, 2019a).

The objectives of the World Bank are focused around providing financial and technical support to developing countries for public sector projects such as investments in infrastructure, education, and financial and private sector development. The IBRD focuses on middle-income countries and the IDA focuses on the poorest countries worldwide. Both WB organisations support development projects in the public sector, and they work together with the central bank in a given country or a comparable national agency. The World Bank uses three lending instruments: Investment Project Financing (IPF), Development Policy Financing (DPF),[2] and Programme-for-Results (P4R) (Peck, 2012; Eurodad, 2019). Investment lending covers the largest part of WB lending. DPF, which replaced structural adjustment lending in 2004, makes up about one-quarter of World Bank lending and has been heavily criticised by external stakeholders such as trade unions due to the conditions attached to the loans and grants. In the past, these conditions included, for example, economic policy reforms such as privatisation of state-owned assets and trade liberalisation, which often have a negative impact on the poorest people in society (Peck, 2012; Eurodad, 2006). Eurodad (2019) more recently examined the conditions attached to DPFs and found evidence that loan conditions reflect the WB's 'own strategic approaches and ideological preferences', such as by promoting and enhancing the role of the private sector (Eurodad, 2019: 1).

Organisational structure

The structure of the World Bank is made up of its organisational governing bodies and its technocratic apparatus. The latter includes departments and regional offices which are responsible for the daily business of the organisation.

The main governing body and organisational supreme authority within the WB is the Board of Governors. All member governments are represented within the Board, either through their finance ministers or through their development ministers. The six largest shareholders are mainly represented by their finance ministers. Only Germany and the UK are represented through their development ministers. As the governors, these ministers are 'the ultimate policy makers at the World Bank' (World Bank, 2020 website[3]). Despite the relative autonomy of the WB mentioned earlier, it can be argued that these ministers have a strong influence on the objectives, the organisational programme and the agenda of the organisation as the ministers represent the policies which have been formally decided at the national level (Bretton Woods Project, 2013). In the case of Germany, for example, the Ministry for Economic Cooperation and Development has been headed by the Social Democratic Party since the elections in 2021.

The general tasks of the governors include the admission of new members, the increase or decrease of capital stock, arrangements concerning cooperation with other international organisations, and the distribution of the net income of the World Bank. The Board meets at least once per year, but additional meetings can be requested by member governments (IBRD, 2012). The Board of Governors reflects a 'lot of political contradictions' which can complicate negotiations as regards policy changes (Interview WB01, 2008). In general, there are some countries which are more open to reforms than other countries, for example in relation to issues such as transparency and accountability.

The following figure shows that the Board of Governors is supported by an Advisory Council and Loan Committees. The members of the Advisory Council are selected by the Board. They include representatives from different sectors

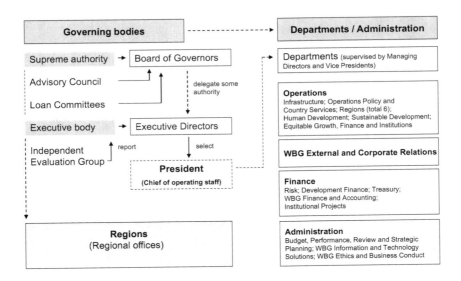

Figure 4.1 Formal Structure of the World Bank

Source: Own illustration, based on the World Bank Organisational Chart (World Bank website, 2020e) and the IBRD Articles of Agreement (2012)

(banking, commerce, industry, labour, and agriculture). The Loan Committees report to the Board on those loans which have been awarded to members.

The executive body at the World Bank is the Board of Executive Directors (EDs), which exercises 'the power delegated to them by the Board of Governors' (IBRD, 2012). Since 2010, there have been 25 EDs which are appointed or elected every two years, and which serve all organisations belonging to the WBG. The members with the largest shares, including the USA and Germany, appoint one ED each. All other EDs are elected by the member governments who represent different groups of countries, so-called multi-country constituencies.[4] The permission given to some countries to appoint their own EDs is based on the number of shares they hold and as such it represents a power imbalance within the World Bank structure.

The EDs are individual actors, and in theory they cannot exercise any power or represent the World Bank without the authorisation of the Board of Executive Directors. However, according to a former ED of the WB, an individual ED can have quite a strong influence on discussions within the Bank and as a result on the Bank's policy decisions. This influence depends to a great extent on an ED's ability to communicate and to convince other EDs (Interview WB05, 2009).

The tasks of the EDs include executive and oversight functions and conducting the day-to-day business of the WB. In this context, the EDs consider proposals on IBRD loans, IDA credits, and IFC investments; they decide on policies which impact on the World Bank's general operations; they select the President who serves as the chairman of the board; they also have the authority to remove him; and they have the power to interpret the 'Articles of Agreement' which is the constitution of the WB. These interpretations are binding for all WB members unless they are overruled by the governors.

Furthermore, the EDs receive the reports of two WB evaluation units, which are the Inspection Panel (IP) and the Independent Evaluation Group (IEG). The Inspection Panel,[5] which was created by the Board of Executive Directors in 1993, provides a complaint mechanism for people and communities regarding any adverse effects of World Bank projects. The Panel has three members appointed by the Board and a permanent Secretariat that provides operational and logistical support. The Panel reports to the Board and only the Board can take the decision to stop a loan if necessary. The Panel is an important mechanism which assists with institutional capacity building in accountability, although its mandates are limited and there are still many people at national level who are not aware of this complaint mechanism (Interview WB01, 2017). Since 2020, the Inspection Panel together with the Dispute Resolution Service forms the WB Accountability Mechanism (AM). The IP is also a member of the international virtual Independent Accountability Mechanisms Network.

The IEG has about 105 full-time staff and assures the accountability of the WBG (IEG, 2019: 25). It reports to the EDs about the WBG strategies, policies, programmes, and activities. The findings of the evaluation group provide new inputs to the EDs and their decision-making processes. Such decision-making processes include, for example, the evaluation of the WB's social and environmental safeguard policies. Nevertheless, even though the IEG has some influence concerning the design of the policy of the WBG, its range of influence has been perceived as limited by the IEG management team in the past.

> IEG's work helps to improve the understanding of Bank Group staff but there is less evidence of direct use of IEG's products to improve policies, strategies, and operations. More can and should be done to encourage learning from IEG's work.
>
> (IEG, 2011: xii)

The IEG aims to provide timely responses to changes within the WBG and the external environment including internal restructuring and reform processes as well as the achievement of the UN 2030 Sustainable Development Agenda. This includes not only a further strengthening of its evaluation and validation work but also an enhanced focus on learning and knowledge sharing.

The day-to-day business of the WB takes place under the leadership of the President, senior staff, and the vice presidents, which are responsible for regions and sectors. In 2019, Jim Yong Kim resigned from his position as WB President and was succeeded by David Malpass, a former official of the US treasury department and investment banker, who was the only candidate nominated to take over from Kim. Despite criticism from civil society organisations worldwide, the so-called 'gentleman's agreement' according to which the USA appoints the WB President and Europe the IMF Managing Director, has been reinforced once more (Barder, 2019). The lack of a fair contest regards the new leader of the World Bank can be considered as 'a setback for an effective, rules-based multilateral system' (Edwards, 2019a, citing Barder, 2019).

The main tasks of a WB President include the day-to-day conduct of the ordinary business of the Bank under the direction of the EDs and the supervision of the operating World Bank staff, including the managing directors and vice presidents. The President's competences include the general organisation, the appointment, and the dismissal of staff and officers. With regard to the recruitment of staff members the geographical spread is important in order to meet staff diversity, which is considered as a strategic business asset and with which the WB tries to secure 'the highest standards of efficiency and technical competence' (IBRD, 2012). The workforce of the WB is structured by ten grade levels which reflect responsibilities, skills, and education. The three main categories are administrative jobs, professional and technical jobs, and managerial jobs. The last stream includes, for example, sector managers, country directors, and vice presidents. Most of the staff is employed on the basis of 'term appointments' (fixed-term contracts) which have a duration between 1 and 5 years. Open-ended contracts are less frequent and only offered on a case-by-case basis.[6]

In 2014, the then acting WB President Kim started to implement a restructuring reform within the WB headquarters in order to make the organisation more efficient and results oriented in fulfilling its mission to tackle global poverty (Provost, 2014). A 'diagnostic' on the 'state of the World Bank', which was published in 2012 by a group of Bank alumni professionals (The 1818 Society), might have contributed to Kim's decision to move forward with a more ambitious internal reform project. The diagnostic report attested to the Bank 'a very cumbersome inefficient internal structure', a low morale amongst staff, and 'the risk of being seen, . . ., as seriously damaged and in decline' (The 1818 Society, 2012: 2). The diagnostic team defined the choice of the new WB President as 'whether to continue to patch a leaky boat or bring it into the shipyard for a much-needed overhaul' (Ibid., 2012: 3).

Kim decided to dismantle existing networks and groupings of WB staff based on the recommendations of the consultancy firm McKinsey & Co. However, the nontransparent reorganisation process and the elimination of about 500 jobs led to staff protests and an increasing climate of fear amongst staff (Rice, 2016; Provost, 2014). Former WB officials considered Kim's autocratic and nonparticipatory approach, which led to a lack of 'ownership' amongst staff and mistakes made during the implementation of the reform, as crucial factors for undermining the success of the reform and the influence of the President (WB01, 2017; WB07, 2019).

WB departments and policies of importance for the Global Unions

The Organisational Chart 2020[7] of the World Bank reflects the institutional changes of the past years. So-called 'global practices' (18 in total) including education, energy, jobs and development, and poverty and social protection have replaced the old matrix management system which was based on functional networks, such as 'human development' and 'sustainable development' (Bretton Woods Project, 2013). The global practices are grouped together under three separate vice presidents responsible for 'Human Development', 'Sustainable Development', and 'Equitable Growth, Finance and Institutions' (see WB Organisational Chart, 2020). The technical staff grouped under 'global practices' work across the six regional units which have been in place since before the reform. In addition to the global practices, five cross-cutting solution areas (CCSA) have been introduced, which comprise smaller teams working on 'Climate Change', 'Fragility, Conflict, and Violence', 'Gender inequality', 'Jobs', and 'Infrastructure and Public-Private Partnerships'. The CCSA on jobs comprises of around 30 staff and is a relatively small unit.

The topics of the CCSAs are applied across countries and sectors, and experts from relevant global practices were also assigned to provide knowledge from their practice. Generally, the idea behind the reforms was to move from a geographical area focus to a focus on subject expertise and sharing technical expertise across all regions (Bretton Woods Project, 2015). According to a former WB official from the jobs group, this was a sensible decision because all sectors are related to the jobs agenda including, the private sector, education, and finance (Interview WB07, 2019). However, structural changes continued after the large re-structuring exercise in 2014 and this led to a situation in which the original ideas of global knowledge sharing, and better coordination have been watered down. As a result, it seems like the Bank has 'come back to what they had before the reforms which is separate global practices, and the sectors are being divided by regions' (Interview WB06, 2019).

The World Bank's job strategy is supported by a 'Jobs Umbrella Multi-Donor Trust Fund' (Robalino et al., 2017). The idea goes back to 2007 when a 'Multi-Donor Trust Fund (MDTF) on Labor Markets, Job Creation and Economic Growth' was created in order to address knowledge and capacity gaps in low-income and middle-income countries and to support policy making with regard to job creation and labour markets in developing countries. Half of the contribution to the fund was then covered by four countries including Germany, Austria, Norway, and Korea (MDTF, 2010). Nowadays, the fund has six donors from five countries comprising the UK, Norway, Germany, Austria, and Sweden and supports the jobs group in the development of 'best evidence-based solutions for job creation' (Robalino et al., 2017: 6).

Regarding the dialogue between the WB and the Global Unions, there are different WB departments involved. The relationship between these departments and the Global Unions is not static and has also been impacted by the WB's structural reform. At the beginning of the dialogue and until 2014, the Civil Society Team (CST) played a major role with regard to providing trade unions with access to the WB. The CST forms part of the Bank's External and Corporate Relations Department, which since the structural reform is directly reporting to the WB President and its vice president and advises the President and senior management on strategic communication and stakeholder engagement. Prior to the reform the external relations department formed part of the 'WBG Integrated Services' and was led by a managing director.

Since the restructuring, the relationship between trade unions and the CST has changed. This is also because one important interlocutor for the trade unions, who in the past played a major role in shaping the WB's relationship with civil society organisations and opened 'a space' for trade unions, left the Bank (ITUC02, 2015).

Nowadays both the global director and the manager of the 'Jobs and Development' unit are the main contacts for the ITUC/Global Unions office in Washington D.C. The unit has its root in the former Social Protection and Labour (SP&L) unit which formed part of the Bank's Human Development Network (HDN) and was intended to bring together various strands of social protection and labour activities, and to overcome the existing 'piecemeal' framework in this area (Holzmann et al., 2009: 1). The HDN was created in 1997 by President Wolfensohn in order to facilitate knowledge sharing and to link staff working in the same sectors throughout the Bank. In this context, labour markets were considered to be 'critical for a sustainable and inclusive development strategy' (Vodopivec et al., 2009: 45).

> A well-functioning labor market is needed to guarantee the success of struc-tural reforms, to maintain social support for those reforms, and to ensure that their benefits are widely distributed. Moving toward a well-functioning labor market will likely be crucial to a more effective implementation of pov-erty reduction strategies and hence progress toward meeting the Millennium Development Goals.
>
> (Ibid., 2009: 45)

In the course of the WB's structural reforms, the SP&L unit was split into 'Jobs and Development' and 'Social Protection' which form two of the 15 global practices at the WB. Both belong to the 'Human Development' cluster and are overseen by the same global director. The jobs group focuses on the creation of new jobs in the formal sector and the increase of job quality. Trade union representatives are largely satisfied with this solution as it ensures direct contact with those WB staff which is concerned with labour issues (Interview ITUC06, 2019). However, as the former director of the ITUC/Global Unions office pointed out,

> So, it's still challenging, I think that what we want is people who are contact points that can put us in contact with the correct people on a quick basis, and really move stuff in the institution.
>
> (Interview ITUC06, 2019)

In addition, some GUFs, such as the BWI and EI, have their own contact points. For example, the BWI maintains relations with the procurement department and the safeguard department and EI with WB representatives responsible for educa-tion policies. The restructuring also impacted the latest secondment of a trade union representative to the WB who found that many staff was very concerned about their work contracts and a lot of competition between staff members (Inter-view ITUC07, 2019).

The evolvement of labour market issues and social protection at the Bank

During the last decades, the WB's awareness and understanding of labour markets and their connection with economic growth and poverty reduction has arguably developed (Vodopivec et al., 2009). The growing importance of social protec-tion and labour is also reflected in the Bank's lending commitments. From 1998 to 2001, the WB lends about US$30 billion to finance social protection and labour programmes in developing and emerging countries. In the years of the international financial and economic crisis (2009–2011), social protection lending increased fivefold, mainly to IBRD countries which already had social protection programmes in place (World Bank, 2012a). However, as the following subchapter aims to demonstrate, publications on the topic still contradict each other, and they often provide evidence that the neoliberal paradigm is still alive.

The WBs involvement in social protection and its work on labour markets goes back to the 1970s but the first strategy on social protection and labour was published in 2001 under the presidency of James Wolfensohn. The 2001 strategy was influenced by the financial crisis in East Asia, Russia and Brazil in the 1990s, and reflected the view that growth and macro-economic policies on their own are not sufficient for poverty reduction (World Bank, 2001a). The 2001 strategy also highlighted the increasing importance of cooperation with partners in the area of social protection. These partners include the IMF, the UN (including the ILO), bilateral donors and 'knowledge partners' (including the OECD and the European Commission), civil society, and trade unions. The work with trade unions was divided into 'knowledge management' (information exchange on the ILO CLS with the then ICFTU and WCL), 'training and institution building' (continued seminars for trade union leaders and seminars for Bank staff on trade unions), and 'operational work' (continued information exchange with trade unions at the country level) (World Bank, 2001a: 44–45).

The WB's social protection and labour strategy 2012–2022 'Resilience, Equity and Opportunity', which was published in 2012, points out that the WB 'supports social protection and labour in client countries as a central part of its mission to reduce poverty through sustainable, inclusive growth' (World Bank, 2012a: I). It stresses that the strategy is not a 'one size fits all' approach and that it aims to 'facilitate informed, country-specific, fiscally sustainable social protection and labor programs and systems' (World Bank, 2012a: II). The strategy provides an overview of the role of different actors in the field of social protection and labour (including jobs) but there is a strong focus on the private sector:

> From a SPL perspective, productive jobs are the main avenue for opportunity, affording people socioeconomic mobility, while mitigating risks through adequate and secure incomes. But such jobs cannot be sustainably created by SPL programs alone. For that, a thriving private sector that demands labor and skills and fairly rewards workers for their productive contributions is needed.
>
> (World Bank, 2012a: 4)

Trade unions, however, are mentioned together with NGOs as important partners regarding the implementation of the strategy which acknowledges that trade union

> engagement in setting the global labor agenda has contributed to shaping core aspects of the strategy, including an emphasis on the global crises of poverty and rising inequality, the need to address coverage of informal sector workers

and labor market issues in LICs, and recognition of gender dimensions of labor market.

(World Bank, 2012a: 44)

In comparison to the 2001 social protection strategy, the 2012–2022 strategy does not define the cooperation with trade unions in more detail. However, the strategy stresses the central role of jobs and the quality and access to jobs which was also reiterated in the 'World Development Report 2013: Jobs' (World Bank, 2012b). The WDR in 2013 pointed out that it is not only 'growth' that is important but also the distribution of income and the 'possibility of redistributing resources through the growth process itself and through government transfers' (World Bank, 2012b: 87). The report acknowledged that workers' rights and the ILO CLS as well as other ILO conventions (such as on social security, occupational safety, and health) are an important foundation for 'good' jobs and that trade unions and collective bargaining have an 'equalizing effect' on wages and help to reduce wage inequalities (World Bank, 2012b: 263). The WDR in 2013 was positively embraced by trade union representatives; however, in 2019, it presented a different perspective, and it was strongly criticised for its focus on flexibility and deregulation (World Bank, 2019a). In their statement to the 2018 annual meetings of the IMF and the World Bank, the Global Unions requested that the World Bank 'put aside the counterproductive proposals in the World Development Report 2019 which promotes failed deregulatory measures and regressive taxation' (Global Unions, 2018: 1), further stating:

> The trade union movement would have welcomed a serious contribution from the World Bank to the debate on the future of work to help counter inacceptable levels of inequality, informality and lack of social protection, as well as the impacts of new technologies and climate change. Unfortunately, the WDR, 2019 does not fulfil that purpose.

(Global Unions, 2018: 3)

Education International responded in an 'open letter' to the World Bank and expressed its concerns as regards the lack of lessons learned from past failures and the lack of alignment between the WDR recommendations and the SDGs (EI, 2018). The examples of the 2013 and the 2019 reports demonstrate the general lack of a consistent approach and message with regard to social protection within the World Bank.

In September 2019, the WB social protection and jobs global practice published a white paper on 'risk sharing policies' rethinking social protection systems and its coverage (World Bank, 2019b). Many of the arguments put forward in the white paper are opposed to the measures suggested by trade unions of how to tackle poverty and inequality. For trade unions this includes 'measures to strengthen decent work, including minimum living wages, collective bargaining, employment protection, and robust labour market institutions' (Baunach et al., 2019). In contrast, the white paper argues that statutory minimum wages are 'slow or unresponsive to changes in market power' (World Bank, 2019b: 145) and that 'reforming the most stringent restrictions on firms' hiring and dismissal decisions should be a priority' (Ibid., 2019b: 149). The latter recommendation is similar to the arguments promoted by the former WB flagship publication 'Doing Business' which often provided related arguments (see World Bank, 2013b, 2020b). The 'Doing Business' report, which was also heavily criticised by the trade unions, will be considered in more detail in the IFC chapter.

Procurement policies

Apart from jobs, labour markets, and social protection, the WB procurement policies are an important issue for the international trade union organisations. Procurement policies are managed by the WB 'Projects and Operations' unit since the restructuring; before that the unit was called 'Procurement Policy and Services Group'. The unit is responsible for the development and the dissemination of the Bank's procurement policies and the development of the 'Procurement Framework'.

Procurement policies and guidance apply to investment loans regarding goods, works, and consulting and nonconsulting services. A borrower (government department) which receives a WB loan must comply with the procurement policies. In 2016, the WBG adopted the new 'Procurement Framework', which replaced the 2011 'Guidelines for the Procurement of Goods, Works and Non-Consulting Services' and Standard Procurement Documents (SPD) (World Bank, 2011b). The old SPD included the user's guide; under the new Procurement Framework, this is a stand-alone document. The procurement guidelines are based on International Competitive Bidding (ICB), which is intended to provide bidders with an equal opportunity to bid for the required goods and works. When a provider of goods and works has been chosen by a government agency on the basis of a competitive bidding process, a bidding document (contract) is signed which sets out the rights and obligations of both parties.

In the last two decades, the BWI (GUF) has played an important role with regard to the adoption of mandatory labour clauses in the SPD for works, as the tender process in construction is very competitive. The winning tender may be a company which pays the lowest wages, has a large proportion of informal workers, and does not comply with health and safety requirements. In 2004, a BWI representative undertook a secondment at the World Bank's procurement department. The secondee focused on the promotion of labour clauses in the bidding phase, as well as capacity building and technical cooperation, in order to promote the understanding of contract compliance by government agencies and contractors. The BWI worked together with the International Federation of Consulting Engineers (FIDIC)[8] and the Confederation of International Contractors' Association (CICA) (Interview BWI, 2009).

The FIDIC represents the consulting engineering industry at global level and aims to be 'the authority on issues relating to business practice' (FIDIC, 2014: 2). Multilateral Development Banks (MDB), including amongst others the WB, the European Bank for Reconstruction and Development (EBRD), the Asian Development Bank (ADB), and the African Development Bank (AfDB), have used the FIDIC construction contracts for many years as part of their SPDs.

In former times, it had been regular practice by MDBs to introduce additional clauses under the section 'Particular Conditions' in its SPDs in order to amend provisions included in the FIDIC contract under the section 'General Conditions'. This led to inconsistencies and variation in the tender documents published by MDBs and created uncertainties amongst the users of these documents. In order to confront the increased risk of disputes, MDBs agreed to harmonise their tender documents at international level and to modify the part of 'General Conditions' in the FIDIC 'Conditions of Contract for Construction' which are mandatory for all contractors. The first harmonised edition of the FIDIC conditions of contract was published in 2005 (FIDIC, 2005), followed by two amended versions in 2006 and 2010. In 2006, clause number 6 on 'Staff and Labour' included for the first time the 'prohibition of forced labour and harmful child labour' (Boswell, 2008). In the following years, the World Bank played a major role with regard to changing the wording of the regulations relating to forced labour and child labour in the FIDIC contract. This was mainly due to the Bank's effort to harmonise the wording of the regulations with the more progressive 'Performance Standards' of the International Finance Corporation (IFC) (WB03, 2009). In 2010, the right of workers to form and join workers' organisations and to bargain collectively, as well as the principles of nondiscrimination and equal opportunity, were included in the FIDIC contract (Charrett, 2010).

The changes in the FIDIC contract were reflected in the 2010 WB SPD for the procurement of large works, which included all the ILO CLS in the section 'General Conditions' for the first time (World Bank, 2012c). In 2016, the WB adopted its new 'Procurement Framework' which aims to support borrowers to 'achieve value for money', meaning a stronger focus on compliant bids which provide the best overall value taking into consideration quality and cost (World Bank, 2018a: 1). The framework clarifies the respective roles of the borrower, lender, client, main contractor and sub-contractors as well as suppliers and engineers. Each SPD (Request for Bids) which relates to 'Works'[9] and the construction context specifies in the section about general conditions the working and labour conditions which main contractors and their sub-contractors must comply with. The WB now requires all borrowers to develop a 'Project Procurement Strategy for Development' (PPSD) which will be reviewed and agreed by the Bank. This document developed by the borrower will also have to include a clause which permits the Bank to 'inspect and audit all accounts, records and other documents relating to the procurement process, selection and/or contract execution' of the borrower and the contractor including sub-contractors (World Bank, 2018b: 8). The latest revision of the SPD of large works in January 2021 incorporated provisions of the disqualification of contractors and proposed subcontractors if projects are assessed as high risk for sexual exploitation and abuse and/or sexual harassment (World Bank, 2021a).

The introduction of these labour clauses in the FIDIC contract and the WB SPDs was clearly related to the lobbying activities of the BWI (Interview BWI, 2009) and the 'openness' of the then WB President James Wolfensohn towards labour standards and his willingness to listen to trade unions (Interview WB03, 2009). In this context, the secondment of the BWI representative to the WB's procurement department was perceived as very 'useful' by some WB staff, in particular as the analysis and information provided by the secondee seemed to set in motion a process of 'maturation' at the World Bank (Interview WB03, 2009). Furthermore, it can be argued that the World Bank and other MDBs agreed to the incorporation of the ILO core labour standards in the FIDIC contract because the MDBs considered them as not being in conflict with national laws (Interview WB03, 2009). Trade unions also asked for the ILO Convention 94 (Labour Clauses/Public Contracts) to be included in the harmonised FIDIC contract; however, no consensus could be achieved with regard to this convention.

WB safeguard policies

The revision of the World Bank safeguard policies started back in 2012. After several years of consultations, in 2016 the WB approved the new Environmental and Social Framework (ESF) which applies to all IPF projects initiated after 1 October 2018. It is important to note that the ESF only covers investment lending and not policy lending as it means that the framework only covers contractors but not consultancies or consultants who work for governments. The ESF aims to support government agencies in the development and management of environmentally and socially sustainable projects (World Bank, 2017a).

The new framework includes the WB's vision for sustainable development, the environmental and social policy for IPF, and ten environmental and social standards (ESS). For the first time, it states specific labour standards requirements after the old safeguard policies were criticised by governments, trade unions and other civil society organisations as well as the IEG for their lack of labour standards for many years (Bakvis, 2014a). With the new ESF, the WB took the opportunity to streamline and update its safeguards in line with other banks such as the ADB and the IFC (Interview WB01, 2017).

The objectives of ESS 2, which concerns 'Labor and Working Conditions', are closely related to the ILO CLS albeit without including any reference to the ILO. The Bank commits itself to conducting environmental and social due diligence of all projects in order to 'assist the Bank in deciding whether to provide support for the proposed project' (World Bank, 2017a: 7). All borrowers must develop and implement an 'Environmental and Social Commitment Plan' (ESCP) which describes the measures and actions which will be taken in order to comply with the ESS. The ESCP forms part of the legal agreement between the Bank and borrower and the borrower is required to undertake monitoring activities which will be agreed with the Bank, and to provide regular reports about monitoring results to the Bank. It also stipulates that:

> The Borrower will notify the Bank promptly of any incident or accident relating to the project which has, or is likely to have, a significant adverse effect on the environment, the affected communities, the public or workers. The notification will provide sufficient detail regarding such incident or accident, including any fatalities or serious injuries. The Borrower will take immediate measures to address the incident or accident and to prevent any recurrence, in accordance with national law and the ESSs.
>
> (World Bank, 2017a: 22)

The ESF and in particular ESS 2 can provide trade unions at national level with a useful tool to become more involved in the assessment of potential labour rights problems at the project preparation stage and in the implementation and monitoring of labour standards during the operational phase. In 2020, the WB published an implementation update on the ESF which highlighted the need of further capacity development for Bank staff as well as the capacity of borrowers to manage environmental and social issues. It was noted that ESS 2 'is one of the most challenging Standards for staff and Borrowers to implement' (World Bank, 2020c: 18). Despite the identified challenge, the report did not explicitly mention trade unions and their expertise with regard to the enhancement of knowledge and tackling this challenge.

The World Bank's (organisational) identity

According to its own definition, the WB is 'one of the world's largest sources of funding and knowledge for developing countries' (World Bank, 2011a: 3). It considers itself as a 'global development cooperative' which is owned by its members (World Bank, 2012c: 16). According to Woods (2006: 179), the amount of financial and nonfinancial resources provides the Bank 'with a power which other international organisations can only dream'. As stated, and promoted by the Ethics and Business Conduct (ECB) department, the core values of the Bank comprise 'impact, integrity, respect, teamwork, and innovation' (World Bank, 2018c: 2). The Bank has committed itself to the UN SDGs following the goals of ending extreme poverty by 2030 and to boost 'shared prosperity' in a sustainable way (World Bank, 2016: 11). The Bank acknowledges that there is not one solution available which fits all countries and that national circumstances must be considered. In this context, the WB's annual report from 2016 states:

> The fundamentals, however, remain true: countries must grow their economies inclusively, so that everyone benefits; they must invest in their people; and they must ensure that those who have left poverty do not fall back into it.
>
> (World Bank, 2016: 1)

The WB's vision on sustainable development has inclusion at its core. Inclusion can be achieved through policies which promote equality and nondiscrimination, and provide all people with access to education, health services, social protection, infrastructure, employment, affordable energy, and financial services (World Bank, 2017a). This general approach towards inclusion is similar to what trade unions aim for. However, in contrast to the trade unions, at the WB, the notion of capitalism and neoliberalism is still at the forefront, even though there has been some change of perceptions. One former WB staff noted in this respect:

> Our paradigm [*capitalism*] is still the same. We believe that our main job is to promote economic development because without economic development you cannot have poverty reduction, . . . but we think that the kind of growth today has to be within a philosophy of more equity, social equity and environmental sustainability.
>
> (Interview WB01, 2008)

According to this WB staff, the traditional neoliberal paradigm of the WB, which was strongly focused on trade liberalisation and the opening of markets, has changed over time and the Bank has become more sensitive to the criticisms expressed by civil society organisations, including trade unions:

> I think a lot of our policies today are debt policies, are social and environmental safeguards, our gender policies, our participation policies, information and disclosure . . . that has changed so much over sixty years and a lot of that has been because of civil society pressure in the last 20, 30 years.
>
> (Interview WB01, 2008)

Nevertheless, despite this change, the WB remains a bank, and in order to finance its loans, the IBRD is active in the global financial markets where it issues bonds and passes the low interest rates on to its borrowers. IBRD bonds have been given premium rating by the two leading credit rating agencies Moody's, and Standard and Poor's (World Bank, 2016). This means that the WB has one of the highest credit worthiness providing investors with a high level of security that debts will be repaid. In the fiscal year 2016, the World Bank raised an equivalent of

US$63 billion by issuing bonds in 21 currencies. Through the return on equity (mainly paid-in capital and reserves) and the margins made on lending, the IBRD finances operating expenses and supports the IDA. In comparison to the IBRD, the IDA which fights extreme poverty in the world's poorest countries is largely funded by contributions from developed and middle-income donor and borrower governments. Every three years IDA donors and borrowers come together and 'replenish' IDA funds. The replenishment round in December 2019 agreed a historic US$82 billion financing package for IDA countries from 2021 to 2023 (World Bank, 2020a). Its operations at international financial markets characterise the Bank as a bank in the ordinary sense and sometimes there is a dichotomy between its role as money lender and its role as 'development agency' which 'wants to reduce poverty' (Interview WB01, 2008). This dichotomy determines the organisational values which are, on the one hand, market and economy oriented, and on the other hand focused on social development and sustainability.

Over time, the 'direction' and identity of the Bank has been shaped not only by its shareholders but also by the organisational leadership, in particular the different WB presidents. James Wolfensohn, who was President of the WB from 1995 to 2005, introduced a major rethinking and reform process at a time when the Bank and the Washington Consensus faced strong criticism. Wolfensohn launched a 'Comprehensive Development Framework' in 1998 which took a holistic view of development and poverty reduction (World Bank, 2001a). In his address to the IFI annual meetings in 1997, Wolfensohn said:

> The message for countries is clear: Educate your people; ensure their health; give them voice and justice, financial systems that work, and sound economic policies, and they will respond, and they will save, and they will attract the investment, both domestic and foreign, that is needed to raise living standards and fuel development.
>
> How can we in the broader development community be most effective in helping with the enormous task ahead? It is clear that the scale of the challenge is simply too great to be handled by any single one of us. Nor will we get the job done if we work at cross purposes or pursue rivalries that should have been laid to rest long since. Name calling between civil society and multilateral development institutions must stop. We should encourage criticism. But we should also recognize that we share a common goal and that we need each other. Partnership, I am convinced, must be a cornerstone of our efforts.
>
> (Wolfensohn, 1997)

In his speech, Wolfensohn made a pledge for making countries and local stakeholders the 'owners' of their projects, for 'inclusive' partnerships involving labour organisations amongst other organisations, and he encouraged the 'development community' to re-evaluate existing strategies and to 'scale up'. He pointed out that the WB needs to change in order to be more effective in terms of focusing on countries' needs and 'to focus on quality, and to be more accountable for the results' of the organisational work (Wolfensohn, 1997: 7). The 'Strategic Compact' from 1997 provided the blueprint for the organisational and cultural change outlined by Wolfensohn. An assessment in 2001 concluded that the Compact helped to improve the work of the Bank but that 'efficiency gains have been difficult to realize' (World Bank, 2001b: i).

Wolfensohn aimed to transform the Bank into an organisation that is able to deliver on its promises. He encouraged consultations with civil society organisations including trade unions, he launched together with the then IMF managing director Horst Koehler and other partners an initiative to reduce the debt of 22 heavily indebted poor countries, the majority in Africa, and he launched the 'Structural Adjustment Participatory Review Initiative' (SAPRI) together with an NGO network (Peet, 2009; Rich, 2002). As Rich (2002: 37) noted, 'The Bank under Wolfensohn at times appeared to be trying to be all things to all people' and the reform agenda was too ambitious and did not live up to fulfilling the objectives.

Despite a lack of implementation of the reform agenda, many trade unionists have a positive memory of Wolfensohn because of his openness towards the dialogue and his effort to develop a relationship with trade unions (Interview ITUC03, 2009). Wolfensohn's perspectives regard social development and workers' rights, as well as his criticism of defence spending in the developed countries instead of contributing more financial aid to development assistance, put him in a favourable light with trade unionists.

Wolfensohn appears to have played a key role in deciding that the Bank should change its position, acknowledging that the anti-core labour standard stance was both untenable and a major obstacle to any improvement in relations with the labour movement. Beginning in early 2002, Wolfensohn made public pronouncements asserting that the Bank supported promotion of CLS.

(Bakvis, 2005: 635)

Wolfensohn was the president who initiated the idea of secondments of trade unionists to the WB. He made it possible that a small number of unionists, one at a time, became appointed by the Bank for a short period of time to follow the work of a particular department and to work on a particular topic. This was an important step to foster the exchange between Bank staff and trade unionists, even though it only took place on a very limited scale (Interview PSI, 2008). He also took a stand regarding the abolition of 'institutional impediments' to trade union involvement when he overruled influential individual actors, such as one of the former directors of the then SP&L department (Interview ITUC01, 2008).

However, as other authors have argued, despite presenting itself as more flexible and collaborative with a stronger focus on development assistance, the

WB remained 'neoliberal in both rhetoric and practice' (Bazbauers, 2014: 92). Wolfensohn's successor Paul Wolfowitz (2005–2007) maintained the foundations laid down by Wolfensohn and did not introduce any major innovations at the Bank. This may also have been due to the fact that his presidency was very short, and he had to leave office because of the involvement in two scandals (Adams and Goldenberg, 2007).

With the arrival of Robert Zoellick (2007–2012), a more innovative approach and a progressive agenda returned at the Bank. Zoellick called for a modernisation of multilateralism (Zoellick, 2008), but like his predecessor, he was also a strong advocate of free markets and free trade putting his faith in the private sector (Bazbauers, 2014). From the perspective of trade unionists, in contrast to Wolfensohn, both Wolfowitz and Zoellick did not have much time for trade unions (Interview ITUC04, 2009; Interview ITUC02, 2011).

President Jim Yong Kim took over in 2012 and abruptly resigned in January 2019, three years before the end of his second term. In a speech at the George Washington University in 2013, he highlighted the new mission statement of the WBG which had been endorsed by the Board earlier in the same year: to end extreme poverty by 2030 and to promote real income growth for the bottom 40 per cent of the population (Kim, 2013). These two ambitious goals were guiding the new corporate strategy of the WBG which was published in 2013 (World Bank, 2013a). The strategy aimed to 'reinforce the WBG's role as the world's unique global development institution' (World Bank, 2013a: 1) by 'embracing a development solutions culture' (Ibid., 2013a: 5).

Kim was the first president who was not an economist but had held professorships at Harvard Medical School and School of Public Health. At the beginning of his presidency, trade unionists saw Kim quite positively, mainly because of his former engagement with civil society. In October 2012, the ITUC General Secretary Sharan Burrow called on the WB 'to develop a new balanced approach to labour market issues and in favour of decent work inspired by the recommendations of the World Development Report 2013' (ITUC, 2012). Despite Kim's strong rhetoric as regards combatting poverty, little action followed, which led to a considerable level of disappointment amongst many civil society actors. Daar (2019) noted in this context that Kim's tone and language changed significantly over time 'from fighting poverty to economic growth, from health, education and human development to human capital, from citizen engagement to private sector engagement'. He also failed to take stronger leadership in the development of the Bank's new safeguard policies. In so far, one of his main achievements was probably the successful negotiation with WB shareholders for a capital increase and the more efficient use of financial assets, in particular IDA assets (Edwards, 2019b). The trade unions considered President Kim's position towards universal health care as positive but his restructuring programme 'created a lot of internal chaos' which impacted the existing dialogue structures negatively (Interview ITUC02, 2015). Trade unions were also critical about Kim's seemingly stronger interest in promoting private investment instead of supporting development through low-interest rates to governments (Baunach, 2019).

In February 2019, the USA nominated David Malpass for World Bank President. Malpass is known for his criticism on multilateralism and opposing the expansion of financial resources for the IFIs. In 2018, Malpass testified in his role as Under Secretary before the U.S. House Financial Services Subcommittee on Monetary Policy and Trade, that the Treasury pushed for the adoption of a new mechanism which will limit World Bank lending. This resulted in the adoption of a 'new financial sustainability framework' which restricts annual lending commitments of the IBRD in order to achieve 'financial discipline'. Furthermore, measures aimed at the reduction of administrative costs were put in place, including the constraint of growth of staff salaries, the strengthening of performance management and efforts 'to remove low performers' (Malpass, 2018). In October 2019, Malpass presented his vision and ideas for the WB at the 1818 Society's annual meeting. In this context, he indicated a further strengthening of private sector involvement in a wide range of countries, a greater focus on lending activities concerning global public goods, the environment and global climate change, and a stronger focus of the Bank on knowledge sharing (The 1818 Society, 2019). In his first address of the IFI annual meetings, Malpass stated:

> The private sector must play a pivotal role in development. With official development assistance stagnant and public-sector debt growing in many countries, it's critical that we pursue private-sector solutions and establish an environment that attracts private investors.
>
> (Malpass, 2019a: 8)

In summary, since its foundation in 1944, the Bank has changed in its focus, key objectives, activities, and implementation strategies. At the very beginning the Bank focused on rebuilding Europe and the necessary institutional foundation, and later the support of countries in Africa, Asia, and Latin America took centre stage. The underlying structural reason for poverty in these continents led to an extension of the Bank's 'paradigm' over the years, which one former Bank staff considers now as more 'holistic' (Interview WB01, 2008). A central and enduring characteristic of the Bank is the organisational dichotomy referred to earlier, on the one hand its role as a bank and on the other hand its role as a development agency (Interview WB01, 2008). The Bank aims to distinguish itself from other MDBs by embracing a 'development solutions culture' which is informed by organisational experiences and knowledge (World Bank, 2013a: 5). The solutions culture focuses on the delivery of customised solutions to countries and the integration of knowledge and financial services. This includes an emphasis on country ownership and developing policies which focus not only on economics but also on other topics as well such as health, education, and corruption (Interview WB01, 2008).

Knowledge management and learning

The creation and dissemination of knowledge and the provision of expertise play a strategic role for the Bank and its approach towards development. The Bank's normative power is based on its key role as 'a producer, customizer, and connector of knowledge' and its 'specialized role as key contributor to global development knowledge' (World Bank, 2011c: 1, 2). The WB's explicit knowledge can be divided into three areas. It includes knowledge available for clients (such as technical advice, procurement guidelines), knowledge for internal use (such as ESF guidance notes), and knowledge for the public (such as regular publications, e.g. the annual World Development Report). The Bank aims to produce knowledge which is 'cutting-edge and operationally relevant' (World Bank, 2011c: 10). In its function as knowledge producer, the Bank is focusing more strongly on technical assistance to countries. In practice 'knowledge customizing' means a focus on collaboration between different Bank teams, government representatives, civil society, and academia in applying global knowledge. However, this kind of cooperation depends on agreement as regards what is considered to be common global knowledge. For example, the IFIs and the trade unions hold different views on minimum living wages and collective bargaining and their importance in combatting poverty and inequality.

With regard to producing and sharing knowledge, staff skills and talent as well as staff learning are considered as key enablers by the Bank. Knowledge is created by individual actors, including WB officials (governors) and staff members, which store information in their minds and make part of this knowledge available to other individual actors through direct individual interaction. In the 1970s the Bank also started to hire public policy experts, sector specialists and social scientists to address the increasingly complex development challenges (World Bank, 2011c). The Bank is well aware of the importance of tacit knowledge developed by staff, clients, and other organisations that they work with and there are ongoing discussions about how this kind of knowledge can be captured and codified and about 'designing mechanisms to ensure it stays alive and current, transmitted and developed from year to year and from staff member to staff member – through mentoring, debriefing, and peer learning' (World Bank, 2011c: 23). In the past, knowledge transfer between departments and country offices concerned with regional work has been limited. The former WB President Kim saw one of the reasons for this in the bureaucratic structure of the organisation stating that 'Bureaucracies sometimes operate in ways that keep people away from each other' (Kim, 2013). As a result, 'self-enclosed areas of influence' emerge which develop into 'silos' over time. The structural and cultural changes within the Bank, the creation of 'Global Practices' and 'Cross-Cutting Solutions Areas', were aimed to support and enable a better knowledge flow across the organisation. In 2016, President Kim launched the Open Learning Campus (OLC) which is open to staff, clients and global partners. The OLC provides a broad range of online sources relating to development learning and offers free online courses in a variety of subjects (World Bank, 2016).

An important driver for organisational change at intra-organisational level is the IEG whose influence and impact are influenced by the WBG's organisational structure and culture. The annual 'Client Survey' conducted by the IEG in 2014 revealed an increased relevance and influence of the produced evaluations and reports within the organisation, in particular amongst Board members (IEG, 2015). The IEG aligns its strategic framework with the overall strategic framework of the WBG, reflecting strategic priorities such as the Covid-19 response. In 2021, the IEG conducted a self-evaluation exercise which highlighted potential further areas for improvement including its own visibility and the 'quality, timeliness, relevance and accessibility of its products' (IEG, 2021: 23).

External drivers for change are global economic developments including international and regional crises, technological developments and pressure from individual and corporate actors, such as civil society organisations or the G-20 (Interview WB01, 2008). More than a decade ago, Birdsall (2007: 52–53) related the increasing pressure on the Bank to the 'erosion of the Bank's legitimacy as an institution, loss of faith in its effectiveness (in reducing poverty and promoting "balanced and externally oriented growth"), and its apparent growing irrelevance'. Adler and Varoufakis (2019) argued that middle-income countries are now able to borrow cheaply on international markets and new development banks are growing, which creates further challenges for the Bank, including the potential danger of fading into irrelevance. However, crises such as the international financial crisis and more recently the Covid-19 pandemic and the war in Ukraine, help to renew the WB's image as an influential political actor on the world stage. Yet it is questionable whether the changes which have occurred at the Bank so far have been the result of deeper organisational learning or just the visible outcome of temporary innovation and adaptation strategies developed and prescribed by top management. The perception of some trade unionists and World Bank staff is that it takes a long time before a different way of thinking or focus of action introduced at the headquarters level works its way through to the departmental and country level. For example, one trade unionist observed that after Wolfensohn declared human and labour rights as important for Bank activities, there were still directors of WB country offices which argued against these rights (Interview ITUC03, 2009).

Power (re)sources and intra-organisational challenges

The WB's material and nonmaterial resources and its importance as lender for many governments provide the organisation with a considerable amount of power to influence global policies as well as governments. The Bank considers itself as a global 'standard-setter' in different areas, including sustainability, transparency, and accountability, which underpins its normative influence (World Bank, 2019d).

In comparison to other organisations, the Bank's costs of mobilising financial and personnel resources are relatively small because of its standing in the capital markets and reputation as an employer. In fiscal year 2019, the World Bank spent US$45.1 billion across 351 projects covering about 100 countries (World Bank, 2019d). Both the IBRD and the IDA employ 12,283 full-time staff and 5,097 short-term consultants whereby 43 per cent of the staff are not based in the head-quarters (World Bank, 2019d: 71). The majority of employees have an economics background, and all employees are meant to contribute to the extension of explicit and tacit knowledge of the Bank. The Bank's Staff Association represents the majority of employees across the Bank and voices their concerns about organisational changes, health coverage, and occupational health matters. Staff on consultancy contracts is not covered by health care provisions and other protection. The influence of individuals within the Bank varies although spontaneous actions are not desirable, and neither are actions which diverge from organisational norms, and which could harm the organisational reputation. In 2019, the EBC department launched a new 'Code of Ethics' which outlines expected behaviours for all WB staff (World Bank, 2019c). Regarding the intra-organisational level, the governance structure and political power imbalances at the WB have been criticised for a long time, in particular the influence of some very powerful member countries such as the USA. All member countries are directly represented through the Board of Governors which convenes twice a year, but all major decisions are made by the Executive Board. At the IBRD and the IDA, the USA has the largest percentage share of voting power (15.60 and 9.86 per cent[10]). The weighted voting system of the Bank means that the relative economic power of member states determines their influence with regard to policy making and negotiations through the Executive Board (Murphy, 2014). The 2010 'voice reform' included an increase of basic votes in order to benefit the poorest countries, the introduction of a 'quota framework', and an additional Executive Director for African countries (Vestergaard, 2011a, 2011b). However, the lack of a clear formula made the 'calculation underlying the allocation of IBRD quota shares completely intransparent' (Vestergaard, 2011a: 26). As a result of the reform, China became the third largest shareholder of the IBRD, and some other countries, for example India, Brazil, Turkey, Poland, and Spain, also benefited. The weighted voting system and the representation of countries through multi-country constituencies create unequal power relationships between members from the northern and the southern hemisphere within the Bank, which tends to shape decision-making processes in favour of the countries from the northern hemisphere (Vestergaard and Wade, 2013). The reform did not help to overcome large voting power imbalances caused by the historic voting system and to resolve the 'rather undemocratic aspect of internal governance' (Strand and Retzl, 2016: 436).

The influence of the USA within the Bank is also intensified by the historic gentleman's agreement between Europe and the USA according to which the Bank is led by an American national and the Fund by a European national (Bretton Woods Project, 2019a). Despite the fact that since many years civil society organisations have demanded a merit-based and transparent election process, it is yet to materialise. However, a former staff member of the WB cautions that even though the Executive Board is still dominated by some European countries and the USA, which is not fair in terms of representation, it is the northern countries which are the most advanced when it comes to reforms regarding, for example, the environment, gender issues, and civil society engagement (Interview WB01, 2017). There are still many countries in the world with autocratic governments which are not accountable to their own people, and which refuse to engage with civil society. In this context, voting shares influence the Bank's underlying political direction and a more equal presentation could create a different set of challenges for societies and at the intra-and inter-organisational level.

The International Finance Corporation

The IFC, which was established in 1956, is one of the five organisations which constitute the WBG. The IFC is a separate legal entity with its own constitution, share capital, and staff. In contrast to the World Bank, it focuses exclusively on the private sector in developing countries.

> The purpose of the Corporation is to further economic development by encouraging the growth of productive private enterprise in member countries, particularly in the less developed areas, thus supplementing the activities of the International Bank for Reconstruction and Development.
>
> (IFC, 2020a: 1)

The IFC acts as global development organisation, and at the same time, it is characterised as a company with different 'business segments', which are investment, treasury, and advisory services. The lending portfolio of the IFC is quite broad as it provides loans to banks (and other financial institutions) and leasing companies, and it invests in companies' equity and private equity funds (MarketLine, 2019). The main investment products of the IFC are loans, equity investments, debt securities, and guarantees. With regard to equity investments, the IFC invests directly in companies' equity and through private equity funds (IFC, 2019b). In 2009, the IFC set up a wholly owned subsidiary, the IFC Asset Management Company (AMC), which mobilises third-party funds (e.g. from pension funds in wealthy countries) and invests them in private companies in IFC client countries (IFC, 2016).

The IFC considers itself as a 'brand' which 'has built up a strong brand identity over six decades of experience' (IFC, 2016: 14). The importance of the IFC has increased during recent decades, in particular as the WBG and the IMF consider the private sector as a key contributor to development and developing economies. In 2012, the Development Committee stated in a discussion note that 'the private sector is a critical driver of — and partner in — economic development' which is responsible for 'about 90 percent of employment in the developing world, including both formal and informal jobs' (Development Committee, 2012: 1). In FY 2019, the IFC spent over US$19.1 billion in long-term investments supporting 269 long-term finance projects in developing countries (IFC, 2019b). In 2021, the IFC spent US$23.3 billion. As a development organisation the IFC works in cooperation with the WBG member organisations on the achievement of the two goals of the WBG strategy, which are to end extreme poverty and to promote shared prosperity. In its 'Road Map FY 15–17', the organisation pointed out that the focus will be on sectors where the greatest impact can be achieved, including infrastructure, agribusiness and the food supply chain, health and education, and financial markets (World Bank, 2014). In terms of regions, Sub-Saharan Africa, South Asia including Afghanistan and Pakistan and the Middle East and North Africa (MENA) are in focus.

At the beginning of 2017, the IFC set out its new strategic framework called 'IFC 3.0' which describes a more proactive approach with regard to creating 'markets, and mobilise private sector resources at a greater scale' (IFC, 2017: 15). The new framework is based on a much stronger engagement with the World Bank and in line with the WBG wide approach, called the 'Cascade', which aims to maximise finance for development. In this context, the former IFC managing director explained in a letter published in the IFC, 2017 Annual Report:

> Bank Group staff, working with our clients, will first seek private sector solutions to address development challenges — where such solutions are advisable and can be effective — and reserve public financing for projects only when other options are suboptimal.
>
> (IFC, 2017: 15)

The 'Cascade' approach is linked to the 'Maximizing Finance for Development' (MFD) approach which aims to leverage the private sector. MFD was launched in 2017 and is considered as a critical instrument to reach the 2030 SDGs. The WBG supports its members to increase economic activities (crowding-in) by providing technical support and advice regarding policy and regulatory reforms, for example with regard to infrastructure (World Bank, 2018d). Trade unions see this development in a very critical light, in particular as policy loans and technical support are not covered by the WBG's environmental and social safeguard policy. The ITUC General Secretary Sharan Burrow stated in this context:

> The Sustainable Development Goals framed a necessary and universal agenda for 2030. This could have been a decisive moment for the Bank to change

course, finally repairing the toxic legacy of Structural Adjustment Programmes. Instead, the World Bank, IMF and multilateral development banks stridently promoted a narrative in which the Sustainable Development Goals could only be financed by rolling out the red carpet for private investors.

(ITUC, 2020a: 5)

The new framework has also an impact on the IFC's business model and its organisation of work. More recently, the IFC has introduced 'country strategies', 'upstream units' (with a focus on the creation of new projects), the roll out of an 'Anticipated Impact Measurement and Monitoring' (AIMM) system for the assessment of the development impact, and an 'Accountability and Decision-Making Framework' in order to enhance operational efficiency (IFC, 2019a: 7).

Organisational characteristics

The IFC is owned by 185 members, and membership is only open to those countries which are also members of the World Bank. Similar to the WB, the IFC has a regional structure and a strong presence in all the regions. The four major regions, which are each led by a regional vice president, include Latin America and the Caribbean (LAC) and Europe; Africa; Middle East, Central Asia, Turkey, Afghanistan and Pakistan; and South Asia, East Asia and Pacific. The paid-in capital in 2019 by member countries was about US$2.57 billion whereby the USA holds the greatest percentage of the capital stock (22.18 per cent) (IFC, 2019a). Other influential shareholders are Japan, Germany, France, the UK, India, Russia, Canada, Italy, and China. In 2019, the IFC employed 3,744 staff, the majority in the more than 100 country offices outside the USA. Similar to the WB, the IFC also employs many consultants but in contrast to the WB, many staff have a banking background. The IFC managerial level is still dominated by male staff (IFC, 2019a: 103).

In 2014, the IFC underwent an organisational reform with the objective to 'simplify' the organisational structure and to deepen the engagement with the World Bank (Stephens, 2014). These changes were introduced without staff consultation and input of the WBG Staff Association. In this context, it is worth noting that the IFC Annual Report 2015 no longer included a reference to the 'IFC Way' which defined the IFC's corporate culture for many years:

A strong corporate culture is central to any organization's ability to succeed and adapt to new challenges. The IFC Way is a way of being, defining, and solidifying IFC's culture and brand, and a process that engages staff at all levels and in all regions to inform management decision making. It includes our vision, our core corporate values, our purpose, and the way we work.

(IFC, 2014: 73)

The most influential governing bodies of the IFC are the Board of Governors and the Board of Directors. The representatives on both boards are the same as at the World Bank; however, the voting power of the EDs depends on the countries relative shareholding and is therefore not the same as at the IBRD or IDA (Vestergaard, 2011a).

The governors decide on such matters as the admission and suspension of members, the capital stock, and the operations of the IFC. This includes, for example, cooperation arrangements with other international organisations. The Board of Directors is responsible for the conduct of the general operations of the IFC and appoints the Managing Director (President) of the IFC on the recommendation of the World Bank President (IFC, 2020a). In March 2021, Philippe Le Houérou was succeeded by Makhtar Diop who, like his predecessor, also has a long-standing career at the WB. The managing director is responsible for the operating staff of the IFC, their appointment and dismissals, and the daily operations of the organisation (IFC, 2020a). The activities of the IFC are evaluated by the IEG.

The IFC also has an independent accountability mechanism, the Compliance Advisor Ombudsman (CAO), through which individuals and communities which are affected by IFC projects can raise their concerns. The CAO was established in 1999 and reports directly to the WBG President. In 2019, the

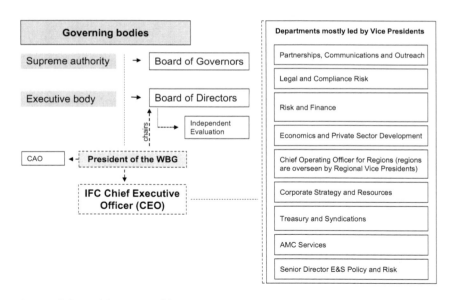

Figure 4.2 Formal Structure of the IFC

Source: Own illustration, based on the IFC Organisational Structure (2020) and Articles of Agreement (2020)

CAO handled 60 cases in 35 countries including 12 new complaints. More than half of the complaints were supported by civil society groups and only 5 per cent were initiated by the CAO (CAO, 2019a). Most complaints were recorded in the infrastructure sector (24 per cent), oil, gas mining, and chemicals (22 per cent), financial markets (18 per cent) and manufacturing (16 per cent) (CAO, 2019b). The CAO has established its own monitoring and evaluation system which is based on stakeholder feedback. However, it needs to be noted that the CAO has no power to enforce IFC compliance with its recommendations (Bretton Woods Project, 2019c).

Accountability to stakeholders and shareholders plays an important role for the IFC. In order to further strengthen its environmental and social advice and risk management, in 2019 the Environmental, Social and Governance (ESG) Advice and Solutions department moved into operations and the IFC created a new Environmental and Social Policy and Risk (CES) department which reports directly to the CEO (IFC, 2019a).

The IFC's identity and knowledge development

The IFC is the world's largest global finance organisation which focuses on the private sector. It considers itself as an investor, adviser, and 'influencer' regarding the way of thinking on private sector development (IFC, 2019a). In the past, some Bank staff perceived the World Bank and the IFC as culturally different organisations and the IFC as 'less conservative and more innovative' than the Bank (Interview WB03, 2009). Nowadays, trade unionists still regard the IFC as more accessible and the level of exchange as deeper than with the WB.

In comparison to the WB, the IFC acts 'much more as a financial institution' although it is not a commercial bank in the traditional sense (Interview IFC03, 2017). The IFC is a bank but with some advantages in comparison to ordinary banks. One advantage is the immunity it has from taxation and customs duties, which include its assets, income, property and operations (IFC, 2020a). As a bank, the IFC offers a great variety of financial products and operates on a commercial basis focusing on 'for-profit' projects in developing countries (IFC, 2019a: 78). Loans for financing projects, companies, and financial institutions represent the greatest part of financial commitments by the IFC, which in FY 2019 comprised US$7.1 billion (IFC, 2019a). Furthermore, the IFC invests directly in the equity of organisations and financial institutions and in private-equity funds, as well as in trade and commodity finance. The IFC is one of the 'biggest players' in emerging market private equity (IFC, 2015: 3). The organisation focuses on three kinds of funds, including growth equity funds, small equity funds and venture capital funds, in order to provide SMEs in the developing world with access to finance. The IFC cannot target SMEs directly but only through financial intermediaries, which creates an extra layer between the IFC as financial investor and the beneficiaries (TUDCN, 2018). The third Conference on Financing for Development,[11] which took place in Addis Ababa in 2015, welcomed the work of the IFC in this area and the significant growth in national private activities in the last two decades (UN, 2015). In the IFC Annual Report 2017, the then IFC President Le Houérou described the AAA Agenda as a 'new vision' of the development community 'in which the private sector plays a central role in delivering development solutions while public resources are used strategically to develop projects, mitigate risks, and enable the private sector to invest sustainably' (IFC, 2017: 19). The Civil Society Forum on Financing Development, of which the trade unions form part, expressed strong concerns with regard to the Addis Ababa Agenda and the central role which has been given to private finance in promoting sustainable development. Amongst other things, the Civil Society Forum took a critical stance regarding public–private partnerships (PPPs) and stressed that 'Essential public services that implicate States' duties to guarantee the human rights to water and sanitation, education, and health should be excluded from private sector partnerships' (Civil Society Forum, 2015: 5). This statement has particular importance as the IFC's advisory work focuses on structuring public–private partnerships (IFC, 2019a).

Knowledge development and knowledge-sharing in relation to private-sector development play a strategic role for the IFC (IFC, 2016). The organisation aims to make some of the tacit knowledge of staff available to the public by providing, for example, 'SmartLessons' papers in which not only staff but also clients present and discuss their experiences with regard to specific topics. Other knowledge distribution mechanisms are, for example, the IFC annual 'Sustainability Exchange' which focuses on economic, environmental and social challenges in emerging markets, and which brings together practitioners and executives from companies, civil society, government and academia, as well as the quarterly journal 'Handshake' which showcases best-practice examples of PPPs (IFC, 2016).

In all its investment decisions, the IFC 'gives weight and attention to environmental, social, and governance risks' (IFC, 2019a: 100). Borrowing organisations value the reputation of the IFC and the impact this has with regard to their own reputation. This benefit or value addition which the IFC brings to a client defines its distinctiveness in comparison to other banks, which is recognised as such by staff members. Since the organisational reform in 2014, the IFC's corporate culture and identity seem to be closer aligned with the World Bank. However, the fact that the IFC is a smaller organisation which focuses directly on the private sector enables the IFC to move faster when it comes to labour issues as the 'Performance Standards' (PS) have demonstrated (Interview IFC01, 2008).

The 'sustainability framework' and 'performance standards'

Since the 1990s, the IFC has increasingly focused on the issue of sustainability and considers itself as a standard setter in this area (IFC, 2016). These developments are connected to the business case of sustainability according to which businesses which address environmental and social issues achieve better growth rates, save costs, improve their brand and reputation, and strengthen stakeholder relationships (IFC, 2012a). The IFC Sustainability Framework is based on three pillars, including the IFC's commitment to environmental and social due diligence and monitoring of clients (Policy on Environmental and Social Sustainability), the 'Performance Standards' which aim to support clients in designing projects in order to avoid negative impacts on the environment and broader community, and the organisational commitment to transparency (Access to Information Policy) (IFC, 2019a). The IFC considers sustainability as an 'integral part' of its external and internal business operations.

> We hold ourselves accountable to the same environmental and social standards we ask of our clients. This commitment connects IFC's mission with how we run our business.
>
> (IFC, 2019a: 102)

In 1998, the IFC adopted its 'Environmental and Social Safeguard Policies' procedures, and in 2003, several development banks adapted a version of the IFC safeguard policies which they called the 'Equator Principles' (IFC, 2016). The Equator Principles is a voluntary risk management framework regarding environmental and social risks which has been adopted by currently 105 financial institutions in 38 countries including Banco Santander S.A., Barclays plc, Development Bank of Japan, and Swedbank AB. In 2006, the safeguard policies were replaced by the 'Policy on Social and Environmental Sustainability' and the 'Performance Standards'. The trade unions were strongly involved in the development of the Performance Standards and its implementation:

> (. . .) we had significant engagement with the unions while we were putting the standards together. So, I would like you to remember that because that's probably unprecedented within IFC's history that we had so much specific policy discussions with the labour unions, and it is not just the ITUC, but it was also with AFL-CIO and the sector unions.
>
> (Interview IFC01, 2008)

This involvement dates back to the beginning of the 2000s when the ICFTU (now ITUC) and ITGLWF (now part of IndustriAll) informed the IFC about labour rights violations at Grupo M, a clothing manufacturer in the Dominican Republic. The trade union complaints led to the inclusion of the 'freedom of association' condition into the loan agreement between the IFC and Grupo M in 2004 (Bakvis and McCoy, 2008).

The IFC updated its 'Policy on Social and Environmental Sustainability' in 2012 after a consultation process with stakeholders including trade unions. The Policy stipulates that proposed investments 'that are determined to have moderate to high levels of environmental and/or social risk, or the potential for adverse environmental and/or social impacts, will be carried out in accordance with the requirements of the Performance Standards' (IFC, 2012b: 1). The Policy is aimed to put the commitment of the IFC with regard to addressing climate change, human rights, and gender equality into practice. The Performance Standards (PS) comprise eight standards and each PS is accompanied by a 'Guidance Note'. All direct investment projects have to apply the PSs (IFC, 2012c). PS 1 refers to the assessment and management of environmental and social risks and impacts on projects. It requires every client to establish an 'Environmental and Social Assessment and Management System' (ESMS) which helps the business to identify and manage environmental and social risks on an ongoing basis. PS 2 'Labour and Working Conditions', which is of particular importance to the trade unions, is guided by the eight ILO core conventions and the UN conventions. It promotes fair-treatment, nondiscrimination, and equal opportunities for workers and the promotion of safe and healthy working conditions. The standard applies to workers which are directly employed by a client, workers contracted by a third party which performs essential core work for the project, and workers employed by a primary supplier (IFC, 2012c). With regard to third parties, clients have to undertake 'commercially reasonable efforts' to make sure that these organisations are 'reputable and legitimate enterprises and have an appropriate ESMS that allow them to operate in a manner consistent with the requirements of this Performance Standard [*PS 2*]' (IFC, 2012c: 16). However, this excludes the requirements as regards retrenchments and supply chains.

PS 2 requires that the IFC client provides workers with documented information about their rights under national labour and employment law and about applicable collective agreements. Furthermore, clients have to employ migrant workers on 'substantially equivalent terms and conditions to non-migrant workers' (IFC, 2012c: 13). In accordance with the requirements set by PS 2, client companies must comply with national law when it explicitly stresses the rights of workers to freely choose and join workers' organisations and to bargain collectively. Otherwise, if national law is restrictive and workers want to develop alternative mechanisms to protect their rights with regard to working conditions, then companies should not influence or control these mechanisms:

> (. . .) the client will not discourage workers from electing worker representatives, forming or joining workers' organizations of their choosing, or from bargaining collectively, and will not discriminate or retaliate against workers who participate, or seek to participate, in such organizations and collective bargaining. The client will engage with such workers' representatives and workers' organizations and provide them with information needed for meaningful negotiation in a timely manner. Workers' organizations are expected to fairly represent the workers in the workforce.

(IFC, 2012c: 14)

IFC clients are also obliged to establish a grievance mechanism for workers and trade unions, through which they can raise workplace concerns. Despite their far-reaching demands, the Performance Standards seem to be widely and positively received by IFC clients. One IFC representative explained:

> We've done many client surveys on their perception, their perception of incremental cost imposed by the Performance Standards, and we were quite surprised that a lot of clients felt that the incremental cost was not so serious that it would stop them from coming back to the IFC.
>
> (Interview IFC01, 2008)

All IFC project investments are evaluated by the IFC Environmental and Social team (E&S), which amongst others assesses every project against the PSs and helps to identify potential risks. The team includes people with different professional backgrounds such as environmental engineers, sociologists, and biologists. There is awareness within the IFC that some sectors such as the textile sector have a high risk for potential labour issues. If a client had issues with trade unions in the past, the IFC team gets in touch with the relevant Global Union and asks for their point of view. In addition, the Global Unions and their constituents can also raise concerns about a project at any point of time (Interview IFC03, 2017). For each project, the E&S Review Summary (ESRS) is publicly available. The IFC E&S team, which comprises around 90 staff, also monitors the implementation of agreed action plans throughout the loan agreement (Interview IFC03, 2017).

Despite the improvement of processes, the enforcement of the standards presented in PS 2 remains challenging for trade unions. A more recent example is Bilt Paper B.V., a pulp and paper manufacturer in India and Malaysia, and its subsidiary Sabah Forest Industries (SFI) in Malaysia.[12] In 2014, the IFC approved a US$250 million debt and equity investment in Bilt Paper B.V. and its subsidiary SFI including loans of up to US$150 million to SFI (CAO, 2018). On several occasions, the BWI (GUF) made the IFC aware of SFI's failure to recognise an independent trade union. Workers at SFI fought for nearly three decades for an independent trade union and the negotiation of a collective agreement, which until 2018 had been regularly denied by the company (BWI, 2018). In August 2014, the BWI filed a formal complaint through the IFC online labour portal, and in September 2014, the BWI filed (together with the state-wide Sabah Timber Industries Employees Union [STIEU]) a complaint to the Office of the CAO. According to the BWI,

> The pre-investment review [*from the IFC*] did not identify any FoA [*Freedom of Association*] related issues as a significant risk, despite more than two decades of workers' struggle to form a union at SFI. Neither did it include an analysis of FoA risks associated with the country and sector'.
>
> (BWI, 2018: 5)

The 2018 report from the CAO revealed that the delay of trade union recognition and issues relating to working conditions at SFI can be attributed to shortcomings in the IFC's reviews and the supervision of its investment in SFI:

> CAO finds that IFC did not discharge its supervision duty in relation to the Freedom of Association issues raised by the complainants: (a) during the initial stages of supervision (2014/15), because IFC did not conduct the analysis necessary to determine the client's compliance; (b) during 2015/16 because IFC suspended supervision at the client's request; and (c) post 2016, because IFC did not exercise remedies in relation to a client that it acknowledged was in breach of PS 2, and was unwilling to accept IFC advice on the issue.
>
> (CAO, 2018: 4)

This case demonstrates the potentially negative impact on workers if risk assessments neglect to review information from organisations such as the ITUC and the ILO and to 'determine whether there is a history of workers' organization conflict' (CAO, 2018: 22). In 2018, the PSI (GUF) and two Indonesian civil society organisations held a meeting in Bali alongside the annual meetings of the World Bank and the IMF, and representatives agreed on the need to support a binding treaty to hold TNCs and the IFIs accountable (PSI, 2018). In the light of the fact that the IFIs play a leading role in shaping international and domestic development policies and 'possess considerable power in the decision-making process within member states' (Apodaca, 2017: 218), the IFIs need to be accountable to their responsibility to citizens and not only the objective of state economic growth.

'Doing business' – measuring the business environment

In contrast to the IFC Performance Standards which support workers' rights and a more worker-friendly behaviour of companies, for a long time the annual WBG flagship publication 'Doing Business' (DB) provided a contrasting message. 'Doing Business' was a co-publication between the WB and the IFC which was published first in 2003 and discontinued in 2021. The origins of the publication go back to the 'Investment Climate Group' which was founded at the beginning of the 2000s by the then vice-president for 'Private Sector Development' and chief economist of the IFC. The group developed the 'Doing Business' indicators based on the 'Index of Economic Freedom' from the Heritage Foundation, a conservative think tank based in Washington D.C. (Bakvis, 2009a). Doing Business ranked countries in relation to the business environment for SMEs in the largest business city of a country considering the extent to which national regulations promote or hinder business activities (World Bank, 2017b). It covered 12 areas of business regulations including 'starting a business', 'dealing with construction permits', 'registering property', and 'paying taxes', which counted towards the 'ease of doing business score' (World Bank, 2020b: 17). The 'Employing Workers Indicator' (EWI) did not count towards the scoring, but it was always a big concern for trade unions as it measured flexibility in the regulation of hiring, working hours, and redundancy rules and costs. DB, 2010 stated that it measures these indicators in a 'manner consistent with the conventions of the International Labour Organization' and that an economy 'can have the most flexible labor regulations as measured by Doing Business while ratifying and complying with all conventions directly relevant to the areas that Doing Business measures' (World Bank, 2010a: 22). With regard to the ILO conventions, the Bank's IEG reported 2008:

> The employing workers indicator is consistent with the letter of ILO provisions, but four measures do not reflect their spirit. Beyond these minimum standards, the DB criteria give lower scores to countries that have opted for policies of greater job protection.
>
> (IEG, 2008: 52)

Countries with the lowest level of workers' protection often ranked highest. For example, the first DB report in 2003 rated all those countries lower which 'were considered to have excessive labour market rigidity' – this included countries that 'provided for a working week on any less than 66 hours, a weekly day of rest, a minimum wage exceeding 25 per cent of average value added per worker, any recourse for appeal or severance pay in case of dismissal, or any limit on the use of term contracts' (Bakvis, 2009a: 424). Bakvis (2009a) pointed out that the 'Hiring and Firing' indicator was not based on academic or scientific research but merely on the argument that Anglo-Saxon law traditions provide for more flexibility and are more business friendly than civil law traditions as common in, for example, continental Europe. The argument of flexibility was also supported by Botero et al. (2004: 1378), who conducted a study supported by the WB and concluded that 'more protective labour laws lead to higher unemployment, especially of the young'. However, a more recent study from Sarkar (2020), which examined the impact of labour regulations on general employment and youth employment in 108 countries including highly developed countries, former Socialist countries and developing countries over a time span from 1996 to 2013, arrived at the opposite conclusion. According to this study, labour laws which protect workers do not negatively impact on the long-term employment perspective for workers including the youth.

A former director of the ITUC/Global Unions office stated that one of the main criticisms of DB by trade unions was that the report never allowed to measure the 'benefits' of regulations and promoted a labour market deregulation agenda instead (Interview ITUC02, 2015). This view was in alignment with the IEG evaluation from 2008. A similar argument was also brought forward by a former WB ED who described the DB report as a 'two-edged instrument' as on the one hand, it aims to motivate developing countries to improve their regulations for businesses in terms of facilitating business but on the other hand, it does not provide any benchmark for the quality of change in a country (Interview WB05, 2009). The ICFTU, later ITUC, sent ten statements to the WB between 2004 and 2008 and produced three detailed analyses of the EWI shedding light on its methodological flaws (Bakvis, 2009a). DB also was one of the major themes during the high-level meetings in 2009 in Washington D.C. The discussion during the meeting contributed to the decision of WB management to suspend the EWI in 2010 and to announce its removal from 'Country Policy and Institutional Assessments' (CPIA) (Bakvis, 2009b). However, DB continued to collect and publish data for the EWI (Bakvis, 2014b).

In 2012, an independent panel was appointed by the WB President to review 'Doing Business' and the director of the ITUC/Global Unions office acted as advisor to the panel. The final report of the panel recommended maintaining Doing Business as 'annual flagship report' but to reform its underlying methodology and to make it more transparent (Independent Panel, 2013: 4). In the years to come, the recommendations were not implemented, and in 2018, the ITUC General Secretary called on the Bank 'to decide once and for all that Doing Business has no business in the World Bank' (2018d). The trade unions received support from some academics such as McCormack (2018: 650) who suggested that 'the DB project should not survive, at least in its present form, because of the theoretical and methodological deficiencies inherent in its conception and implementation'. One of the issues was, for example, that the reports were based on standardised case scenarios focusing only on the largest city in a country and not considering variations within countries (World Bank, 2020b).

Despite the criticism which the publication had received over the years, the last DB report in 2020 highlighted again the importance of flexible labour regulation and the USA as a model to follow. It stated that flexible labour regulation 'provides workers with the opportunity to choose their jobs and working hours more freely, which in turn increases labour force participation' (World Bank, 2020b: 58). It also highlighted the importance of easing redundancy procedures in order to enable businesses to allocate their resources more efficiently:

> Restrictive steps for dismissing workers cause managers to divert their attention from performing more productive tasks and investing time in innovation as well as research and development.
>
> (World Bank, 2020b: 64)

These findings and recommendations, however, did not present new information. They were also presented in the 2013 report which welcomed the increase of fixed-term contracts and the reduction of redundancy costs in the Czech Republic, Portugal, the Slovak Republic, and Spain as these measures supposedly helped to facilitate employing workers (World Bank, 2013b).

In December 2019, two years before the report was discontinued because of 'data irregularities', the WB President confirmed that the labour indicator will no longer be included in rankings and that no data will be collected and included in the DB data set in the future (Malpass, 2019b). It took nearly two decades until the labour movement in cooperation with other civil society organisations achieved the removal of the EWI. However, it is likely that this has been a short-lived success because in 2022 the WBG announced a new approach of assessing the business climate renaming 'Doing Business' into the 'Business Enabling Environment' (BEE) report. The data and report aim to fulfil a twofold purpose which is to advocate for policy reform and to inform economic research and policy advice. The topics of analysis will include, amongst others, labour and taxation. The first report is targeted for autumn 2023 (World Bank, 2022). The Global Unions pointed out in their statement to the IFI spring meetings in 2022 that BEE should not consider labour market policies and that this topic should be handled separately as these policies are complex and complicated to measure (ITUC, 2022b).

Organisational development and learning

In comparison with the WB, the IFC is a smaller organisation. However, it is the largest global development organisation in the world which focuses exclusively on the private sector in developing countries and due to the number of financial resources which it provides, the IFC can be considered as an important authority with the power to set standards for companies. Lending commitments increased from US$4 billion in 2000 to more than US$23 billion in 2018 and represent almost one third of the total financial commitments of the WBG (Dreher et al., 2019). In March 2020, the IFC increased its Covid-19-related funding to US$8 billion in order to support private companies and to tackle the economic fallout caused by the pandemic (IFC, 2020b). In terms of shaping the policy at the IFC, some member governments are more influential than others, depending on the share of capital they hold within the organisation. In this context, the study from Dreher et al. (2019: 253) concludes that companies have a higher probability to receive a loan from the IFC if the government of their home country is represented at the IFC Board of Directors. The finding of this study can help to explain the 'IFC's focus on supporting projects in middle-income countries and companies from high- and middle-income countries'.

Since its foundation, the organisation has gone through several change processes, and it is continuously aiming for innovation and improvement in its services and its way of working. For example, back in 1981, the IFC coined the phrase 'emerging markets' and created the first 'Emerging Markets Data Base' which was followed by a substantial change of how financial organisations perceived developing countries (IFC, 2016: 19). The adoption of the safeguard policies in 1998, which became a benchmark for the Equator Principles and the basis for the IFC

Performance Standards in 2006, also exemplifies the innovative potential of the organisation. The IFC was the first organisation which took the initiative to make sure that its rhetoric and practices concerning the CLS were consistent (Bakvis, 2005). In this context, IFC management played a major role and there was a 'political commitment from the top from the beginning' (Interview BWI, 2009).

There are different factors which can be considered as important with regard to the promotion of change and organisational learning within the IFC. These factors include the size of the organisation, its culture, and the role of the top management. In contrast to the WB, the smaller size of the IFC, its more centralised structure, and its culture which actively promotes innovation allow for more flexibility regarding the introduction of change processes which comprise all organisational units. Furthermore, since the IFC deals with the private sector, it is possible to raise certain issues such as the CLS on a project-by-project basis, which gives the organisation considerable leverage before disbursing loans. The IFC does not face the problem of the World Bank which deals with government agencies, that is that it is not allowed to get involved with domestic political agendas (Interview IFC01, 2008).

In terms of organisational learning, communication and exchange of information through sector and regional meetings, as well as the documentation of information and feedback by project teams, play an important role in making knowledge available for others. In addition, formal training sessions (provided, e.g. by external labour experts) ensure that 'people are always kept up-to-date and up to speed on basics, and on key challenging issues, of which the labour unions and freedom association are obviously often a topic' (Interview IFC03, 2017).

> Everyone is responsible for all eight performance standards, which is quite a lot to cover, so it's critical to have that baseline training and familiarity, but then also to make sure that there are resources and additional support available when something might be particularly tricky on one topic, then people need to know where to go to try to get more support so that they're not just left.
> (Interview IFC03, 2017)

The E&S team, for example, also has a yearly meeting where worldwide staff get together and share information. Information sharing, training, and knowledge development at the IFC happen through multiple mechanisms, and it is driven by individual actors and organisational processes.

In terms of the content and implementation of the performance standards, the IFC has become a 'benchmark' for the WBG and other regional development banks (Interview ITF, 2008). The positive attitude of senior managers and members of the IFC Board of Directors with regard to the CLS, and their interest in bringing forward the social and environmental safeguards and in strengthening the organisational credibility of the IFC in this field, were major drivers behind these developments (Bakvis, 2005). In other words, it was the IFC which started to breathe life into the dialogue with the Global Unions in the sense of taking the necessary 'action'. However, it needs to be noted that these changes happened during the time when the WB was led by James Wolfensohn who in comparison to other presidents 'developed some clearly more enlightened positions in several areas, not the least on the recognition of workers' rights' (Bakvis, 2005: 633).

The International Monetary Fund

The IMF is the third organisation which participates in the dialogue with the Global Unions. It was established at Bretton Woods in 1944 and has 189 members. The IMF has a diverse agenda, which includes the promotion of international monetary cooperation and exchange stability, the expansion and growth of international trade, 'the promotion and maintenance of high levels of employment and real income', the financial support of members, policy advice, and capacity development support (IMF, 2020: 2). The largest borrowers of the IMF are Argentina, Ukraine, Greece,[13] and Egypt (IMF, 2019a). In the last decades, the IMF has played a key role in managing cross-border financial crises and its role as 'lead crisis lender has transformed it into one of the world's most powerful multilateral institutions' (Copelovitch, 2010: 3). In particular, the outbreak of the international financial and economic crisis in 2008 'put an end to the notion that the IMF was redundant' (Reinhart and Trebesch, 2016: 3).

Apart from lending, the capacity development (CD) work plays a large role at the IMF and has been performed in all 189 members over time (IMF, 2020c). Capacity development is one of the three core functions of the IMF to which the organisation commits around one third of its total spending. The main objective is to support members with the development of strong national institutions which help to promote economic stability and growth. The advice and training which is provided on request by member countries is, in accordance with the IMF Article of Agreements, directly related to the IMF's core competences and expertise. These areas include, for example, 'public financial management', 'financial supervision and regulation', and 'tax policy' (IMF, 2019b: 4).

The IMF is a much smaller organisation than the WBG. In April 2019, it employed 2,765 staff, who are primarily economists with expertise in macroeconomic and financial policies (IMF, 2019d). In comparison to the WB's mandate, which focuses on long-term economic development and poverty reduction and targets specific national sectors, the IMF follows a more holistic approach focusing on the stability of national economies. However, there is a strong cooperation between the IMF and the WB at different organisational levels. For example, during the IFI annual meetings, the boards of governors consult on international and financial issues and determine priorities for both organisations. The WB President and the IMF Managing Director also have regular consultations and issue joint statements, and staff from both organisations cooperate closely with regard to country assistance and policy issues (IMF, 2020b). In other words, both organisations are closely connected with each other although they are different in relation to some of their organisational characteristics.

The organisational structure

The IMF's structure was negotiated between the USA and the United Kingdom prior to the Bretton Woods Conference in 1944. Back then, the decision was made that each member of the IMF would pay a quota according to its relative size in the world economy. The quota determines the financial commitment to the IMF and its relative voting power within the organisation (Mountford, 2008). This decision created a power imbalance right from the beginning giving the greatest decision-making power to wealthy countries and in particular, to the IMF's biggest shareholder the USA. The USA has always had the largest voting share and a veto over major policy decisions (Chorev and Babb, 2009). The most influential shareholders with the largest percentage of total votes are the USA (16.51 per cent), followed by Japan (6.15 per cent), China (6.08 per cent), Germany (5.32 per cent), and France and the UK (each 4.03 per cent).[14]

Like the World Bank, the IMF is governed by a Board of Governors which consists of one governor (usually the finance minister) and one alternate governor from each member country. The Board of Governors is the highest decision-making body and 'ultimate political authority' in the Fund (Mountford, 2008). It delegates power and authority to the Executive Board which makes decisions about the acceptance of new members and establishment of their quotas, the suspension of membership, increases in the quotas of existing members, amendments of the Articles of Agreement, the appointment and nomination of Executive Directors, and the creation of advisory committees (Mountford, 2008). The governors meet once a year during the annual meetings which are held jointly with the governors of the WB; however, meetings can also be called by the Executive Board or requested by 15 members or by members having one quarter of the total voting power (IMF, 2020a).

The Board of Governors is advised by the International Monetary and Financial Committee (IMFC), which was established in this form in 1999, and by the Development Committee, which was established in 1974. The IMFC has 24 members who are governors of the IMF member countries. The members are central bank governors, ministers, or other individuals of comparable rank (IMF, 2019c). The committee meets twice a year (before the IFI spring and annual meetings), and some international organisations, such as the World Bank and the ILO, participate as observers in the meetings. The IMFC supervises the management and adaptation of the international monetary system, considers proposals from the EDs to amend the Articles of Agreement and deals with sudden disturbances to the international monetary system. In its communiqué in relation to the IFI spring meetings 2020, the IMFC welcomed the IMF's crisis response package and reaffirmed its commitment 'to a strong, quota-based, and adequately resourced

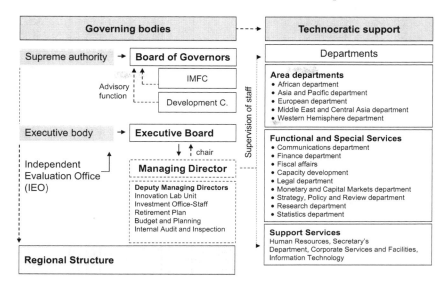

Figure 4.3 Formal Structure of the IMF

Source: Own illustration, based on the IMF Organizational Chart (2020) and Articles of Agreement (2020)

IMF at the centre of the global financial safety net' (IMF, 2020d). Although the IMFC has no formal decision-making and voting powers, it has become the 'main source of ministerial-level advice, guidance, and feedback to the Executive Board on all the main issues facing the Fund' (Mountford, 2008: 8). The Development Committee is similar in size to the IMFC (25 members), and it advises the Board of Governors of both the World Bank and the IMF on development issues including the transfer of resources to developing countries. Its members are governors of the WB and the IMF. The development committee does also meet during the IFI spring and annual meetings and issues communiqués.

The Board of Governors can decide to increase or decrease the number of Executive Directors before each election (IMF, 2020a). The Executive Board is responsible for conducting the day-to-day business of the IMF and activities include the preparation and follow up on board meetings, informal interactions with management and staff, and informing and advising member governments (Mountford, 2008). The Executive Board is chaired by the IMF managing director who is the 'main public face of the Fund' (Mountford, 2008: 21), and composed of 24 EDs who are elected either by individual member countries or by a group of countries (multi-country constituencies). The countries which appoint their director directly and have the largest share of voting power include the USA, Japan, China, Germany, France, UK, and Saudi Arabia.[15] Multi-country constituencies often have a large size (between 2 and 23 countries) which means that some EDs represent a great number of countries. Several challenges have emerged regarding multi-country constituencies, including the inadequate representation of the views of all members of a constituency by one ED (Portugal, 2005). Furthermore, EDs who are appointed by single countries have a 'greater incentive to be politically attuned and responsive' because their behaviour is more likely to be brought into question by national authorities such as by parliaments or the national central banks (Woods and Lombardi, 2006: 510). Governments assure the loyalty of appointed EDs through frequent turnovers and short tenures. Most of the EDs do not spend more than one term (two years) on the IMF board. Martinez-Diaz (2008: 13) concluded in his study about executive boards in international organisations, that the IMF Executive Board' capacity as political counterweight has noticeably increased over the years meanwhile its roles as 'strategic thinker' and 'democratic forum' have weakened (Martinez-Diaz, 2008: 13). The latter is a result of the remaining unequal voting power, which is particularly important in view of the fact that most decisions only require a simple majority.

In 2008, the IMF Board of Governors adopted a 'Quota and Voice Reform', which became enforced in 2011. The reform included an updated quota formula, an increase in quotas for 54 member countries, a tripling of basic votes, and an entitlement for those multi-country constituencies which exceed 19 members to appoint a second alternate ED (IEO, 2018a). In 2009, the G20 agreed to further reforms of the IMF governance structure. The 'Quota and Governance Reforms' were approved by the Board of Governors in 2010 and entered into force in 2016. The reform included the completion of the 14th General Review of Quotas, which provided a doubling of quotas and a realignment of quota shares and led to the recognition of Brazil, China, India, and Russia amongst the IMF's ten largest shareholders. Furthermore, the 2010 reform included a transfer of two ED positions from advanced European countries to emerging markets and developing countries. The IEO (2018a: 22) evaluation report concluded:

> (. . .) the balance of the IMF's governance structure remains weighed in favor of effectiveness and efficiency, while accountability and voice have continued to raise concerns which if unaddressed could affect IMF legitimacy and, ultimately, effectiveness.

The 15th General Review of Quotas, which aimed to agree a new quota formula and an increase in quota shares of dynamic economies, was blocked by the USA in December 2019 because of a likely increase of vote shares in favour of China (Bretton Woods Project, 2020a). The majority of the EDs supported a quota increase and further progress on the governance reform and expressed their disappointment about the outcome (IMF, 2020e).

In comparison to the WB, the IMF is a quite centralised organisation, which implicates that 'the show is run from the headquarters' (Interview IMF02,

2008). In July 2011, Christine Lagarde displaced the former Managing Director Dominique Strauss-Kahn as the first woman in this position. In October 2019, another woman, Kristalina Georgieva, a Bulgarian national who acted previously as CEO[16] at the World Bank, assumed the position. Shortly after her arrival, the longest serving First Deputy Managing Director David Lipton left the position before the end of his term and was replaced by Geoffrey Okamoto who previously acted as Assistant Secretary to the US Treasury (Bretton Woods Project, 2020b).

In January 2020, Georgieva acknowledged in a blog post that inequality was a rising challenge and that this would require a rethinking of fiscal policies and progressive taxation as well as social spending policies.

> Progressive taxation is a key component of effective fiscal policy. At the top of the income distribution, our research shows that marginal tax rates can be raised without sacrificing economic growth. . . . Second, social spending policies are increasingly relevant in tackling inequality. When done right they can play a fundamental role to mitigate income inequality and its detrimental effects on inequality of opportunity and social cohesion. Education, for example, prepares young people to become productive adults who contribute to society. Health care saves lives and can also improve the quality of life. Pension programs can allow the elderly to preserve their dignity in old age.
>
> (Georgieva, 2020a)

In order to tackle inequality, Georgieva aims to promote the cooperation of the IMF with other organisations such as the ILO, civil society, think tanks, and trade unions. The statement above does interlink with the demands of the Global Unions that the IFIs should support countries in making public investments and to cease the promotion of regressive taxation (Global Unions, 2019a).

The IMF has 18 departments which are subordinated to three general departments: the Area departments (administration of the regions), Functional and Special Services departments (including the Communication department, Finance, Capacity Development, Legal department, Strategy, Policy and Review department, Research, and Statistics), and Support Services (such as the HR department). The trade unions communicate mainly with the Communication department (public affairs) where they have a focal point. Partly because the IMF is a much more centralised organisation in comparison to the World Bank, communication is fairly straight forward for the trade unions when an issue arises with regard to a particular country or topic and the public affairs department helps to 'get people to the table' (Interview ITUC06, 2019). In former times, there was also some exchange with the Strategy, Policy, and Review department (Interview IMF01, 2008). In addition, at the highest organisational level, the managing director of the IMF and some deputy managing directors also interact with the ITUC at senior levels. In 2009, in the shadows of the international financial crisis, the first meeting between members of the Executive Board and the ITUC took place.

The work and policies of the IMF are evaluated by the Independent Evaluation Office (IEO), which was established in 2001. The IEO operates fully independently from IMF management and staff and plays a crucial role in enhancing organisational knowledge development and internal learning with regard to IMF policies and activities (IMF, 2019d). The office employs 18 staff, and its work programme and evaluation topics are decided in cooperation with the Executive Board, IMF management and staff, and external stakeholders including civil society. The 2019 work programme included, for example, a first pilot for an evaluation format focusing on the IMF and its collaboration with the WB. The final report was released in 2020 and found that there was a lack of consistency in Bank – Fund cooperation on macro-structural issues (IEO, 2020). The IEO itself is evaluated by an external panel every five years. The latest evaluation was led by the former president of the African Development Bank. The panel noted in its report that the IEO's evaluation work has contributed to greater transparency and accountability of the IMF. However, it also concluded that the IEO has too little impact in the IMF and that the 'Board has missed the opportunity to effectively use the IEO as an oversight and governance tool' (Kaberuka et al., 2018: 4).

Organisational knowledge development and learning

Knowledge development and knowledge sharing with government institutions (e.g. finance ministries) play an important role for the IMF and the IMF considers itself as a learning organisation. Organisational core competencies include revenue administration, public financial management, financial supervision, macroeconomic frameworks, and tax policy. At intra-organisational level, CD activities in connection with funding and surveillance form a key pillar of IMF activities. One of the underlying core principles for CD is 'country ownership', in other words, 'letting countries lead, including in defining their own strategies and priorities' (IMF, 2018: 8). The Executive Directors provide strategic direction and oversight regarding the CD management, including reviews and policy guidance as well as budget and risk management (IMF, 2019b). CD activities involve exchanges between IMF staff and member countries on aspects of policy design and implementation. According to the IMF, in this context, the strengthening of individual capabilities and the development of analytical skills of organisational representatives are important for the analysis of economic developments and the formulation of 'effective macroeconomic and financial policies' (IMF, 2019b: 4). In addition, the IMF runs regional capacity development centres[17] such as the Africa Training Institute (ATI), AFRITAC East (AFE), or the South Asia Regional Training & Technical Assistance Center (SARTTAC) which are financed by the IMF, external partners, and member countries. All regional centres aim to promote regional integration and knowledge sharing under the guidance of the IMF headquarters.

In 2018, the Executive Board concluded in its review of the IMF CD strategy that these activities need to be further integrated with surveillance (policy advice) and lending activities, and that internal information sharing needs to be increased (IMF, 2018). Surveillance includes the monitoring of national, regional, and global economic and financial developments. In accordance with the IMF constitution Article IV, 'the Fund shall exercise firm surveillance over the exchange rate policies of members' (IMF, 2020a: 6). During the so-called 'Article IV consultations', IMF mission teams discuss the economic situation and policies with national governments and authorities, its impact on the country's stability, and 'desirable policy adjustments'. In this context, IMF staff are encouraged to focus on 'the issues and themes that are relevant for stability with clear advice on an appropriate mix of policies' (IMF, 2015: 5). The latter are not limited to conventional fiscal-monetary policies but can also include financial, structural and exchange rate policies. Structural policies should be considered when they are 'macro-critical', in other words, if they affect domestic or global stability. The guidance notes for IMF staff regarding the Article IV consultations recommend that staff should first determine the extent to which a structural issue is macro-critical and then the availability of in-house expertise. Structural issues are identified 'obstacles' which hinder the efficient production of goods and services and the efficient allocation of resources. Such 'obstacles' may arise from, for example, public finance, state-owned enterprises, labour market regulations, and social safety nets. For example, high social security contributions or a high minimum wage can lead to increased hiring costs and unemployment rates (IMF, 2015). The guidance states that when the IMF is lacking expertise:

> staff should analyze the issue, drawing on expertise from other organizations (e.g. the OECD on product markets, the ILO and OECD on labour markets, and the World Bank on the structural aspects of the health and education sectors, and infrastructure needs). Staff is not expected to provide specific policy advice in these cases.
>
> For macro-critical structural issues that are important to a critical mass of members but where Fund expertise is lacking (e.g. labor market reforms), the Fund will further develop in-house expertise so staff can provide the necessary policy advice, while continuing to draw on other institutions' expertise.
>
> (IMF, 2015: 36–37)

During the Covid-19 pandemic, the IMF provided a supplement to the guidance note which gave IMF staff the option of flexible and focused follow-up discussions with governments on past Article IV recommendations (IMF, 2021). The IMF also doubled its emergency response and suspended debt repayments for the poorest countries. However, the question which still needs to be answered is which long-term policy recommendations will be given by the IMF to countries during the recovery phase. For example, a study published by the ILO in 2013 analysed IMF policy recommendations through Article IV consultations to European countries from 2008 to 2011 and concluded that the consultations underestimated the severity of the recession triggered by the international financial crisis. The given recommendations mainly focused on expenditure cuts and deregulatory measures (Weisbrot and Jorgensen, 2013). This time it seems like the IMF aims to grasp the opportunity provided by the Covid-19 crisis and to reshape economies and 'build a better world'. The IMF Managing Director stated in the IMF's flagship magazine '*Finance & Development*' that the focus should be on a 'greener' and 'fairer' recovery and that investments in education and social programmes 'will need to be funded by more equitable taxation' (Georgieva, 2020b).

The process of knowledge creation by operational staff is complemented and supported by the IMF 'Research Department' and the 'Statistics Department'. The research department is led by the IMF chief economist and coordinates, amongst others, the interdepartmental review and analysis of world economic developments for the flagship publication 'World Economic Outlook' (WEO), which is published twice a year. The basis for the report forms the information which IMF Article IV mission teams gather through their consultations with member countries. The WEO from 2019 projected a very low growth rate and 'difficult headwinds' for the global economy (IMF, 2019f: 22). In recent years, the research department has also published some working papers which consider the relationship between inequality and labour market institutions such as the paper from Jaumotte and Buitron Osorio (2015). However, although some research links the rise of inequality with declining unionisation rates, there is no consistent integration of these findings into recommendations of labour market reforms at national level (Interview AFL-CIO, 2017).

In addition to internally driven knowledge development, external circumstances and organisations also impact the creation of knowledge and learning within the IMF. An example is the ILO and inclusive growth. In recent years, the IMF began to engage more strongly on inequality issues and inclusive growth and to acknowledge the importance of social spending in this context (IMF, 2019e). Social spending comprises social protection (social insurance and assistance), education (primary and secondary), and health spending (basic health services) whereby private sector engagement is considered as a potentially 'important complement' (IMF, 2019e: 24). In 2018, the ITUC discussed together with other organisations, including the ILO, the FES, the WB, and the IMF, challenges for financing social protection at the 'Global Conference on Financing Social Protection' (ITUC, 2018e). The ITUC has a critical view on the IMF's strategic framework on social spending because of its narrow focus on social assistance and lack of alignment with international standards:

> The institutional view is thin on details about health, education and essential forms of social protection beyond assistance, such as pensions. Cooperation is particularly foreseen with the World Bank, which has a record of promoting

pension privatisations that ended in declining or stagnating coverage and fiscal failure.

(ITUC, 2019b)

Despite social protection is being part of IMF loan programmes nowadays, social protection floors are often limited to selected social assistance benefits. In this context, the Global Unions have demanded repeatedly that IMF social spending floors are aligned with the ILO 'Social Protection Floors Recommendation' (No. 202) and the ILO 'Social Security Convention' (No. 102) which cover on minimum standards of social security (Global Unions, 2022).

With regard to organisational learning, the IEO plays a vital role. The IEO evaluation reports stimulate debates within the IMF and provide staff with the opportunity to engage through commenting on draft reports and during the implementation phase of IEO recommendations. However, Schwartz and Rist (2016) point out that the use of new knowledge depends strongly on the receptivity of individuals and their attitudes towards new knowledge, the conditions established for intra-organisational learning by the organisational culture, and the role of management as facilitator. For example, in 2015, the IEO assessed self-evaluation activities at the IMF, which are undertaken by management, staff, and the Executive Board with the objective to learn from experience and to improve the quality of work. The evaluation concluded that, although considerable self-evaluation takes place, 'the IMF takes an ad hoc approach to self-evaluation' and that self-evaluation practices 'do not reflect a strategic assessment of learning and accountability priorities' (IEO, 2015: 22). In their response to the report, EDs acknowledged the findings and the potential benefits of a strategic approach to self-evaluation but the majority preferred to build on existing processes instead of establishing a new organisation wide framework (IMF, 2016). The latest external evaluation of the IEO noted a relatively low level of awareness amongst IMF staff as regards the IEO work, and that IMF staff is not engaging sufficiently with IEO reports (Kaberuka et al., 2018). In order to improve the efficiency of the IMF and to enable the IEO as 'change agent', the Executive Board, management, and the IEO itself need to 'reboot' their commitment to independent evaluation.

Organisational power – where does the IMF stand today?

Prior to the international financial crisis in 2008, the IMF had lost some of its relevance due to the substantial decline in macroeconomic volatility in advanced economies. Its role was largely defined by surveillance activities, and lending activities focused mainly on low-income countries (IEO, 2013). However, the 2008 crisis prompted a re-evaluation of the IMF, and despite being a much smaller organisation than the WB in terms of its workforce, the crisis transformed the IMF to become one of the most powerful actors within the system of global governance. A decade later, the economic crisis caused by the Covid-19 pandemic made a large number of poor and middle-income countries turn to the IMF for financial help and reaffirmed its importance as world player (Elliott, 2020). In contrast to the WB, IMF resources originate primarily from its members through the payment of quota. The IMF can receive additional resources from a number of member countries through the 'New Arrangements to Borrow' (NAB) and 'Bilateral Borrowing Agreements' (BBA). In 2019, the IMF had access to about US$ 1 trillion for nonconcessional loans (IMF, 2019d: 88).

Its financial and nonfinancial resources make the IMF a powerful intergovernmental actor which is influenced by its members, and which seeks influence over its members. The IMF exercises power over members through its surveillance activities and political advice. Potential conflicts arise for the IMF in respect of its dual roles as 'global watchdog' and 'trusted advisor', in particular at the bilateral level. A former IEO evaluation revealed that the Article IV consultations are considered by many government officials as 'formalistic rituals' which focus on information gathering and not on in-depth policy discussions (IEO, 2013: 7, 13). Furthermore, many government authorities believed that advice is 'overly generic' and guided by the Washington Consensus (IEO, 2013: 21).

Those member states which are reliant on financial support have conditions attached to their loans which impact policy outcomes. Quantitative conditions are related to macroeconomic issues such as the fiscal deficit of a government, whilst structural conditions refer to institutional and legislative policy reforms such as privatisation, trade liberalisation, and judiciary reforms (Eurodad, 2006). Before 2000, 'more than half of the conditions, of structural conditions of the Fund, were outside of the core radius of the Funds knowledge' which decreased to one third later on (Interview IMF02, 2008). By attaching conditions to loans, the IMF diffuses 'neoliberal policies worldwide' (Chorev and Babb, 2009: 469), and during the Euro crisis in 2010, structural conditionality was 'far more extensive than in other contemporaneous IMF-supported programs' (IEO, 2018b: 7). Despite a reform of the organisational approach regarding structural conditions, national authorities still perceive a lack of ownership and there is little transparency in staff reports about how structural conditionality has been designed in areas where the IMF lacks expertise (IEO, 2018b).

Trade unions are particularly concerned about structural conditions targeting national labour markets, which include, for example, a reduction in pensions and minimum wages and the shrinking of the public sector as employer. The study from Rickard and Caraway (2019) confirmed that governments which face public sector loan conditions introduce deeper cuts to the wage bill than governments under IMF programmes without these conditions. However, trade unions have some leverage to influence the implementation of conditionality, for example by increasing the political costs of reforms (Gunaydin, 2018: 891).

At intra-organisational level, the asymmetric power structure which becomes, amongst others, reflected in multi-country constituencies, provides some members with a high level of influence in decision-making processes and others with very little influence. Highly influential members such as the USA and European members use the IMF to monitor and control international financial and economic developments, and to 'pursue its own foreign policy objectives' (Darrow, 2003: 28; Ortiz and Cummins, 2019). Furthermore, EDs are not accountable to the members of their own constituency. They are not obliged to vote in accordance with the instructions and the views of their members, and their vote is not necessarily legitimated by the majority of members (Woods and Lombardi, 2006).

Since its foundation, the IMF has undergone several changes and innovation processes such as regarding its lending instruments and internal voting. However, its democratic accountability is still weak, and despite the last voting reforms in 2016, 'the distribution of voting power remains severely imbalanced in favour of the USA, European countries and Japan' (Bretton Woods Project, 2019a: 3). The IMF's work on inequality issues has improved over the last years but there is still a long way to go. For a long time, both the IMF and the WB continued to push for macroeconomic policies which focused on fiscal consolidation (austerity) including the privatisation of social services and the weakening of labour rights (Bretton Woods Project, 2019a). Internal and external research have confirmed the negative effects of these measures on employment, private demand and GDP growth; however, the Washington Consensus seems to persist (Ortiz and Cummins, 2019). It therefore remains to be seen if the latest crises lead to a more profound change of organisational policies and their implementation, although some predictions present a less hopeful vision in this regard (Ortiz and Cummins, 2021).

Notes

1 Source: IMF Members' Quota and Voting Power (2019) http://www.imf.org/exter nal/np/sec/memdir/members.aspx
2 DPF is also referred to as Development Policy Lending (DPL)
3 Source: World Bank (2020) https://www.worldbank.org/en/about/leadership
4 The appointed and elected Executive Directors of the IBRD, the IDA, the IFC, and MIGA are available on the following website: https://www.worldbank.org/en/about/leadership/votingpowers
5 Source: WBG (2022) https://www.worldbank.org/en/programs/accountability/brief/the-inspection-panel, also see annual report FY 2021 https://www.worldbank.org/en/programs/accountability/publication/world-bank-inspection-panel-annual-report-fy2021
6 Source: WBG (2020) 'Employment Policy' https://www.worldbank.org/en/about/careers/employment-policy
7 Source: WB (2020) http://pubdocs.worldbank.org/en/404071412346998230/The-World-Bank-Group-Organizational-Chart-English.pdf
8 The FIDIC was established in 1913 and has currently 102 member associations worldwide which represent more than one million engineering professionals. Member associations include, for example, the American Council of Engineering Companies (USA) and the Association for Consultancy and Engineering (UK) (FIDIC, 2019).
9 See: Procurement Framework and Regulations for Projects after 1 July 2016 https://projects.worldbank.org/en/projects-operations/products-and-services/brief/procurement-new-framework#SPD

10 Source: Allocation of Votes by Organization (2022) https://www.worldbank.org/en/about/leadership/votingpowers

11 The Conference adopted the Addis Ababa Action Agenda (AAA Agenda). All participating governments agreed to end poverty and hunger and to promote sustainable development by respecting human rights, ensuring gender equality and enabling full and productive employment and decent work

12 Malaysia has ratified the ILO Convention (C098) on the Right to Organise and Collective Bargaining, but it has not ratified the ILO Convention (C087) on Freedom of Association and Protection of the Right to Organise.

13 Greece paid off the IMF bailout loans in April 2022.

14 IMF members' quotas and voting power (2020) https://www.imf.org/external/np/sec/memdir/members.aspx

15 Source: IMF (2020) https://www.imf.org/external/np/sec/memdir/eds.aspx

16 The position of CEO at the World Bank was created by WB President Jim Yong Kim in 2016.

17 The IMF website on CD provides a complete and updated overview of the regional centres and offices https://www.imf.org/en/Capacity-Development/how-we-work

5 The International Labour Organization and its cooperation with the World Bank and the IMF

The ILO was founded in 1919 with the objective to establish international labour standards and to ensure social progress and decent employment and working conditions alongside economic growth (Rodgers et al., 2009). It is the only tripartite organisation in the UN system which gives a voice to workers, employers, and governments at international level, and it is the only UN organisation where trade unions have direct access and an institutional seat underpinned by seats in the governing body as well as constitutional and statutory roles.

> The Organization as a whole, in its intention and in its essence, is a global assembly of the representatives of the world of work.
>
> (Rodgers et al., 2009: 11)

The 'Bureau for Workers' Activities' (ACTRAV) is the main link between the ILO and the trade unions. In this role, ACTRAV provides support to trade unions regarding the promotion and defence of labour rights, and it ensures that concerns of organised labour are taken into consideration in the policy development and activities of the ILO. The equivalent to ACTRAV for employers' and business organisations is the 'Bureau for Employer's Activities' (ACT/EMP).

For workers and the trade unions, the ILO 'is a major instrument to pursue their goals' (Rodgers et al., 2009: 16). Both the ITUC and the ILO confer legitimacy and recognition on each other (Cotton and Gumbrell-McCormick, 2012), in particular through ACTRAV, and in this regard, the ILO is more sensitive to trade union concerns than other intergovernmental organisations. Furthermore, some GUFs such as EI work together with the ILO on specific topics such as education, child labour, and decent work. In the past, EI made regular proposals to the joint ILO-UNESCO 'Committee of Experts on the Application of the Recommendations concerning Teaching Personnel' (CEART) (Interview EI (GUF), 2008, 2019).

In 2019, the ILO celebrated its centenary and adopted the 'Declaration for the Future of Work' during the 108th session of the International Labour Conference. With the Declaration, the ILO aimed to renew its mandate and to reflect on the

DOI: 10.4324/9781315458410-5

report and recommendations of the 'Global Commission on the Future of Work'. The former UNI General Secretary and member of the Commission stated that:

> the ILO Global Commission report, and its respective pillars, give a kind of a lighthouse or a roadmap for the ILO to follow in the future (. . .) the future of work has got a pretty strong place in government reflections about what their future labour market policies will be, and the ILO is meant to be a basis for this.
>
> (Interview UNI, 2019)

The ILO plays an important role with regard to framing the transformations in the world of work caused by climate change, migration, digitalisation, and inequality. However, the latest Declaration cannot hide the fact that the ILO is also facing serious challenges and struggles to redefine its position within the global governance system. It also highlights the increasing influence of the employer side within the ILO once again (Silva, 2021). The following chapter provides an overview of the ILO's history, organisational structure, identity and its cooperation with the IFIs including the IMF and the World Bank.

Historical 'milestones' of the ILO

The foundation of the ILO was a response to 'war and revolution' in the 20th century, drawing on the belief that 'peace and justice go hand in hand' (Rodgers et al., 2009: 2–3). This belief is reflected in the preamble of the ILO constitution which states that 'universal and lasting peace can be established only it is based upon social justice' (ILO, 1997). After more than a century, this statement has not lost in relevance, in particular in view of recent global economic developments that have led to rapidly growing inequality across countries.

The ILO's constitution formed part of the Treaty of Versailles in 1919 and has been amended six times since. In 1944, the highest governing body of the ILO, the International Labour Conference (ILC), adopted the 'Declaration of Philadelphia' which became an integral part of its constitution in 1946, the same year that the ILO became a specialised agency of the UN. The 1944 Declaration reaffirmed the fundamental principles of the ILO, including that 'labour is not a commodity', that 'the freedom of expression and association are essential to sustained progress', and that 'poverty anywhere constitutes a danger to prosperity everywhere' (Rodgers et al., 2009: 251). In addition, it expanded the organisational mandate and vision as established in the Treaty of Versailles beyond the field of labour conditions by addressing all human beings and their participation in 'social process', highlighting the role of social and economic policies (Perulli, 2018: 4–5).

The ILO Constitution and the Philadelphia Declaration define the ILO's normative foundation and mission and neither of them has lost their relevance in the past decades (Supiot, 2020). In order to achieve its normative mission, the ILO designs and sets international labour standards through the creation of conventions and recommendations. Conventions can be described as 'hard' standards which become legally binding when member states ratify them and are subject to international supervision. Recommendations are not legally binding and can therefore be described as 'soft standards' (Hepple, 2005: 4), although in many cases, they accompany conventions. Yet there are 189 conventions which can be divided into 'technical', 'fundamental', and 'governance' conventions depending on their nature (Rombouts, 2019). Technical conventions concern the safety of workers such as expressed in the 'Maximum Weight Convention' (No 127) from 1967. Fundamental conventions, also called core labour standards (CLS), are stated in the 'Declaration of Fundamental Principles and Rights at Work' (ILO, 1998) and all ILO members are required to respect these standards. Governance conventions aim to ensure the functioning of the international labour standard system and include, for example, the 'Labour Inspection Convention' (No 81) from 1947. The latter stipulates that each ILO member should maintain a system of labour inspection in industrial workplaces. However, although the organisation encourages members to ratify conventions, ratification is heavily dependent on the commitment of member states. In this regard, the indicative nature of recommendations has always put a constraint to the normative system of the ILO (Kott, 2019).

In addition to conventions and recommendations, declarations provide another important instrument to the ILO and its normative capacity (Jakovleski et al., 2019). Key declarations are the 'Declaration of Philadelphia' (1944), the 'Declaration of Fundamental Principles and Rights at Work' (1998), the 'Declaration on Social Justice for a Fair Globalisation' (2008), and the 'Centenary Declaration for the Future of Work' (2019). All Declarations promote the principle of social justice. The 1998 Declaration, which presents 'universally acknowledged human rights' (Perulli, 2018: 5), draws on the aspiration of people for social progress and has a promotional character (Kellerson, 1998). The 2008 Declaration, which was updated in 2022, promotes 'Decent Work' and redistribution by focusing on employment, social protection, social dialogue, and the fundamental principles and rights at work (ILO, 2008). It states:

> Other international and regional organizations with mandates in closely related fields can have an important contribution to make to the implementation of the integrated approach. . . . As trade and financial market policy both affect employment, it is the ILO's role to evaluate those employment effects to achieve its aim of placing employment at the heart of economic policies.
>
> (ILO, 2008: 8)

In 2016, the ILO General Conference evaluated the impact of the 2008 Declaration and confirmed its commitment and the significance of the Declaration, in particular with regard to the implementation of the UN 2030 Agenda for Sustainable Development.[1] However, it also noted several remaining challenges including the achievement of policy coherence with regard to the implementation of the decent work agenda and the monitoring of the progress in member countries (ILO, 2016a).

The 'Centenary Declaration for the Future of Work' (2019) highlights the importance of decent and sustainable work and urges ILO constituents 'to seize the opportunities and address the challenges to shape a fair, inclusive and secure future of work' (ILO, 2019c: 2). The 'human-centred' approach of the agenda and its increasing prominence in the international discourse is considered by some ILO representatives as an opportunity to take leadership in the discourse and to promote its implementation and understanding by governments and other international organisations (Interview ILO10, 2019). Some trade union representatives already observed a 'spill-over effect in broader thinking' such as in the OECD (Interview UNI, 2019). An example is the OECD Employment Outlook (2019b) which highlighted the importance of employment and social protection and the important role of governments for creating an inclusive future of work. In the light of the Covid-19 pandemic and its negative impact on employment and working conditions across countries (Baunach, 2020), the implementation of the 2019 Declaration could offer an opportunity to revive multilateralism.

Organisational structure

The governance system of the ILO is based on four pillars: tripartism, the adoption of international conventions and recommendations, a monitoring system to ensure the enforcement of laws and regulations, and the collaboration with international organisations (Rodgers et al., 2009). The principle of tripartism and the adoption and ratification of international labour standards are distinctive characteristics of the ILO in comparison to other intergovernmental organisations such as the World Bank and the IMF.

> Tripartism is consistent with a liberal reformist vision that seeks to correct the asymmetric power relations between workers and employers intrinsic to the employment contract through the organization of collective bargaining.
>
> (Kott, 2019: 26)

Although tripartism, which ensures that governments, employers, and trade unions alike are represented in organisational decision-making processes, is considered by many as providing legitimacy to the organisation, it has faced many challenges over the years. Long-standing tensions between employer and worker representatives became particularly obvious in 2012 and 2013 when the employer side attacked Convention 87 which recognises the right to strike (La Hovary, 2015) and during the negotiations of the Centenary Declaration:

> When we started the Global Commission work in 2017 the employers were saying that there wouldn't be a declaration, they didn't see a need for a

declaration, that what we had was enough, and they were kind of dampening expectations.

(Interview UNI, 2019)

The challenge around the principle of tripartism is also linked to developments at the national level, which has been acknowledged by the Director-General in the past:

> (. . .) the strength and legitimacy of tripartism and its actors depend on mutual recognition and respect of rights and roles. Refusal by any part to engage in social dialogue at national level can only be detrimental to that legitimacy. Equally, non-recognition of representative organizations for purposes of collective bargaining erodes the representational function of organizations. . . . In that light, the idea that individual contract arrangements could be an equal and equivalent alternative to collective bargaining between representative organizations cannot easily be squared with the ILO's 'unique advantage' of tripartism and social dialogue.
>
> (ILO, 2013b: 17)

Despite all its challenges, tripartism characterises the ILO's governance. The ILO's main governing body is the 'General Conference of Representatives of the Members', also called 'International Labour Conference' (ILC). The ILC represents all ILO member countries (currently 187) whereby each country is represented by two government delegates – one worker representative and one employer representative. The conference takes place every year and is responsible for the adoption of international labour standards in form of conventions and recommendations and its supervision at national level. It is important to point out that the negotiation and decision on conventions is done by all ILO members and their representatives including government, employer, and trade union representatives. ILO staff provides input, background materials, and analysis but is not involved in the negotiations themselves.

> (. . .) it's an international negotiation, it has its rhythm, its dynamics, and its tensions quite frankly, both between the employers and the workers organisations but also between governments with either different levels of development or different political orientations, so that really determines the negotiation of conventions.
>
> (Interview ILO09, 2018)

Regarding the supervision of labour standards, the ILC examines member reports in which governments outline their compliance with ratified conventions. Further tasks comprise the examination of the 'Global Report' submitted by the Director-General as well as a discussion of the annual report. All delegates are entitled to vote individually on all matters considered by the ILC. However, if a member country fails to nominate one of the two nongovernment representatives, which it is entitled to nominate, the available nongovernment representative is allowed to speak but not to vote. All decisions are taken by a simple majority of the votes. Once the ILC adopts a proposal, it stays with the conference to decide if the proposal should take the form of a convention or a recommendation. The adoption of a convention or recommendation requires a majority of two-thirds of the delegates votes (ILO, 1997). The General Conference also adopts the organisational budget. In 2018, the ILO's income was US$708.3 million whereby the main income sources were assessed contributions from member states (55 per cent) and voluntary contributions (37 per cent). The expenses (US$742.0 million) exceeded the income (ILO, 2019a). The ILO budget is the same in real terms than it was over 30 years ago, which has an impact on staffing levels and aid budgets that are available for projects (Interview ILO06, 2016).

The ILO's executive organ is the 'Governing Body', which is elected by the ILC, and which meets three times a year. It consists of 56 delegates (so called titular members) whereby 28 represent governments and the other 28 delegates are split equally between workers and employers. With regard to the 28 government members, ten are appointed by the countries of 'chief industrial importance'[2] which hold these seats on a de facto permanent basis. The other 18 are elected by government delegates to the ILC every three years excluding the ten countries of chief industrial importance. Most elected members retain their seats for at least two terms which allow them to accumulate knowledge and expertise, expand their social networks within and outside the organisation and to increase their influence. However, the permanent seats hold by industrialised countries and their decision-making power as well as the marginalisation of African countries continues to remain a source for internal conflict (Louis, 2019). The Governing Body is responsible for overseeing the International Labour Office, and it has a number of functions on its own, including the settlement of the agenda for the ILC, the election of the Director-General, and the filing of a complaint against a member country if necessary (ILO, 2019b).

The work of the Governing Body is structured through five sections and segments which are reflected in the agenda of each session hold by the Governing Body. The 'Policy Development Section' (POL) is divided into four policy segments (Employment and Social Protection, Multinational Enterprises, Social Dialogue, and Development Cooperation) and considers, for example, policies and activities in the fields of employment, training, working and employment conditions, social security, and social dialogue. The 'Legal Issues and International Labour Standards Section' (LILS) comprises two segments (Legal Issues, International Labour Standards and Human Rights) and considers, for example, the status of the ILO in member states as well as legal agreements concluded with other international organisations. The other three sections comprise the 'Programme, Financial and Administrative Section' (PFA), the 'Institutional Section' (INS), and the 'High-Level Section' (HL) (ILO, 2019b). Furthermore, the Governing Body

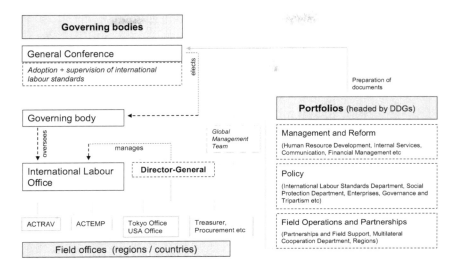

Figure 5.1 Formal Structure of the ILO

Source: Own illustration, based on the ILO structure and organisation (ILO, 2021c website) and the ILO Constitution (1997)

organises some of the work through committees and working groups, such as the 'Committee on Freedom of Association' (CFA) which was established in 1951 or the 'Working Party on the Social Dimension of Globalization'.

The third organisational body is the International Labour Office, the permanent secretariat, which is located in Geneva and managed by the Director-General and controlled by the Governing Body. It employs approximately 2,700 employees in Geneva and the 40 field offices around the world. The principle of tripartism is also reflected in the Office which since the 1990s comprises ACTRAV and ACT/EMP (Kott, 2019). According to Maupain (2009), an effective administrative structure of the ILO as a whole and the analytical capacity of the International Labour Office are key for the implementation of declarations at organisational level. In 2013, the then recently elected Director-General Guy Ryder announced changes in the Office structure in order to make the organisation more effective (ILO, 2013a). In this context, three 'portfolios' were introduced comprising 'Policy' (International Labour Standards Department, the Employment Policy Department, the Social Protection Department), the 'Management and Reform Portfolio' (e.g. Financial Management and Human Resources Development), and 'Field Operations and Partnerships'. The latter includes the 'Multilateral Cooperation Department' which 'leads, coordinates and promotes the ILO's active involvement in the UN system' (ILO website, 2020[3]). Each portfolio is headed by a Deputy Director-General (DDG) which together with the Director-General forms the Global Management team that ensures coordination, cohesion, and efficiency between different policy areas and across the organisation (ILO, 2013a). The newly created structure aimed to overcome the organisation's 'fragmented' approach and the DDG of the Policy portfolio provides 'guidance at a high level to all of the ILO policy staff, in other words to all of the experts who deal with economic, legal, social policy' (Interview ILO09, 2018). Furthermore, the Policy DDG also plays an important role in the G20 context as ILO Sherpa interacting with the Sherpas from the WB and the IMF. In addition to the three portfolios, the new structure comprises eight units which report directly to the Director-General including the 'Bureau for Workers' Activities' and the 'ILO Office for the United States'.

In general, job expectations and descriptions for ILO Office staff vary and can be driven by employer or by worker interests (Interview ILO01, 2008). The responsibilities of the Office include the collection and distribution of information relating to international labour relations and working conditions and the preparation of documents which are relevant to the General Conference. In March 2022, the Governing Body elected Gilbert Houngbo, the former ILO Deputy Director-General for Field Operations and Partnerships, as new Director-General. Yet no woman has held this position. Houngbo succeeds Guy Ryder who held the post since 2012. In his opening remarks to the Centenary Conference in 2019, Ryder acknowledged the profound changes in the world of work and confirmed the main objectives of the organisation which are the promotion of social justice and decent work. However, he also pointed out that the organisation needs to reflect on how to tackle future challenges.

> (. . .), are not called then to review or revise, or even to add, to the objectives which the ILO was established to pursue, this great social contract for peace and social justice. But we certainly do need to subject to rigorous examination exactly how we intend to realize these objectives. . . . Impossible that our organization would be best served by unreflecting business as usual. What worked well yesterday may not work well tomorrow.
>
> (Ryder, 2019)

Based on these reflections, the ILO and its new Director-General will need to evaluate how to embrace future decades and to enhance organisational capacity and governance.

Organisational knowledge development and identity

The ILO's main objectives comprise the promotion of workers' rights and labour standards, social justice, and awareness that labour is not a commodity and not tradable (Perulli, 2018; Evju, 2013). These objectives are directly linked to knowledge creation, for example through labour inspectors which examine the application of national labour standards in the workplace, research activities on labour and employment issues, and technical cooperation including the support of countries regarding their social protection response. Key documents such as the ILO flagship reports the 'World Employment and Social Outlook', the 'Global Wage Report', and the 'World Social Protection Report' help to disseminate explicit knowledge. Furthermore, the ILO publishes a 'Research Paper' series which provides evidence-based analysis of policies at national, regional, and international level; 'Working Papers' which present preliminary findings in relation to work and employment issues, and 'Research Briefs' which provide policy advice.

The ILO acts as a knowledge creator and standard setter and both tasks define the normative role of the organisation in the multilateral system (Maupain, 2013). Amongst the best-known conventions, which describe the organisation's 'ethos', are the conventions on discrimination (No. 111), freedom of association (No. 87), collective bargaining (No. 154), and social security (No. 102) (Standing, 2008: 358). Over time the ILO's focus has gradually changed towards development cooperation and the agreement, and ratification of conventions has slowed down (Royle, 2010; Baccaro and Mele, 2012). Since 1998, only nine conventions have been adopted by the ILC of which two were protocols to existing conventions (Jakovleski et al., 2019). The ratification of conventions remains challenging, and even some developed countries such as the USA, which is one of main donors to the ILO, are lagging behind with ratifications. The USA has only ratified 14 conventions to this day whereby 11 are technical conventions.[4] According to a representative from the AFL-CIO, the USA confronts serious challenges with regard to the fundamental right to organise 'that are written into our laws and how our laws are organised' Interview AFL-CIO, 2017). An example is the Hoffman Plastic Compounds labour law decision from 2002 which denied the undocumented worker Jose Castro an award of pay back after being laid off for participating in a union organising campaign.

The 'Migration for Employment Convention' (No 97) from 1949 which is highly relevant in a global context has been ratified by fewer than half of the ILO member countries. According to Baccaro and Mele (2012: 196), the relatively low level of ratification and implementation of newly adopted conventions is in 'stark contrast to the organization's stated goal of providing universal and uniform rules regulating labour conditions around the world'. However, despite this large ratification gap, in August 2020, the ILO achieved a milestone, when for the first time in its history, one international labour convention (Worst Forms of Child Labour Convention, No. 182) became universally ratified by all member states. This is an important achievement, in particular as the Covid-19 pandemic is likely to push millions of more children into child labour (ILO, 2020a).

As with other organisations, changes in knowledge development and identity at the ILO are driven by internal factors (such as top management and the Director-General) and external factors (such as political and economic changes). For example, the former Director-General David Morse (1948–1970) promoted internal changes of the ILO focusing on development and technical assistance. In 1969, the ILO launched the 'World Employment Programme' which was led by Louis Emmerij and 'would become the agency's largest-scale intervention around development issues' (Benanav, 2019: 114). The programme aimed to support governments in the reduction of unemployment by promoting measures such as rural development, infrastructure projects, and the reduction of capital intensity in relation to other production factors. The objective was to level employment rates with economic growth rates. In the same year the ILO received the Nobel Peace Prize for the promotion of social security in the western world.

In the 1970s, economic conditions changed and oil and energy crises resulted in petroleum shortages and elevated prices and led to a halt of full employment in developed countries. Although later in the 1980s international organisations and governments restored the 'economic growth paradigm', the objective of full employment was abandoned despite the criticisms of the ILO. During the rise of political and economic neoliberalism and its principles of labour market deregulation and flexibility, the ILO missed the opportunity to position itself. One example is the institutionalisation of the neo-liberal paradigm in the World Bank's structural adjustment policy, in which case:

> The ILO . . . failed to produce its own critique of structural adjustment, as an official policy document or recommendation. The first UN criticism of structural adjustment was produced not by the ILO but by UNICEF.
>
> (Benanav, 2019: 121)

Some authors such as Standing (2008) argue that a lack of confidence amongst senior officials of the ILO and the objective to receive funding from the Bank for future technical assistance projects were driving the limited response.

As a result, in the 1970s and 1980s, the instrumental power of the ILO in terms of framing economic developments started to diminish. The organisation failed to develop a coherent response to the supply-side economic model which is underpinned by the idea of labour market flexibility and privatisation and to position itself with regard to the informal sector although it was promoting the concept of informality (Benanav, 2019; Standing, 2008). At the beginning of the 1990s, after the end of the Cold War, the ILO was unable to defend and promote labourism and to criticise the World Bank's approach on labour policy in former communist countries (Standing, 2008).

The 1998 'Declaration on Fundamental Principles and Rights at Work', which prioritises some selected conventions and the endorsement of the 'Decent Work Agenda' in 1999, was an attempt to regain influence at international level. The 1998 Declaration was positively embraced by different stakeholders including governments, in particular the US government and employers. One of the reasons for this welcoming attitude was the fact that the selected conventions do not present social or work rights and with this any pressure on employers or liberal governments (Standing, 2008: 367). In 2022, the ILO added safety and health to the fundamental principles of the 1998 Declaration based on the conventions concerning occupational safety and health (No 155 and No 187). In the past, the 1998 Declaration has been considered critically by many authors and law scholars, such as Philip Alston. Alston and Heenan (2004: 223) expressed their concerns about the narrow focus of the declaration and the organisational move

> towards an approach that is fundamentally promotional, rather than grounded in firm legal obligations and involving targeted institutional responses to violations of labour rights.

They and others highlighted the potential negative consequences for the organisation by focusing on 'a core set of largely procedural and essentially civil and political labour rights' which are in line with the preferences of a neoliberal economic approach (Alston and Heenan, 2004: 223), and the neglect of economic rights including work safety, maternity provisions, and pension and disability benefits (Standing, 2008). Although there is some agreement that the declaration has weakened the supervisory mechanism of the ILO further by fostering a promotional approach (Royle, 2010; Standing, 2008), there are authors and ILO representatives who highlighted positive outcomes. For example, Maupain (2005) highlighted an increase in the ILO's capacity to protect fundamental workers' rights and Marginson (2016) noted a rise in the ratification of the eight core conventions although he remained critical about the fact that the ILO has no sanctions to apply when countries breach ratified conventions.

The Decent Work Agenda aims to embed decent work in the ILO's organisational structure and to synthesise 'rights at work, employment and social protection into an overall vision, pursued through social dialogue' (Rodgers et al., 2009: 10; ILO, 2010). The agenda is based on four strategic pillars (employment creation, social protection, rights at work, and social dialogue) and acknowledges the importance of work and rights of workers beyond formal wage employment including informal, self-employed, domestic, and voluntary workers (Deranty and MacMillan, 2012). In 2015, the agenda became an integral part of the 2030 SDGs. However, the SDGs targets for decent work have not been aligned to the four strategic pillars of the ILO agenda, which some authors consider as a missed opportunity to bring 'policy coherence to the agendas of the ILO, the UN human rights system, and the 2030 global development agenda' (Frey and MacNaughton, 2016: 10).

The ILO and its relationship with the IFIs

In the Centenary Declaration, the ILO underlined the importance of multilateralism with regard to the future of work and declared the promotion of workers' rights as key to inclusive and sustainable growth (ILO, 2019c). The ILO plays an important role in the multilateral system, and the promotion of coherency and solidarity amongst different stakeholders in the global governance system is one of its constitutional duties (Supiot, 2020). In this regard, it is the ILO's responsibility to consider international economic and financial policies and to evaluate its contribution to social progress and justice (Rodgers et al., 2009; Perulli, 2018). This becomes even more important as many stakeholders including trade unions consider the multilateral system as weak (Baunach, 2020). The ITUC has called repeatedly for a reform of the World Bank and the IMF and a 'new social contract' which 'puts people back at the centre of multilateralism' (ITUC, 2021 website[5]).

Since 1946, the ILO has signed 86 partnerships with international organisations, including the 'Better Work' programme (2006) and the 'Let's Work' (2013) global partnership with the IFC. The 'Better Work' programme is seen by others in the UN as a model for working with the WBG. Based on an innovative financing model, the programme led to an increase in productivity whilst implementing labour standards (Interview ILO07, 2017).

In comparison to the World Bank and the IMF, the ILO has limited resources available (Carbonnier and Gironde, 2019) and a limited political influence at global level despite its normative power (Supiot, 2020). Since the 1990s and in particular since the disappearance of the former communist regimes, the ILO has struggled to promote its own social agenda and to develop a counterweight to the deregulatory policies promoted by the World Bank, the IMF and the OECD (Kott, 2019). In the 1990s an attempt to integrate a social clause in the World Trade Organization (WTO) and to link trade with labour rights failed due to the objections of developing countries (Chan and Ross, 2003). Nevertheless, as one trade union representative expressed it:

> (. . .) one of the things you can't do is ignore the role of the ILO in terms of the work of the Bank and the IMF; but also, more broadly for us, the need . . . to have the ILO at the table. . . . The IMF can do its work and the Bank can do its work, but you can't put the leverage for growth in place, whether it's the global level or the national level, if you don't actually deal with labour markets. And when you deal with labour markets, you need to deal with the ILO and with the unions and employers. So, it's just a fundamental analysis that you must have the ILO at the table.
>
> (Interview ITUC03, 2009)

In the past decades, the ILO undertook an effort to develop a stronger connection and exchange with the IFIs which will be considered in more detail later.

Cooperation with the IMF

In 2000, the ILO established the 'international policy group' which focused on relations with other international organisations. In 2002, the unit became a department on its own; the 'Policy Integration Department'. The department focused on the integration of policies internally, in particular regarding the decent work agenda and the communication of policies to organisations like the IMF and the World Bank. Under Director-General Guy Ryder, the department became part of the then newly created portfolio structure. Nowadays the 'Multilateral Cooperation Department' (MULTILATERALS), coordinates and manages the involvement of the ILO in the UN system and the cooperation with other multilateral organisations and the IFIs. In addition, the ILO has an 'ILO Office for the United States' in Washington D.C. which also focuses on 'partnerships' including with the IMF and the World Bank. The office promotes cooperation in relation to joint programmes, the ILO labour standards, and maintains a continuous information exchange with the IMF and the World Bank.

Since the mid-1990s, the ILO has a 'seat' (observer status) at the IMF IMFC which advises and reports to the IMF Board of Governors. It addresses these meeting through written statements in which it provides its own position on economic and financial developments and policies. For example, in October 2020, the statement of the ILO Director-General that was presented to the IMFC outlined current global trends, focusing on employment issues such as substantial losses in labour income and rising unemployment levels. It proposed measures to reduce poverty and inequality including the development and strengthening of social security systems and public and private investments in job creation and skilling (ILO, 2020b). The statement referred to the 'human-centered' approach as outlined in the ILO Centenary Declaration and the SDGs. Generally, the ILO aims to 'catch' the current debate at the IMF and to provide some input during these meetings (Interview ILO06, 2017). However, the former director of MULTILATERALS noted in this context:

> I suppose the best analogy is, it is water dripping on a stone. If you don't do it then the implication is that you're happy with the way the world affairs are going, so you have to do it.
>
> (Interview ILO06, 2017)

It took some time until the ILO started paying attention to the IMF, despite its constitutional mandate as outlined in the Philadelphia Declaration to consider international economic and financial policies. In the 1980s, trade unions started criticising the IFIs structural adjustment lending. The social consequences of the debt crisis in Latin America and Africa contributed to the IMF's acknowledgement 'that the trade unions were potentially a rather loud voice which could be making it much harder for the government to deal with them' (Interview ILO06, 2016). At this point of time, the IMF experimentally started to meet with trade unions and the meetings were eventually joined by the ILO. The engagement with the IMF was perceived critically by some ILO employer representatives which considered macro-economic and financial issues as the 'job' of the IMF (Interview ILO06, 2016).

From the perspective of some ILO representatives, the cooperation between the ILO and the IMF was driven by the trade unions which pushed the ILO towards getting involved. The trade unions were also a key driver in the following decades. For example, during the high-level meetings in 2009, the then president of the Australian Council of Trade Unions (ACTU) stated that the international financial crisis is a good starting point to promote a partnership between the IMF and the ILO (Observation Minutes High-Level Meetings, 2009). A senior adviser from the IMF responded that the IMF strives for more international cooperation, even though this is difficult for the organisation due to a lack of available resources (Ibid., 2009). In recent years, a more formal dialogue has developed and there is a 'willingness to listen and to engage on the part of both institutions' (Interview ILO10, 2019).

The promotion of cooperation also depends on the organisational leadership. Although traditionally the IMF managing director comes from a European country and has some experience with trade unions, the attitudes of managing directors towards cooperation with trade unions and the ILO vary. For example, Dominique Strauss-Kahn had a stronger interest in a working relationship with trade unions and was 'prepared to be much more adventurous' than his successor Christine Lagarde (Interview ILO06, 2016). Strauss-Kahn promoted cooperation in particular in the aftermath of the international financial and economic crisis in 2008. He spoke at an ILO high-level meeting in 2008 on the social consequences of the crisis, and in 2010, the IMF and the ILO held their first joint conference in Oslo. The negative impact of the crisis on jobs is considered as one of the key drivers for cooperation back then:

> I think it was very much a mutual awareness that the jobs consequences of the financial crisis would be severe and that in some ways turning around and getting out of crisis had to be both fiscal but also jobs, you needed to generate the jobs to get the wages, to get the economy turning in the opposite direction. Strauss-Kahn was very much aware of that; I think he was also aware that just managing the crisis would require social dialogue, so whether or not the dialogue led to turning the economy around – just to contain the tensions of the crisis it was important to talk, almost for the sake of talking, so he was also aware of that.
>
> (Interview ILO06, 2016)

The joint conference on 'The Challenges of Growth, Employment and Social Cohesion' was attended by senior government leaders, trade unionists, employers, and academics. One of the outcomes was an agreement between the IMF and the ILO to cooperate in two policy areas including social protection floors and job growth and both organisations acknowledged the important role of social dialogue in the context of tackling existing challenges (IMF, 2010).

The cooperation in the area of social dialogue included the selection of three pilot countries: Zambia, Romania, and the Dominican Republic. However, in particular in Romania, stakeholders held different perspectives with regard to monetary approaches which limited the potential positive outcomes of social dialogue (Interview ILO06, 2016). In recent years, the IMF acknowledged the relevance of social dialogue more extensively and its research department has published some studies which underline the importance of social dialogue. Nevertheless, there are still fundamental differences between both organisations, and for example in 2020, the IMF blocked the establishment of a regulatory frame in Greece which would have helped to re-establish social dialogue and sector level bargaining (ETUI, 2020).

In the area of social protection, the three pilot countries comprised Mozambique, Vietnam, and El Salvador. In Mozambique, the ILO and the IMF reached some agreement on the costing and the basic elements of a social protection system but generally the pilot projects were not further developed. This was mainly due to the ILO's engagement with the UN system and the implementation of the 2030 Agenda for Sustainable Development which since its adoption in 2015 has a high level of 'political legitimacy' (Interview ILO06, 2016). Like on social dialogue, both organisations hold different views with regard to social spending and protection. In 2019, the IMF published a policy paper on its engagement on social spending including social protection, education, and health. The policy paper outlines and comments on the recommendations received by civil society organisations and trade unions. Both point out that the IMF has limited expertise in the areas of social spending and protection and should therefore step back from taking on a leading role. In this context, the ITUC called for a 'more regular, structured cooperation [*of the IMF*] with other international organisations with mandates and expertise in the area of social policy, including the ILO' (ITUC, 2018f: 1). During the high-level meetings in 2021, the IMF Managing Director acknowledged shared concerns between the IMF and the ILO about the impact of the Covid-19 pandemic and jobs recovery and announced plans for joint country pilots on social protection (ITUC, 2021b).

Despite some progress in the area of social spending, IMF conditionality, which is considered as 'critical for program success' by the IMF itself (IMF, 2019g: 13, 15), remains a concern for trade unions and other civil society organisations. Conditions to loans are attached to all spending categories including education, health, social assistance, unemployment benefits, and pensions. The latest IMF review of conditionality highlights the increase of structural conditions and recommends 'to build expertise in critical shared areas of responsibility' (IMF, 2019h: 42). Such shared areas include for example reforms relating to pension systems, the health and education sector, civil service and public employment, public enterprises, and privatisation. However, despite the ILO's and trade union expertise in these areas, a potential cooperation is not explicitly considered in the review document.

Apart from the high-level cooperation, the ILO and the IMF have a stable and regular exchange of working papers and knowledge in research. Over the years, the IMF has published some working papers about labour market institutions and inequality which were welcome by the ILO and the trade unions. For example, the paper from Jaumotte and Buitron Osorio (2015) highlighted the fact that an erosion of labour market institutions leads to increased income inequality. Blanchard et al. (2013: 20) concluded in their paper that 'implications of alternative structures of collective bargaining are poorly understood' and therefore advised the IMF to carefully consider its policy advice in this area. These two papers were published under the then IMF chief economist Olivier Blanchard and his influence on the IMF research department was considered positively by ILO representatives and trade unionists, especially as Blanchard seemed to 'share' the same language with the ILO and trade unions (Interview ILO06, 2016). Still, despite his positive influence the challenge of intra-organisational decoupling within the IMF persists, and country mission teams rarely consider the global perspective at national level that is provided in studies of the research department.

In summary, the cooperation between the ILO and the IMF has increased although the focus is on research. Different perspectives and approaches between the two organisations remain, which can be related to the organisations' different natures and missions. In the case of the ILO, social justice and social protection define its mission, but these principles are not part of the IMF's mandate. Although the IMF has acknowledged the importance of social protection and its contribution to macroeconomic development, action has been limited despite joining the UN Social Protection Floor initiative in 2009 (IEO, 2017). In 2018, the then special rapporteur on extreme poverty and human rights Philip Alston presented a report to the UN Human Rights Council on the IMF highlighting that:

> No international institution exerts greater influence than the IMF over issues such as distribution, including social protection. But for many years, it took the position that these issues were not its concern; it could take account only of macroeconomic issues narrowly defined. Other institutions were left to pick up the pieces in the social area but could only do so within the confines of the fiscal space, if any, left open after IMF prescriptions had been adopted.
>
> (UN Human Rights Council, 2018a: 3)

The IMF's limited work in the field of social protection can be explained by the lack of a general agreed position of IMF staff regarding the IMF's role in social protection and the lack of a consistent organisational approach and strategy (IEO, 2017: 2):

> (. . .), while the IMF's preferred approach of targeting social protection to the poor and vulnerable was aligned with the World Bank's approach, it meshed less well with the rights-based approach to social protection espoused by the International

Labour Organization and UN agencies which emphasizes universal benefits and targeting by category (e.g. demographic group) rather than income

The IEO (2017: 36) report recommended that the IMF 'should engage actively in inter-institutional cooperation on social protection' and that 'it must rely heavily on other agencies for in-depth expertise'.

However, there is not only a discrepancy in organisational approaches relating to social protection, social justice, and conditionality, but also the understanding of 'macroeconomic policy' in general. The definition promoted by the IMF has a strong fiscal and monetary focus which does not consider the declining labour share, income disparities and unemployment in relation to economic growth (Interview ILO06, 2017). For some years, the ILO has been arguing that the shift and decline in labour income share matters macro-economically. In 2019, a research study of the ILO Department of Statistics concluded that the global labour income share is declining and countercyclical and that 'within countries, relative increases of labour income at the upper end of the distribution are associated, on average, with relative losses for the rest' (ILO, 2019d: 39). According to Piketty (2015), it is important to analyse the reasons for labour income inequality in order to determine suitable and effective redistribution instruments such as the taxation of top incomes, fiscal transfers, and minimum wages.

Despite all the limitations and challenges, the political dialogue at the leadership level is perceived as 'cordial and respectful' and knowledge exchange between research departments is moving forward, although one ILO representative stated, 'we could do more things together' (Interview ILO08, 2017). The question that arises in relation to the functioning of the multilateral system is whether international organisations have a choice regarding cooperation. In the case of the ILO-IMF cooperation, there is some recognition from both sides that mutual dialogue is necessary and the only way forward, or as one former ILO representative expressed it:

> I think the ILO is condemned to, we have to deal with the IMF because it is the place, the macro-institution, but then I think the IMF has to deal with us too, because it can't do its job unless there is some social environmental dimension to what it is doing, and that I think has become much more evident and recognised, in part because of what we did.
>
> (Interview ILO06, 2016)

The UN special rapporteur Philip Alston recommended that the IMF should collaborate with the ILO 'in a much more concerted and meaningful way', specifically on issues such as social protection in which it lacks own expertise (UN Human Rights Council, 2018a: 19).

Cooperation with the World Bank

Similar to the IMF, the ILO cooperates with the WB in several areas and on several levels (e.g. high level and technical level) and both organisations undertake joint initiatives (Interview ILO08, 2017). Since around 2015, the ILO and the Bank meet every year in a 'more organised collaboration framework' (Interview ILO07, 2017). Areas of cooperation encompass, amongst others, data compilation and research activities, social protection, consultation processes, and third-party monitoring. At the beginning of the cooperation between the ILO and the WB, the focus was, however, on the development of mutual understanding:

> (. . .) there's been lots of scepticism in building the relationship, it's like any person, there is mistrust because of the things that were said in the past, so we have first learnt to know each other without any label behind.
>
> (Interview ILO08, 2017)

The WB is represented at the 'International Conference of Labour Statisticians' (ICLS), which is hosted by the ILO, and which acts as standard setter in labour statistics. The ICLS takes place every five years, and in 2018, it agreed a major review and extension of labour and decent work statistics such as new job classifications, and the measurement of the status of women at work and labour rights within the 2030 SDGs agenda. Furthermore, the ILO Department of Statistics also supports the WB in the implementation of new measurements and surveys (Interview ILO07, 2017).

Another topic of cooperation is social security. In 2012, the ILO adopted recommendation No 202 on Social Protection Floors which provides guidance to ILO members regarding the establishment and implementation of social protection floors and the provision of basic social security. In the same year, the ILO and the World Bank started co-chairing the 'Social Protection Inter-Agency Board' (SPIAC-B), which aims to coordinate social protection activities of its 20 members including the IMF and the OECD. However, the fact that the World Bank did not refer to the ILO core labour standards in its new ESF has been considered as problematic by the ILO and the trade unions. The ILO made the Bank aware that approaches and definitions of labour issues must be consistent between organisations in order to enable cooperation (Interview ITUC02, 2015). In general terms, both the ILO and the WB understand universal social protection as an integrated set of policies designed to ensure support to all people across the life cycle as well as income security (ILO and WBG, 2015). The trade unions are supportive of SPIAC-B and the ITUC has an observer status, but they are also aware of the fact that the WB's definition of 'universal social protection' differs to some extent from the definition of the ILO which has implications regarding the implementation of social protection:

> I think it [*SPIAC-B*] is a very important venue for conversations to happen that move towards some sort of coherence between organisations and donors, so I think that's been quite productive. It's not that they're always going to come to an agreement but at least there's a conversation happening that's open and

honest about what recommendations are being made, rather than having all these different donors run around and do whatever they want, that are giving mixed messages. So, it's not the mixed messages have been resolved yet, but I think that there is a really promising venue to make sure that people are talking to each other within the multilateral system, which too often doesn't happen.

(Interview ITUC06, 2019)

The importance of social protection for the WB has also been expressed in the White Paper on risk-sharing policies and protection of people in low- and middle-income countries (World Bank, 2019b). The Covid-19 pandemic exposed social protection gaps in many countries and the newly appointed UN special rapporteur on extreme poverty and human rights Olivier de Schutter pledged to base social protection systems on human rights and called on all stakeholders to support a Global Fund for social protection (De Schutter, 2020). The ITUC strongly supports the idea of a Global Fund but objects to the involvement of the private sector. From the ITUC's perspective, 'the ILO should be the main UN body involved in operational proposals for the development of the Global Fund, given that it is responsible for overseeing the implementation of international labour standards on social protection' (ITUC, 2020c: 5). The idea of a Global Fund was also discussed during the virtual Civil Society Policy Forum in March 2021. During this event, the WB director for Social Protection and Jobs acknowledged the coverage gap for social protection and agreed that more resources are needed. The acknowledgement supports the wider organisational recognition of social protection and labour market issues in the WB since the international financial and economic crisis in 2008. However, it must be noted that this recognition has not developed evenly within the WB and the 'old rhetoric' is still present amongst some staff (Interview ILO08, 2017). In this context, the restructuring process within the Bank seems to have empowered classical orthodox perceptions in the organisation (Interview ILO09, 2018).

Collaboration between the ILO and the WB also takes place in consultation processes. Like the ITUC, the ILO was strongly involved in the consultation process about the new WB safeguards which began in 2012. There was disappointment that the final document lacked reference to the ILO and the CLS. However, the ILO reiterated its intention to work with the Bank and to help them to implement the ESF without compromising its position on the international labour standards (Interview ILO07, 2017). This specific consultation process also highlighted the challenge of having different institutional representatives involved at board level. This became apparent when the finance ministers at the Board of Governors in the WB and the ministers for labour affairs representing governments at the ILO lacked an efficient exchange of information (Interview ILO07, 2017). In addition, internal issues at the Bank complicated the process further. However, the safeguards consultation process can be considered as a positive signal from the WB to apply a more participatory approach despite the remaining power struggle (Interview ILO08, 2017). As one ILO representative expressed it, 'we are both UN specialised agencies' and 'as an institution we have a mandate and a requirement, we will work together' (Interview ILO07, 2017). The ILO aims to support the ESF implementation process by providing the Bank with access to databases on supervisory mechanisms and complaints which have been made in relation to, for example, child labour, forced labour, and working conditions, as well as information in relation to ratified conventions, industrial sectors, and training (Interview ILO07, 2017).

Another example of consultation involving the ILO and the ITUC is the WB staff manual on labour market regulations. The guidebook provides some general guidelines and principles for the design and implementation of labour regulations in the areas of employment contracts, minimum wages, dismissal procedures and severance pay, and unemployment benefits (World Bank, 2015). The ILO considers the manual as highly relevant and as a step towards convergence between the ILO and the WB, but there is awareness that its use depends on the view of the WB leadership and the 'political wind' blowing in the organisation (Interview ILO09, 2018).

> (. . .) from an ILO perspective we can endorse every page, in fact we helped write every page, and so it was a lot of work but there was a real convergence. That manual still exists, it's still out there for WB staff who want to use it.
>
> (Interview ILO09, 2018)

Generally, as highlighted by the examples of social protection and consultation, the ILO aims to promote international labour standards and decent work through joint dialogue and collaboration. Third-party monitoring offers a further opportunity for the ILO to promote decent work and to mobilise additional financial resources for existing projects. One example is the cooperation in the cotton harvest and production in Uzbekistan which was formalised between the ILO and the WB by a 'Memorandum of Understanding' in 2014. The third-party monitoring project was financed by a WB Multi-Donor Trust Fund and included capacity building and awareness raising regarding child and forced labour in the cotton sector (ILO, 2018). The project was successful, and in 2020, the ILO reported the abolishment of 'systematic or systemic child labour' during the cotton harvest in Uzbekistan and a reduction of forced labour (ILO, 2020c: 4). From the ILO perspective, there is scope for organisational 'alignment of interests' if the Bank determines 'gaps' with regard to occupational health and safety, working conditions, and the development of grievance mechanisms (Interview ILO07, 2017).

The examples elucidate that the outcome of cooperation between the WB and the ILO is strongly determined by the nature and content of projects, organisational characteristics, and external factors such as economic and political crisis.

Regarding organisational characteristics, structural and cultural differences, and different organisational approaches and priorities, 'political dynamics' and the 'position in the overall geopolitical reality' need to be taken into account (Interview ILO09, 2018; Interview WB01, 2008).

> The ILO is a tripartite agency and so I would say it is partly on the left of the international finance, international organisations' community, and the Bank tends to be more corporate and more on the right.
>
> (Interview WB01, 2008)

Despite these differences, there are some commonalities such as the fact that the ILO and the WB share largely the same membership in terms of countries (although board members are linked to different national institutions), and both aim to achieve 'shared prosperity' (Interview ILO08, 2017).

> The Bank is a big, complicated place and you will find people whose political views are more aligned with the majority of the people in the ILO, and people who aren't, . . ., their policy is that in principle we have the same development goals, we want shared prosperity, inclusive growth, the problem is, it [*the Bank*] is not a monolith, nor is the ILO necessarily.
>
> (Interview ILO07, 2017)

On the ILO side, there is awareness of the complex structure of the WB, its internal challenges, and the importance of leadership. For example, under Jim Yong Kim's leadership, the ILO increased its effort to develop joint projects with the Bank because Kim was considered as an 'easier person to deal with than his predecessor' (Interview ILO06, 2016). However, the restructuring process at the WB undermined the establishment of a more stable and trust based inter-organisational relationship. As a result, the initial convergence of the WB towards ILO positions and 'international consensus' under Kim changed to a more divergent position later (Interview ILO09, 2018). In particular, the WB's 'World Development Report' from 2019 revealed an increasing level of divergence of the WB moving away from a socially oriented consensus and the position of the ILO and the ITUC (World Bank, 2019a).

All these factors make it difficult for ILO representatives to assess the impact and outcomes of cooperation and there is agreement that political commitment within the IFIs needs to be transferred from the high level to the departmental level:

> (. . .) you can do a lot of hard work with the Bank, find people in the Bank who are very amenable to working with you, and you're never quite sure what the real impact is.
>
> (Interview ILO06, 2016)

I think if they [*IFIs*] don't move into looking internally at their core business, then this function between the theory or the speech or the nice presentation of things in research, will not be translated into action. . . . So, the sustainability does not only depend on the level of political will and commitment that you see at the leadership; it goes hand-by-hand with the staff, with the structure, and there is where you hit rock.

(Interview ILO08, 2017)

In addition to internal factors, external factors such as the international financial crises from 2008 and the Covid-19 pandemic influence cooperation. The impact of the financial crisis created a window of political opportunity for the ILO of which the organisation took advantage, for example by developing its cooperation with the WB in the area of social protection further (Interview ILO09, 2018). Despite the remaining challenges, there is an overall agreement at the ILO and the ITUC that the engagement with the IFIs is necessary and useful. One ILO representative highlighted that not working together is not an option, but it is about 'how we can best work together and find a better alignment and just keep moving things forward' (Interview ILO07, 2017).

Challenges and future tasks for the ILO

The ILO is the primary 'designer' of international labour standards (Rombouts, 2019) and has a normative influence in the global governance system. Charnovitz (2015: 95) suggests that the ILO's normative capacity is not only state-centred and that the ILO 'could become more prescriptive for international organizations, the private sector, and voluntary bodies'. According to a former deputy director general for policy, the ILO has become more holistic and integrated in its internal work and analysis and it has become more ambitious in putting forward its analyses and proposals (Interview ILO09, 2018). An example is the ILO's focus on exploring issues about the future of work in a more holistic way long before other stakeholders followed (Interview ILO10, 2019).

(. . .) our approach to the future of work is not simply how many jobs will be created, how many jobs will be lost, but what are the policies that we need to harness, the trends that we see for a human-centred approach in which the social contract that is really at the heart of the ILO is both, reinvigorated and where it perhaps it doesn't yet exist, where policies are put into place that start to develop that social contract. I do think this is a very important moment for the ILO.

(Interview ILO10, 2019)

However, the ILO operates and functions 'within the overall geopolitical context of the world' and at intra-organisational level some governments exert a high level of influence (Interview ILO09, 2018). This challenge becomes also reflected in the ongoing debate amongst academic scholars and practitioners about the future of the ILO and its capacity to implement mission goals. Capacity translates into organisational legitimacy and power which, to some extent, have been undermined by internal and external factors in the past decades (Marginson, 2016). At intra-organisational level identified challenges are, for example: the ILO's organisational structure, the functioning of the principle of tripartism, the growing influence of the employers' side, the engagement in public–private partnerships, the limitation of financial resources, the promotional approach regarding international labour standards, and the lack of proper monitoring and sanction mechanisms. The limited financial resources also determine the amount of expertise which can be directed towards dealings with the IFIs:

> It is a very high skilled area because you're mixing your economic knowledge with political savoir faire, to be able to know who to talk to, when and how to get the agreements, and where people are coming from, so it's quite a high skilled area. So, I think the ILO could do more, but how to generate the resources to be able to do that is very hard.
>
> (Interview ILO06, 2016)

The growing influence of employer representatives within the ILO and tensions between employers and trade unions is not a new challenge. For example, back in 2011, the then acting president of the German Trade Union Confederation (DGB) Michael Sommer called for a renewal of the ILO and criticised the increasing radicalisation of employer representatives following the neoliberal ideology (Sommer, 2011). The power imbalance between employers' and workers' representatives has an impact on the work of the ILO as it fuels internal disagreements. An example is the interpretation of international labour standards by the independent 'Committee of Experts on the Application of Conventions and Recommendations' (CEACR), which became particularly apparent in the right to strike conflict in 2012 (La Hovary, 2015). The employers rejected the role of the CEARC in providing clarification to international labour standards, in this case on the right to strike, and the crisis shook the 'the very foundations of tripartism within the ILO' (Ibid., 2015: 234).

Indirectly, the growing influence of employers can also be linked to public–private partnerships in which the ILO started to engage more systematically about a decade ago. The engagement fulfils two objectives: the promotion of decent work and the mobilisation of financial resources. The latter is important as financial contributions from major donor governments such as the USA and the UK are not sufficient. From 2008 to 2015, more than 56 per cent of the ILO PPPs were with private companies and only 4.4 per cent with social partners (ILO, 2016b). However, these partnerships are not without criticism and in 2018 the IUF (GUF) and the ITUC condemned publicly that McDonalds signed up to the

ILO 'Global Initiative on Decent Jobs for Youth'. The company has a poor labour rights record in the private sector and since 2014 it has been the target of a global corporate campaign which aims to increase wages and improve working conditions (Royle and Rueckert, 2020).

There are different suggestions for the ILO on how to move forward including the creation of a 'new "policy paradigm" for global labour governance' (Thomas and Turnbull, 2018: 538) and 'the amelioration of its persuasive capacity, by way a more integrated implementation of its objectives, and a more judicious use of the means available to pursue them' (Maupain (2013: 16). Standing (2008: 379) argued that the ILO has reached an impasse and 'is trapped in its governance structure' and 'its deeply ingrained orientation to labourism as a model of work organization'. The restructuring of the ILO office attempted to address some of these issues and to promote a 'more integrated approach to the policy issues that affect work and working people, working families, and enterprises everywhere' (Interview ILO09, 2018). However, several issues remain including the resourcing question and the challenge that the ILO's organisational mandate seems to be contradicted by 'legal powerlessness' (Supiot, 2020: 125). Member states can freely choose the standards they want to obey, and some authors argue that recommendations, declarations, and overarching policy frameworks 'represent a weakening of legally binding commitments' (Jakovleski et al., 2019: 85). Nevertheless, the normative influence of the declarations should not be underestimated. Rombouts and Zekic (2020: 356) argue that the universalistic notion of the decent work principle based on the Decent Work Agenda and the fundamental rights at work 'led to a closer alignment between labour rights and human rights in recent decades'. According to the authors:

> (. . .), the international community considers the Declarations of the ILO formal and authoritative statements that outline key principles on how the world of work should be organized in order to cope with contemporary challenges.
> (Rombouts and Zekic, 2020: 327)

Global crisis and challenges require a coordinated global governance response and approach towards regulations. This kind of response is influenced by geopolitical tensions and government leaders which impact the internal and external functioning of intergovernmental organisations and inter-organisational cooperation. In this context, the critical position of the US government towards multilateralism under the Trump administration posed a challenge to both the ILO and the IFIs. However, despite all the existing internal and external challenges, the ILO's expertise and authority with regard to labour markets, employment, and social protection remains unquestioned, for which reason all stakeholder groups should have an interest in strengthening the organisation's influence in the global governance system.

Notes

1 The 2030 Agenda for Sustainable Development includes 17 goals. Goal 8 'Decent Work and Economic Growth' promotes full and productive employment and decent work for all people including people.
2 These countries comprise Brazil, China, France, Germany, India, Italy, Japan, the Russian Federation, the UK, and the USA.
3 Source: ILO (2020) https://www.ilo.org/integration/lang-en/index.htm [Accessed 18 September 2020]
4 In the USA, the ratification process is complicated by the fact that both the executive and legislative have to be aligned before ratification can go ahead. This means that international treaties will only be ratified if national laws are already in conformity with these treaties.
5 Source: ITUC (2021) https://www.ituc-csi.org/multilateralism?debut_documents_645=18

6 The dialogue and cooperation between the Global Unions, the ILO, and the IFIs

The establishment of the dialogue

The rise of Structural Adjustment Programmes (SAPs) in the 1980s, which promoted the self-regulatory capacity of national markets, was the starting point for the Global Unions to express their concerns to the IFIs (Interview ITUC02, 2008). The SAPs intended to stimulate and maintain economic growth and obliged borrowing governments to adopt internal policy changes such as fiscal discipline, financial and trade liberalisation, privatisation of state-owned companies, and deregulation of labour markets (Easterly, 2005). The economic and social outcomes of these programmes were often limited and had a negative impact on workers and the provision of public services. From the perspective of an Education International representative, the implementation of the SAPs in the 1980s lowered the quality of public education in many African countries. The introduction of school fees resulted in the exclusion of poorer children, bigger class sizes, public underinvestment in teacher training and the closure of teacher training colleges, which altogether led to a shrinking quality of public education:

> (. . .) if you look at Senegal today, the majority of teachers are not trained at all, the majority of teachers in Mali are not trained at all etc. So, the damage, the impact on the quality of these countries' education systems has been tremendous. In short, these examples illustrate the impact of the policy advice of the WB and the IMF on developing countries, which is actually littered with mistakes. And then the same WB . . . turned around towards the end of the nineties and said, 'oh yeah, abolishing fees can get more children to school', after they had told some countries to introduce fees, the same Bank, complete turnaround.
>
> (Interview EI, 2019)

The example demonstrates the impact of the SAPs on public services, and that on many occasions, the programmes did not lead to a 'simultaneous achievement of economic growth and advancement in protection of economic and social rights of citizens' (Abouharb and Cingranelli, 2007: 227).

DOI: 10.4324/9781315458410-6

In the 1990s, representatives of the ICFTU, the WCL, and some GUFs started to discuss macroeconomic policies with IFI officials and took part in policy dialogue sessions at the WB where they criticised the SAPs. The beginning of the dialogue was supported by internal organisational changes of the IFIs including an organisational shift towards greater transparency, a provision of information to the public and an opening up towards civil society organisations. At the end of the 1990s, high-level meetings between the international trade union organisations and the IFIs started to take place on a regular basis, and in 2002, the trade unions and the IFIs adopted an agreement concerning a regular enhanced dialogue based on a formalised structure. From the beginning, it was important for the Global Unions to ensure that their national affiliates were able to participate and intervene in the process, particularly as the WB is a decentralised organisation (Interview ITUC02, 2008). During a joint meeting in October 2002, the then WB President James Wolfensohn told trade unionists that the WB is 'no longer dogmatic on the question of privatization' and that the Bank 'promotes social justice and human rights through its work on equality, education, health and labour rights' (World Bank, 2002: 1). Wolfensohn felt that 'unions and the Bank should be allies on most questions' and offered to finance secondments of trade union officials to the Bank through the President's contingency fund. The WB also suggested that cooperation between the organisations could comprise the engagement of trade unions in the Poverty Reduction Strategy Paper (PRSP[1]) process as well as technical meetings on pensions and labour market reforms and HIV/AIDS. In addition, the Bank welcomed trade union involvement and support in the implementation of national social sector reforms. At the same time, the IMF showed a more reserved response to a potential cooperation at international level. The then IMF Managing Director Horst Koehler stated 'that IMF missions are urged to meet with unions' but 'that it would be difficult to institutionalize dialogue on the international level beyond the framework that has already been put in place' (World Bank, 2002: 8). However, in the following two decades, the involvement of the IMF in the dialogue and its openness towards civil society organisations did increase further (Interview WB01, 2017).

Until February 2002, the two international trade union confederations ICFTU and WCL had separate relations and meetings with the IFIs, which they then merged into one joint approach. In 2007, all stakeholders involved in the dialogue undertook a review of the activities which had taken place since the adoption of the protocol in 2002 (World Bank, 2007). The review considered the dialogue at the country level, sector level and headquarters level. At country level, an IMF survey revealed that mission teams met frequently with trade unions, and according to IMF staff, 'there was a significant impact of the meetings on their policy advice', and the meetings helped 'shaping the missions' views in many areas, such as monetary policy and wage policy' (World Bank, 2007: 2–3). The survey conducted by the World Bank revealed a more mixed picture of staff perceptions. Although there was an acknowledgement that trade unions are 'knowledgeable counterparts', trade union leaders were perceived as 'not prepared in economic matters', and consultations with trade unions were considered as 'less helpful' than those with other civil society organisations (World Bank, 2007: 3). The survey conducted by the ITUC amongst national affiliates also revealed a mixed picture whereby trade unionists perceived the dialogue with the WB more positively than the dialogue with the IMF. Generally, the surveys identified a 'lack of negotiating skills and perceived arrogance of World Bank staff, combined with perceptions of political agendas and the lack of technical knowledge of unions' as the main impediments to a better understanding between WB staff and trade union representatives (World Bank, 2007: 3). Over the years mutual perceptions softened, although at national level the dialogue between trade unions and WB staff still depends to a large extent on the attitude of the WB country office director. A former General Secretary of the ITUC-TUCA noted that WB country directors have the 'real power' at the WB (Interview TUCA, 2009). This influence was also confirmed by a former WB representative who commented that there is no enforcement mechanism for formal consultations at national level; consultations largely depend on the influence of national and local trade unions and their relationship with the WB office. Nowadays the attitude of the responsible WB representatives at country level, the policy agenda, and the sensitivity of a particular issue have a strong impact on consultations (Interview WB06, 2019). In this context, a former ITUC secondee to the WB was asked by some WB staff to help to promote the exchange with trade unions at country level as only few WB staff do reach out to trade unions (Interview ITUC07, 2017).

Although the international financial crisis in 2008 did not have a major impact on the exchange at national level, it led to an increased high-level exchange between the Global Unions and the IFIs. In 2009, a first meeting with the Executive Board of the IMF and trade unionists took place and in 2013 the dialogue protocol was amended. The ITUC and the IFIs agreed that both parties would benefit from an early exchange of information about IFIs projects. This goes back to the demand of the trade unions to receive project-related information as early as possible in order to be able to contribute their views:

> Staff of the IFIs acknowledge the importance of consultations with trade union organizations on labour-related issues in individual countries, regionally, or globally with regard to ongoing and new projects, programs and policies. Where feasible, consultations between the ITUC and IFIs could prove useful if undertaken before projects, programs or policies are finalized.
>
> (ITUC, 2015: 1)

The updated dialogue framework confirms the existing structure of the dialogue and it 'identifies the ITUC as a core trade union interlocutor at the multilateral level' (ITUC, 2015: 1). The amendment of the protocol can be considered as a further step in expanding the influence of the Global Unions in the global governance system; however, it needs to be noted that IFI staff are not obliged to consult with trade unions on projects which affect labour.

How does the dialogue work?

The formal dialogue between the Global Unions and the IFIs takes place at three levels: the country level, the sector level, and the HQ level. The country level dialogue includes exchanges between the trade unions and IMF mission teams and trade unions and World Bank offices. The sector level dialogue is related to the different sectors which are covered by the GUFs including the private industry/sector and the public sector. Some GUFs operate a 'thematic focal point' with a particular department of the WB with the objective of establishing an effective exchange of information on policies and projects initiated by the World Bank. For example, in 2004, Education International and the World Bank established a focal point which focused on training and education.

The HQ level dialogue takes place between the headquarters of the ITUC, the GUFs, the WB, the IFC, and the IMF. Trade union delegations are normally quite large and diverse (around 65 representatives) and include representatives from the ITUC and the GUFs, their regional organisations and national affiliates as well as the TUAC. Organisational representatives are general secretaries, presidents, chief economists and sector and policy specialists, as well as at least one representative from the ILO Washington D.C. office. The IFI representatives include senior economists and directors of research and policy units which are relevant for the dialogue, such as from the IMF research department and the WB social protection and jobs unit.

The high-level meetings take place every two years and focus on an agenda which covers a broad range of topics not specific to a particular industrial sector. The agenda for the high-level meetings is developed jointly between the representatives from the ITUC/Global Unions office in Washington D.C. and the WB and IMF representatives who are responsible for maintaining the contact with the trade unions (Interview IMF03, 2017). The high-level meetings usually take place for two and a half days which means that topics need to be chosen carefully because of the time constraints (Interview ITUC06, 2019). Face-to-face meetings are translated into five languages and trade unionists have an allocated speaking time of three minutes (Minutes high-level meeting, 2009), during the Covid-19 pandemic some meetings were held virtually, for example, the high-level meetings in March 2020 and October 2021. Those meetings also applied a regional focus covering Africa, the Americas, Asia Pacific, Europe, and Central Asia. The high-level meetings are supported by technical meetings and interim meetings. During technical meetings, which normally take place over a period of one or two days, the focus is on specific issues such as pensions or labour market reforms. The technical meetings in February 2022 took place virtually and brought together more than 60 trade union representatives (economists and policy specialists) from

32 countries and representatives from the TUAC and the IFIs. The meetings concentrated on labour market trends, social protection, and the reduction of inequality. Interim meetings serve to follow up the implementation of the commitments from the high-level and technical meetings and are held by a relatively small group of trade unionists and representatives of the IFIs.

Since 2014, there is more exchange between staff from the ITUC/Global Unions Washington office and the 'jobs group' of the World Bank (Interview ITUC02, 2015), which is 'the primary partner' and 'official contact point' at the WB for the ITUC/Global Unions office (Interview ITUC06, 2019). Beyond the formal dialogue, trade union and IFI representatives also maintain informal contacts which help to prepare the way for formal commitments. Informal contacts play a more significant role between representatives of the organisational headquarters and depend strongly on individual attitudes towards cooperation. For example, the BWI has been working for several years with WB procurement and safeguard representatives and informal relationships play a crucial role with regard to arranging support at country and project level (Interview BWI, 2017). From the BWI perspective, after many years of cooperation, it is relatively 'easy' to have meetings with the WB, and WB representatives are said to be 'kind of open' towards the BWI (Ibid., 2017).

The HQ level dialogue, which is the focus of this book, shares some of the characteristics of *social dialogue* and *lobbying*. Overlaps with social dialogue are, for example, its focus on long-term gains, the enduring political will of all parties involved to achieve commitments and the exchange of organisational views and information. However, social dialogue is rooted in the European continent and goes back to the 1950s when the concept of social dialogue was built into the European Coal and Steel Community (ECSC) treaty. It takes place between employers' organisations and trade unions (bipartite dialogue), or it involves employers, workers, and governments, or EU institutions (tripartite dialogue). Bipartite social dialogue 'may take the form of collective bargaining or other forms of negotiation, cooperation and dispute prevention and resolution', whilst tripartite social dialogue includes discussions of public policies and laws which impact on workplaces, workers and employers' interests (ILO, 2013c: 5). In comparison to the dialogue between the Global Unions and the IFIs, social dialogue has a much longer history and broader scope and the relationship between social partners is clearly defined. Furthermore, the outcomes of social dialogue can be legally binding or take the form of joint agreements and directives which is not the case in the dialogue between the Global Unions and the IFIs.

The HQ level dialogue bears a resemblance to lobbying as it can be considered as a form of advocacy aimed at influencing policy processes and approaches at the IFIs (Baumgartner et al., 2009). However, in a narrower sense, lobbying relates to 'government decision-making' and is 'motivated by a desire to influence government decisions' (John, 2002: 8). Professional lobbyists receive payment for lobbying activities, which they conduct on behalf of the organisation which hires them.

In contrast, the HQ level dialogue does not include a third party which represents the interests of either the IFIs or the Global Unions. Furthermore, the dialogue has a formally institutionalised structure and the parties involved (Global Unions and IFIs) have a continued interest in the exchange of information and not only at a particular point of time (Interview ITUC02, 2008).

In conclusion, the dialogue differs in several aspects from social dialogue and lobbying, and therefore requires its own specific definition. It can be classified as a form of international policy dialogue based on an institutionalised communication process taking place between organisations which are active at the global policy level. The organisations involved do not act as social partners and they do not negotiate specific agreements. Rather, this form of dialogue serves to exchange views on specific topics, to develop a better understanding of each other's approaches and to identify possible areas of cooperation. The dialogue is based on the development of a long-term relationship and trust between the involved stakeholders, whereby the HQ level dialogue includes information sharing mainly on a formal level, and to a minor extent, on an informal level. The dialogue is more holistic in its approach in comparison to lobbying, although for the trade unions it is also about acquiring policy commitments from the IFIs.

Two decades of dialogue – expectations and outcomes

The expectations of dialogue stakeholders and the development of communication

The first officially recorded three-day high-level meeting took place in October 2000. Trade union representatives met with the World Bank President, the IMF Managing Director, and the Executive Directors from the WB and the IMF. This first dialogue served to discover topics of joint relevance and to initiate a discussion about the development of a future consultation mechanism. Both the leaders of the World Bank and the IMF acknowledged the broad membership of trade union organisations worldwide and their representative legitimacy. In 2000, the then WB President James Wolfensohn welcomed the increased dialogue with the ICFTU and argued for a 'frank dialogue in order to determine areas of agreement and disagreement and how both institutions could move forward together' (World Bank, 2000: 1). Wolfensohn was a driving force for the development of the dialogue, and the former IMF managing director Horst Kohler, who was new in this position at the time, also considered the dialogue with trade unions as 'necessary and useful' (World Bank, 2000: 1).

However, from the beginning of the dialogue expectations varied between the different stakeholders and there remains an expectation 'gap' between trade union and IFI representatives. The trade unions, and in particular the ITUC (former ICFTU), which initiated the dialogue, pursue clearly defined objectives and have explicit expectations for the dialogue's outcomes. For example, the Global Unions focused continuously on the integration of the CLS in WB and IMF operations and in the past, they had promoted the development of a platform for the consultation of trade unions in the Poverty Reduction Strategy Paper (PRSP) process (World Bank, 2001c). In contrast, for the IFIs, the dialogue presents an opportunity to develop and practice their diplomatic relationships with trade unions as part of a general opening towards civil society.

The ITUC, supported by the TUAC and in coordination with the GUFs, takes the lead in the dialogue because of its strong political focus. The engagement of the GUFs in the dialogue varies, depending on the sector which they cover and the impact of the WB policies on the sector. However, there is a close coordination within the international trade union movement regarding joint political statements and the ITUC's profile building work is highly acknowledged:

> (. . .) there is generally good consultation between the respective secretariats to ensure that the view that we have, our worries and our concerns, are reflected in the statements that are made at the UN, at the level of the G20, at the level of the OECD, and in the other global institutions. So, I think that this overall political message is important to us, and to our members. Our members want to see where we are situated in the global kind of political picture, and my sense has been that our own affiliates welcome this kind of profile that the ITUC has developed, and they see that we are engaged also in the process.
>
> (Interview UNI, 2019)

The expectations of the different organisations which take part in the high-level dialogue can be divided into two areas: first the process of the dialogue itself that is dealing with each other during the meetings, and second, the outcomes of the dialogue. Organisational expectations are closely linked with the expectations of individual actors who drive the dialogue and vice versa. The expectations of the individual actors involved in the dialogue are influenced by three factors: first, the level of direct involvement of their organisation in the dialogue; second, their personal commitment and attitude towards the dialogue; and third, their perception of the dialogue partners. Individual and organisational perceptions and their associated expectations are not static; they can change and evolve over time influenced by, for example, knowledge sharing and positive experiences through cooperation.

From the beginning the Global Unions expressed the expectation that the IFIs should develop an understanding of the role and function of trade unions, and that they should consider trade unions as serious dialogue partners which deserve a 'seat on the table'. In terms of mutual treatment there was a general expectation that the IFIs should listen seriously to trade union proposals (World Bank, 2002) and act on them:

> (. . .) we engage in the dialogue with very specific objectives of changing policy and not for the purpose of simply discussing each other's points of view and getting understanding of what they are doing.
>
> (Interview ITUC02, 2008)

In 2000, the General Secretary of the ICFTU stated that the trade unions want to have a better relationship with the IMF, and that they want to be seen as stakeholders whose views are considered (World Bank, 2000). Over the years this goal has been achieved and the exchange with the IMF has become deeper, more regular, and fundamental for the trade unions. As the former ETUC General Secretary put it:

> The dialogue is very important, also because particularly the IMF has been for a long time our enemy, trying to influence all the macro-economic and social policies in a very wrong way; recommending wage cuts and cuts in public spending and labour market reforms that also introduced some recessive pro-cyclical measures etc. So, having a dialogue with them and trying to change these policies is fundamental for us.
>
> (Interview ETUC, 2017)

The relationship with the WB is more cyclical, and the restructuring reform in 2014 led to a destabilisation of long-established contacts as some trade union-friendly representatives changed jobs or left the organisation. Trade union representatives are aware that policy changes take a long time because of the size and the complexity of the IFIs, including the influence of some significant member governments (Interview ITUC01, 2008). There is little hope that a fundamental change of the organisations can be achieved through the dialogue and according to the ITUC General Secretary Sharan Burrow, there is engagement 'but from a perception that the IFIs would change, frankly, we don't hold that view' (Interview ITUC08, 2018).

Like the Global Unions, the IFIs have an interest in cooperation, and during the high-level meetings in 2002, a WB representative expressed hope that 'the dialogue with unions would not only advance understanding of the other parties' concerns, but also identify new areas of cooperation, such as in health care and education' (World Bank, 2002: 3). In comparison to other civil society organisations, the trade unions are considered to have a special relationship with the WB as the following statement highlights:

> (. . .) from all the civil society constituencies, the trade unions have been the most organised and the most systematic, there is no other constituency . . . that meets systematically and has a protocol like the trade unions.
>
> (Interview WB01, 2017)

The dialogue protocol helped to institutionalise the dialogue in terms of continuity, but it cannot equalise inter-organisational power relations. For example, under the Malpass presidency, trade unionists perceived a general pullback from openness and consultations which they were unable to prevent. The attitudes and behaviours of the organisational leadership and other influential individuals such as the WB country directors are not restrained by the protocol, and at the national level consultations still depend on the will and attitude of country office staff to reach out to trade unions and to facilitate consultations. The expectation of trade unions that the WB would give clear instructions and guidelines to its country offices to consult with trade unions has not materialised. Furthermore, the protocol does not homogenise individual approaches regarding the dialogue and as a result expectations and perceptions towards the dialogue continue to vary between individual WB representatives and departments. In particular, sector level cooperation depends on the corresponding WB department and its decision to get involved with the corresponding GUF.

From the perspective of the IMF's public affairs department the engagement in the dialogue is partly driven by the imperative of 'immediate needs and concerns' (Interview IMF01, 2008):

> The IMF expects a dialogue, a conversation, and that's not an easy thing to achieve always. (. . .) what we are doing is agreeing on having an idea, a focused discussion on relevant crucial issues. Now I think some years the issues are more crucial and more relevant than in other years. When things were going very well in the global economy earlier in this decade [*beginning of the 2000s*] the discussion was maybe driven less by the imperative of immediate needs and concerns. There were always needs and concerns, but the word is 'immediate'.
>
> (Interview IMF01, 2008)

There was also acknowledgement for the need for a bilateral dialogue which goes beyond the high-level meetings and the expectation that the dialogue would transcend to lower levels which feed back into the high-level dialogue:

> (. . .) we think there is an important dialogue to be held outside of the context of the high-level dialogue because the high-level dialogue is 50 or 60 people and that's very different from 10 people, 12 people. So, we think one facilitates the other and hopefully it becomes a positive circle of contacts where the high-level dialogue generates other contacts, which generate a more constructive high-level dialogue.
>
> (Interview IMF01, 2008)

The frequency of meetings between trade unions and the IMF mission teams increased at the beginning of the 2000s, because the IMF management gave instructions to mission teams to meet with trade unions (Interview ITUC02, 2008). Despite the improvement of the frequency of meetings, the quality of consultations is often low, although national trade unions have different experiences. For example, in Germany, trade unions were regularly involved in meetings with the IMF mission teams. According to an IG Metall representative, IMF mission teams have more knowledge about labour issues and trade unions in Germany than they did 20 years ago and there have been very 'engaged conversations' in recent years (Interview IG Metall, 2019). At the global level, cooperation has become more frequent and regular between the Global Unions and the IMF whereby some of the meetings are driven by immediate concerns, such as during the Covid-19 pandemic. According to the IMF's Managing Director the IMF now promotes more of an 'open door' policy, and there is a willingness to listen to other voices at global and national level (ITUC, 2021b).

Dialogue outcomes in relation to specific topics

Over the years, the topics and the focus of the dialogue were adjusted by the dialogue stakeholders in order to reflect further developments and the emergence of new and urgent issues. Meanwhile some issues such as the CLS, labour market regulations, social spending, and debt relief are continuous, other issues such as the PRSP process were abandoned over time. The last major discussion between the trade unions and the IFIs about the PRSPs took place in 2005. Although the IFIs emphasised and encouraged the participation of trade unions and civil society organisations in PRSP consultations, many trade unions felt that their input was not reflected in the final documents (ITUC, 2008). Furthermore, new issues such as climate change, just transition and global social protection were added to the dialogue agenda. The following sections consider four recurrent dialogue topics: the promotion of the CLS, labour market issues and social protection, privatisation and PPPs, and loan conditionality.

The promotion of the Core Labour Standards within IFI policies

The CLS and their integration in WB, IFC, and IMF operations have played an important role since the beginning of the dialogue (Murphy, 2014). The Global Unions ask the IFIs to recognise the importance of the ILO conventions covered by the Declaration on Fundamental Principles and Rights at Work and to ensure that their own policies do not undermine these principles in order to prevent the exploitation of labour. The awareness of the WB and the IFC regarding the CLS started to increase at the beginning of the 2000s (World Bank, 2002). According to the joint report of the 2002 high-level meetings, some Executive Directors expressed the view that there was an 'increasing recognition that these standards do not hinder, but rather support the development process' (World Bank, 2002: 2). Regarding the implementation of the CLS, there was agreement that the cooperation with the ILO is important:

> It was specified that unions are not asking that the IFIs take on the role of monitoring the application of the CLS, but rather that they properly interact

with the ILO when working on labour issues, such as when the World Bank becomes involved in labour market reforms.

(World Bank, 2002: 2–3)

In 2006, the IFC included the CLS in its newly adopted Performance Standards (PS). As already described in the chapter about the IFIs, the trade unions were heavily involved in the development of the standards and in particular PS 2. The pioneering role of the IFC in this context can be partly explained by the type of clients the organisation deals with (private businesses) and by its organisational culture. Private businesses are a point of intersection with the trade unions as the latter are involved in shaping working conditions and negotiating with businesses at national level.

The starting point for the consideration of the CLS by the IFC was the corporate financing of the Dominican private sector employer 'Grupo M' which promoted an export zone in Haiti focusing on garment production. In 2003, the IFC approved a US$20 million loan to Grupo M which had started operating its first factory in Haiti supplying major US brands such as Levis and Tommy Hilfiger (Bretton Woods Project, 2003). The approval of the loan happened during the time when the IFIs turned Haiti into a 'Caribbean sweatshop' by promoting an export-led garment production based on cheap labour (Kennard, 2012). The former General Secretary of the ITGLWF stated that the textiles, clothing, and footwear industry is 'enormously labour intensive' and that there is a 'tendency for the industry to locate in those countries with the lowest standards and with least regulation' (Interview ITGLWF, 2009). Shortly after the factory opening by Grupo M in Haiti, strikes and work stoppages took place which lasted more than two years. One IFC representative stated that the ICFTU, the ITGLWF, and a Dominican trade union had raised serious concerns about the repeated violation of the right of freedom of association and that:

> the charges were serious enough about anti-union behaviour – that people got beaten up, that people were being fired because they wanted to form a trade union etc., so that we [*IFC*] decided we would, as a condition of going to the Board, that we would have a labour investigation done, and that we would implement any remedial actions that came out of that investigation. So having never done any of this before, this predates the Performance Standards on labour that the IFC has.
>
> (Interview IFC02, 2008)

Representatives from the Worker Rights Consortium (WRC), the AFL-CIO, the ICFTU and the ITGLWF cooperated with IFC representatives to resolve the issues. The decision was made to install two observers in the affected company, one appointed by the company and one appointed by the trade unions. However, due to the lack of agreement on observations between the observers, labour mediation was required which resulted in a collective agreement for the factory (Interview IFC02, 2008). The General Secretary of the ITGLWF pointed out that the trade unions never had an intention to stop loans, but to ensure the implementation of decent working conditions:

> What we want is, when there is a request for such loans, that the conditions attached to them will ensure they . . . will provide decent work. You know, it's the same, we have the same approach when there are problems within individual companies. We don't rush out and say 'boycott' to this company. . . . It just somebody else will do it and probably just in the same way, far better to work with the applicant or with the company in question to raise the standards, to ensure that decent work becomes a reality.
>
> (Interview ITGLWF, 2009)

The trade unions considered the case of Grupo M as a considerable success for two reasons: first, because they were able to draw the IFC's attention to a company and its history of labour issues, and second, because they were able to initiate a discussion within the IFC about labour conditionalities and its future design (Interview ITGLWF, 2009). In addition to the factory agreement, labour contractual requirements on labour and freedom of association were included in the loan agreement for Grupo M which was a significant achievement at the time. The labour contractual requirements for Grupo M preceded the IFC Performance Standards and meant a steep learning curve on labour issues for IFC staff. One IFC representative summarised his experience and the perceived challenges as follows:

> I am not trying to personalise this, but I am just trying to put in the context of having had this experience and how formative it was, sort of on behalf of the organisation. I believed in the importance of labour obviously, and on the other hand, I recognised the difficulty in actually doing some of these things. So, it's kind of like, you have to be cautious. It's great. You can be a hero, an REVP [*Regional Executive Vice President*] or VP [*Vice President*] . . . make speeches and get a standing ovation from, you know, a big labour union convention or whatever, and be a hero. But at the end of the day, what matters is your ability to implement this on the ground, day to day in projects. That is where the rubber hits the road. None of it matters if you have the best policy and there are plenty of examples in the IFIs of wonderful policies written to the minute detail, but then you have to look at how are they being implemented. Are they being implemented? I rather have a lower standard, knowing that I can implement that and then be serious about it and then move from there, than I would have the best standard in the world and have a tremendous gap between reality and rhetoric and that does nothing. So that's the challenge, that's the test.
>
> (Interview IFC02, 2008)

In 2006, the IFC adopted the Performance Standards which the then IFC President described as a 'shared opportunity' (World Bank, 2006: 10), and which were considered as a 'major step forward' by the trade unions. From the perspective of the trade unions, the 'political commitment from the [IFC] top' was crucial for the achieved progress (Interview BWI, 2009). The IFC is still committed to the dialogue and finding solutions when a complaint is raised (Interview IFC03, 2017); however, in recent years, some trade unionists are getting the impression that the Performance Standards have become more of a 'check-off exercise' (Interview AFL-CIO, 2017). One example is the IFC investment in the Dinant corporation in Honduras (Interview AFL-CIO, 2017), where in 2017 the US NGO Earth Rights International (ERI) lodged a complaint with the US federal court on behalf of the farmers in the Bajo Aguan valley (Provost, 2017). Despite a report from the IFC's Compliance Advisor Ombudsman about Dinant's failure to protect local communities from violence in 2013 and an action plan, the intimidation and killing of local community members and farmers continued. In 2015, ERI filed a complaint against the IFC in relation to the Tata Mundra Coal Power plant in a US federal court. The complaint was raised on behalf of farmers and fishermen in north-western India and the destruction of their livelihoods. The IFC claimed that it is entitled to absolute immunity from prosecution in the USA referring to the International Organisations Immunities Act from 1945, but in 2019, the US Supreme Court ruled against this claim (Bretton Woods Project, 2019c). Although the decision marks a legal precedent, it is unlikely that it will open the door to mass litigation of international organisations like the IFC. More recently, in June 2022, the IUF called on the IFC to intervene at the Sheraton Grand Conakry hotel in Guinea where workers face economic devastation after the closure of the hotel in 2021 (IUF, 2022). The closure of the hotel followed the decision of workers to submit a strike notice demanding the reinstatement of two elected trade union leaders who were dismissed after raising awareness of fundamental labour rights issues.

Despite the shortcomings in the implementation of the IFC Performance Standards, the standards set a leading example for the WB to reshape its procurement policies and documents. For a long time, the WB only 'recommended' labour standards until it started to move gradually towards a 'mandatory' approach in procurement. The trade unions, and in particular the BWI, were actively involved in the development of mandatory labour clauses in the WB's standard procurement documents from the end of the 1990s. During the high-level meetings in 2006, the director of the WB's Operations, Policy, and Country Services department noted that the Bank 'would soon adopt all four CLS in its SBD' and that the 'WB intended to harmonize the wording of its procurement standards to that of the IFC performance standards' (World Bank, 2006: 10). Four years later in 2010, for the first time in its history the WB included all the CLS in the SBD for the procurement of large works under 'General Conditions' which made the CLS mandatory. The trade unions welcomed the decision but were also cautious, and the BWI stressed the importance of capacity building of national actors in the construction industry and training about national procurement systems for WB staff. Furthermore, from the BWI perspective a proactive approach regarding information sharing and implementation is important, for which reason the GUF aims to bring Bank staff, trade unions, contractors, and clients together at the early stages of a project. The importance of this approach can also be explained by the complexity of the enforcement of labour legislation in the construction sector, which is due to the high levels of subcontracting and outsourcing (Interview BWI, 2009). For example, MNCs involved in building highways within the Pan-European Transport corridors, contract sub-contractors who often ignore national legislation and as a result, issues have arisen in the areas of wages, working hours and health and safety (Interview BWI, 2017).

Another WB document in which both the trade unions and the ILO pursued the integration of the CLS is the WB Environmental and Social Framework (ESF). The framework which became effective in 2018 comprises ten environmental and social standards (including labour and working conditions, ESS 2) and applies to investment project financing. The trade unions' perspective during the extensive consultation phase was mainly represented by the ITUC, and the AFL-CIO pressured the US government to 'stand up and push for strong safeguards' (Interview AFL-CIO, 2017). From the perspective of the AFL-CIO, the framework is a 'fairly large achievement' as it states specific labour standard requirements for the first time, although the trade unions had hoped for a more 'forward looking vision from the Bank' and a clear implementation mechanism. The ILO offered its support to the WB with regard to the ESF implementation process by providing, for example, information with regard to the ratification of ILO conventions at national level as well as training activities (Interview ILO07, 2017).

Both the trade unions and the ILO were not able to achieve the referencing of the ILO and the CLS in the framework itself, but in the guidance notes for borrowers and WB staff. The guidance notes, which were developed with input from the trade unions, state that ESS 2 is in part informed by ILO and UN conventions and list the ILO conventions accordingly. The lack of reference to the ILO within the ESF was a concern for the trade unions, and therefore the guidance notes are considered as a 'compromise' on this issue (Interview BWI, 2017). The guidance notes also include a template form for WB staff and borrowers which supports the identification of concrete labour issues (Interview ITUC06, 2019). In addition, the Bank offers an online complaints procedure through which stakeholders can raise problems which occur at project level, and it aims to establish a group of independent third-party mediators and conciliation specialists. The ITUC/Global Unions office aims to make national trade unions aware of the complaint mechanism, so that more pressure can be created from the ground (Interview ITUC07, 2019); however, the trade unions remain concerned about the lack of trade union involvement in project design and monitoring activities.

With reference to these examples, it can be argued that the dialogue between the Global Unions and the WB and the IFC has played an important role regarding the promotion and implementation of the CLS in some IFI policy documents. At the beginning, the trade unions received very unsatisfactory responses from the IFIs regarding their claim that they should recognise the importance of these standards, and it took a long time and effort to achieve change.

> (. . .) it really took a lot of insistence from our part before they finally started endorsing all of the standards and recognising, that not only were these important standards per se, but rationally should be considered part and parcel of the development agenda.
>
> (Interview ITUC02, 2008)

Despite the partial success, it is important to remember that the WB considers the CLS only in investment project financing and not in other lending instruments such as development policy financing. It is also rather doubtful that this can be achieved in the years to come as some EDs are heavily opposed to the idea. Furthermore, up to now the CLS mainly play a role in relation to the IFC and the WB, and although the IMF has shown a positive attitude towards the ILO and the labour standards discussed within the dialogue, the IMF has never committed to adopting labour standards in principle. Therefore, little has been achieved in practical terms with regard to IMF policies and respective documents.

Labour market issues and social protection

The global health crisis caused by the Covid-19 pandemic exposed once more the weaknesses of labour market institutions worldwide and led to a high level of job losses and a deterioration of working conditions. In 2021, the ITUC Global Rights Index revealed that governments and employers increased the exploitation of workers during the pandemic and violated collective bargaining rights and the right to strike (ITUC, 2021a). The IFIs play an important role with regard to sustainable economic recovery and since the international financial crisis in 2008 labour market recommendations by the IFIs concern developing countries and advanced economies (Blanchard et al., 2013). Although there is an increased awareness of the IFIs regarding labour market issues including minimum wages, skill development, social insurance, and informality, notable differences in terms of policy responses and the design and implementation of labour market regulations between the dialogue partners remain. During the high-level meetings in 2004, trade unions argued that economic growth was insufficient for effective poverty reduction and that growth 'must be accompanied by "decent" job creation and an increase in social security and justice' (World Bank, 2004: 2). In this context, an ILO representative stressed the importance of 'policy coherence' and 'greater consistency between the actions of different international institutions on economic and social policy' referring to the report by the 'World Commission on the Social Dimension of Globalization'[2] (World Bank, 2004: 8). The report of the Commission concluded that although globalisation has the potential to benefit the many, it needs to become fairer and more inclusive and to put people first. In other words, globalisation must include a social dimension, 'which sustains human values and enhances the well-being of people, in terms of their freedom, prosperity and security' (ILO, 2004: 5).

The WBG and the IMF consider the creation of inclusive jobs as key to the reduction of poverty and inequality and the idea of a 'new social contract', as suggested by the trade unions, now receives more attention in their publications than it used to. Yet, in contrast to the Global Unions and the ILO, the IFIs regard the private sector and labour market flexibility as crucial in relation to job creation. Back in 2008, the director of the WB SP&L department stressed that in the context of labour market reforms important issues are the 'strain on employers through severance payments', and the difficulties around 'hiring and firing' (Interview WB02, 2008).

> (. . .) we have countries where, if somebody has been given a job, this person cannot be dismissed ever again, and where a worker has been employed for one year, he receives half a year severance payment. This is something which is not suitable for achieving a more flexible labour market which really creates jobs. I doubt it. We doubt it.
>
> (Interview WB02, 2008)

The issue of labour market regulations matters, because the WB acts as a knowledge producer and disseminates knowledge widely through training and capacity development courses to national policy makers, WB operational staff, and donor agencies. One example is the 'Core Courses'[3] which have focused repeatedly on global social protection and jobs.

In the past, the ITUC/Global Union office in Washington D.C. contributed to some WB training sessions, such as in 2012 when the director of the ITUC/Global Unions office in Washington presented the trade union position on labour market regulation arguing that labour market regulation is not an impediment to economic growth and job creation. He supported his argumentation by referring to the ILO 'World of Work' report (2012) and the OECD report about rising inequality (2011b) which highlighted the problem of growing inequality and the potentially adverse effect of badly designed labour market regulations on employment. According to the ILO report:

> (. . .) the highest employment rates are found in either decentralized (but coordinated by social partners) systems of collective bargaining or centralized and coordinated bargaining systems. The recent trend towards decentralized

collective bargaining, sometimes carried out without sufficient social dialogue or coordination, may therefore affect employment performance.

(ILO, 2012: 36)

In the aftermath of the international financial crisis in 2008, some WB representatives conducted together with ILO representatives a policy inventory of national responses as an organisational learning and didactic exercise. The inventory examined the impact of government interventions during the crisis including macroeconomic and sectoral policies, the practice of social dialogue, and the enforcement of international labour standards. The joint report concluded that social dialogue is an important instrument for building trust and consensus and that governments should encourage the coordination of collective bargaining. Furthermore, it stated that:

(. . .) it is important to increase vigilance to avoid violations of fundamental principles and rights at work. It should be recalled that lowering labour standards, in particular in times of crisis, can encourage the spread of low-wage, low-skill, and high turnover industries.

(ILO and World Bank, 2012: 46)

Regarding the findings of the 2021 ITUC Global Rights Index, it can be concluded that the opposite occurred during the Covid-19 pandemic, and that many governments used the health crisis to dismantle workers' rights and to pursue an anti-union agenda.

The WBG's perceptions and visions on social protection and jobs are not consistent and over the years some publications were seen very critically by the trade unions. For example, for many years, the trade unions urged the Bank to cease its flagship annual publication 'Doing Business' which promoted low taxes and the deregulation of workers' rights and social protection. The report was discontinued in September 2021, but in February 2022, the WB published a pre-concept note on a new publication which is to replace 'Doing Business'. The planned publication with the preliminary title of 'Business Enabling Environment' (BEE) which, amongst others, includes labour and tax indicators is of concern to the trade unions (ITUC, 2022b). It remains to be seen if the fears of those, who argue that the WB aims to continue the deregulation agenda under a different name, will become reality. Another publication which was strongly criticised by the trade unions is the WB's World Development Report from 2019. Although the report states that a new social contract is necessary for improving social inclusion and equality of opportunity, it also argues that a 'restrictive approach to labour regulation is a poor fit with many developing countries' labour markets' as these countries face high levels of informality, and that regulations 'reduce dynamism in the economy' (World Bank, 2019a: 115–116). In addition, the report opposes lower tax rates for basic necessities and employer-financed protection in developing countries. The Global Unions expressed their disappointment about the report and highlighted that the report was in stark contrast to the Bank's ESF. The disagreement about the report also affected the dialogue between the ITUC and the WB's jobs and social protection unit in a negative way.

More recently the WB announced an update on its 'Social Protection and Labour Strategy' (2012–2022) and to develop a 'Social protection and Jobs Compass' which was welcomed by the international trade union movement. The new Compass aims to reflect labour market challenges after the Covid-19 pandemic with a particular focus on universal social protection (ITUC, 2022a). The Compass was also discussed during the technical meetings in February 2022 where WB representatives presented the progress on the new framework. The ITUC urged the WB to have a 'robust consultation with the global labour movement in crafting the Compass and social dialogue as part of all social protection reform and expansion processes' (ITUC, 2022c: 3). This also includes financing of social protection where the trade unions support progressive taxation and the creation of a global social protection fund in order to support the poorest countries.

> Extending social protection is a key priority of the international labour movement, who recognise that social protection is a fundamental human right, enshrined in numerous international instruments and international labour standards. It is moreover an essential component of decent work and a key factor for inclusive economic growth.
>
> (ITUC, 2020c: 1)

Like the WB, the IMF nowadays also focuses more strongly on social spending and protection and pursuing the SDGs. The IMF research department produced some insightful studies about inequality and labour markets in recent years, but in spite of that and the regular and deepened dialogue with the trade unions, both stakeholders continue to follow different economic narratives. For example, whilst the IMF takes a critical stance on wage increases in times of high inflation and promotes deregulation to achieve higher productivity, the trade unions highlight the importance of evidence-based minimum wages, social dialogue, and collective bargaining (ITUC, 2021b). Furthermore, the trade unions repeatedly criticised cuts to public spending and public wage freezes which had devastating effects for education and health and social care in many countries. In their statement to the annual meeting of the IFIs in October 2021, the Global Unions demanded a reform of 'conditionality and policy advice on labour' and an end to the promotion of 'deregulatory reform, discouragement of social dialogue, and decentralization of collective bargaining' (Global Unions, 2021: 5). The fact that the international trade union organisations are still having to repeat these demands demonstrates that progress overall has been limited and many differences remain in this area.

Privatisation and public–private partnerships

Labour market reforms and employment protection are closely related to the privatisation of public goods and services. In 1992, the Director of the WB's Public Sector Management and Private Sector Development Division published a paper which outlined reasons for governments to denationalise state assets. The article suggested that privatisation improves the use of public resources as well as their operating and dynamic efficiency and stated:

> The World Bank aims to help developing countries that are attempting to increase efficiency and cost effectiveness through privatization to do so successfully. . . . The World Bank acts as a catalyst for privatization, helping to finance the technical advice. It also helps countries put privatization in its context and supports a broader program of reforms.
>
> (Shirley, 1992: 32)

Three decades after the article was published, privatisation still plays a significant role for the IFIs. During his time as UN special rapporteur on extreme poverty and human rights, Philip Alston concluded that both the WB and the IMF actively promote privatisation through advice provided to governments and conditions attached to loans:

> Neoliberal economic policies are aimed at shrinking the role of the state, especially through privatization. This agenda has been remarkably successful in recent years and continues to be promoted aggressively by the World Bank, IMF, parts of the United Nations and the private sector. The logic of privatization assumes no necessary limits as to what can be privatized, and public goods ranging from social protection and welfare services, to schools, pension systems, parks and libraries, and policing, criminal justice and the military sector, have all been targeted.
>
> (UN Human Rights Council, 2018b: 23–24)

The promotion of privatisation by the IFIs ignores studies such as conducted by the UK National Audit Office and the European Court of Auditors in 2018 which revealed that private finance is more expensive and less efficient than public finance and that public–private partnerships offer only limited benefits. At the WB, PPPs represent one of the cross-cutting solution areas which require integration across the global practices. This suggests that PPPs have not lost their relevance for the WB (Interview ITUC02, 2015), and that the WB remains to be the 'real driver' on PPPs (Interview ITUC06, 2019). The IMF recognises the fiscal risks associated with PPPs, but it called for advancing the legal basis for PPPs in some instances such as in the case of Tunisia in 2015 (Bretton Woods Project, 2019b).

Privatisation and the resourcing of public services have been contested issues between the trade unions and the IFIs for many years. In September 1999, the WB committed itself 'to increase dialogue and establish a more formal structure for information sharing between the Bank and trade unions on privatization' (World Bank, 2001c: 1). A few years later trade union representatives complained about the WB's lack of engagement with trade unionists on privatisation (World Bank, 2002) and that consultations remained 'ad hoc' (World Bank, 2003a: 1). In this context, a PSI representative stated that 'relevant unions must be involved right from the beginning in privatisation processes', and that the WB only encourages dialogue between governments and trade unions once the decision to privatise has already been made (Interview PSI, 2008). Although privatisation and PPPs have not featured as separate items on recent dialogue agendas, the topics still play an important role in the wider debate about inequality, pension systems, education and social and health care.

For example, in the case of pension systems, trade unions are particularly concerned about the decreasing number of workers likely to receive an adequate pension and the increasing number of workers who may receive no pension at all. The first thematic meeting on the topic took place in 2003 during which WB and trade union representatives agreed that the involvement of social partners in reform processes is necessary and that pension coverage needs to be on the top of the agenda (World Bank, 2003b). Since then, a further thematic meeting took place in 2010 during which trade union and WB representatives consented to the idea that universal coverage and the sustainability of pension systems are important. Nevertheless, disagreement prevailed over with regard to potential solutions, in particular, the role and involvement of private funds (World Bank, 2010b). The issue of pensions is now included in the international debate about social protection floors which describe a set of basic social security rights. For example, the ILO Social Protection Floors Recommendation from 2012 promotes four social security guarantees including basic retirement pensions. The establishment of social protection systems at national level is included in the SDG agenda and the IFIs have increased their work on social spending in the last decade. For the IMF an important guiding principle on social spending is macro-criticality which corresponds to issues and policies that could potentially have macroeconomic implications such as pension systems. In terms of macro-criticality key objectives for the IMF are to maintain fiscal sustainability, spending adequacy, and efficiency (IMF, 2019e). The ILO tripartite round table on pensions highlighted in 2020 that national pension systems face unprecedented challenges caused by aging populations, the growing informality of labour markets and new forms of employment (ILO, 2021a). In this context, the contribution to social security protection and the debate about the creation of fiscal space often lead to disagreement between trade union and IFI representatives; for example, in relation to pension plans, some WB staff recommend individual saving plans and the elimination of employer contributions (Interview ITUC06, 2019). Although trade unions do not condemn individual plans, they argue that responsibilities need to be shared and that adequate state support is crucial for reducing poverty in old age.

The trade unions have repeatedly stressed that social protection and public services require financing by governments and not the private sector. During the high-level meetings in 2021, trade union representatives stated the importance of well-functioning and adequately resourced public services such as care and education (ITUC, 2021b). This is particularly important as the Covid-19 pandemic exposed gaps and problems with low-quality jobs in these sectors. An ILO report on the current state of social protection revealed that more than half of the global population is completely unprotected with no access to social protection benefits such as healthcare, sickness, and unemployment benefits (ILO, 2021b). Since the international financial crisis in 2008 public health spending is in decline and from the trade union perspective PPPs often fail to deliver promised outcomes in terms of costs and quality of services (Observation minutes high-level meetings, 2017).

> I definitely think that they [IFC], like a lot of people, are really enamoured with the private-public partnership and see it as this great model, and obviously, we have attempted to push back on that with plenty of data demonstrating the many instances where privatisation actually does not result in even cost saving, let alone a better provision of the service that you are trying to provide.
>
> (Interview AFL-CIO, 2017)

A similar picture applies to education which trade unions consider as a public good requiring protection from privatisation and commercialisation (EI, 2011). The WB is the largest external financier of education in the developing world. Over the last two decades the WB has put more than US$66 billion into education projects in 160 countries (World Bank, 2021b: 3) and since 2001 the IFC is financing private education projects. EI is regularly challenging the WB on its education policies and advice which are often detrimental to an inclusive approach to skills development.

The bilateral relationship between EI and the WB goes back to 2004 when a focal point was established with the aim to enhance communication 'on projects and policies that involve both parties' (World Bank, 2007: 5). EI provides comments on the reports of the WB whenever they have an impact on education, but as one EI representative stated, 'usually the relation with the World Bank is more a relation of opposition' (Interview, EI, 2008). Some meetings in the past were perceived as successful by trade unionists, such as a meeting on the WB Africa HIV/AIDS programme in 2007 during which EI and WB representatives identified four areas for joint work. However, there was no follow-up meeting focusing on implementation which was partly because of a change of personnel at EI at the time and, partly because of a lack of interest at the WB in continuing and further developing the relationship.

In recent years EI was involved in studies in Uganda and Kenya which revealed that the low spending of private schools on teachers' salaries is related to low pay and failure to provide adequate social security and pension benefits for their employees (Interview EI, 2019). Furthermore, research in Kenya revealed insufficient teacher qualifications, inadequate school infrastructures and a devastating impact of school fees on families and students pushing them into debt (EI, 2016). In 2020, EI and many civil society organisations welcomed the announcement of the IFC to temporarily freeze investment in fee charging private schools, in 2022 the IFC announced an indefinite extension of the freeze of investment basing its decision on the IEG (2022) evaluation report. The report concluded that the resumption of IFC investments in private schools is not advisable without substantial changes to the IFC's business model which overlooked criteria for equitable access and education quality.

EI representatives consider the WB's concept of 'learning poverty' and the focus on reading proficiency by the age of 10 critically because of its narrow focus and the narrowing down of SDG 4 (Quality Education) (Interview EI, 2019). Furthermore, there is still a lack of consultation on education and teacher policies and EI also criticises the WB for imposing programmes such as SABER[4] on developing countries without involving national professionals in the programme design. Generally, EI representatives consider their influence in consultations as limited, and for example, in its 2018 World Development Report on education, the WB largely ignored the recommendations made by EI (World Bank, 2018e). In 2020, a report on education published by the WB during the Covid-19 pandemic missed the opportunity to discuss issues such as labour and education rights, social dialogue, and adequate teacher's support (World Bank, 2020d; Bretton Woods Project, 2020c).

From the perspective of EI, the advice of the Bank is largely driven by ideology and not by evidence. The application of a narrow economic lens, which often gives priority to costs and economic return, can hinder meaningful investments in, for example, technical and vocational training. This also applies to the IMF which EI criticises for its contradictory advice on education systems, public wage bill cuts and freezes on the sector (ITUC, 2021b). However, despite the existing challenges, WB representatives seem to take notice of the comments and criticisms published at the EI website which is perceived as a positive development by EI representatives (Interview EI, 2019). EI hopes to continue and strengthen the dialogue with the WB and the IMF in the future:

(. . .) the dialogue is absolutely necessary, of course it's difficult to change the views of the IMF or the WB, this is where the challenges are. . . . So, it's absolute necessary, in fact this dialogue should continue, and I believe it should be more structured, and the Bank must engage, must actually have the political will and commitment to take the suggestions seriously. . . . So, it must be a structured dialogue on a bilateral and multilateral basis in the context of different Global Unions coming together to engage with the two institutions as it is currently the case, and that should certainly continue. . . . Sometimes we have been involved in consultations and the Bank has not actually taken our views on board, so we need to strengthen that dialogue so that it's really a dialogue and not a one-way process.

(Interview EI, 2019)

The GUF considers 'genuine' consultations and engagement from IFI side as a precondition for the future success of the dialogue (Interview EI, 2019).

Loan conditionality

Lending conditionalities such as cuts to public spending and deregulatory reforms as well as the policy advice of the IFIs have a big influence on borrowing countries and lead frequently to further increases in existing inequality. A study from Blanton et al. (2015: 332) revealed that loan programmes administered by the IFIs 'are negatively and significantly related to collective labour rights, including laws designed to guarantee basic collective bargaining and freedom of association rights, as well as the protection of these rights in practice'. In the aftermath of the international financial crisis in 2008, the IMF promoted austerity policies and labour market deregulation which had a negative impact on workers' and trade union rights and the provision of public services. A review on programme design and conditionality in the period from 2011 to 2017 conducted by the IMF itself found an increase in structural conditions (IMF, 2019h). The findings contrast a statement made by the former IMF managing director Christine Lagarde during an IMFC press briefing in 2014 where she said:

> We provide lending, and, by the way, structural adjustments? That was before my time. I have no idea what it is. We do not do that anymore. No, seriously, you have to realize that we have changed the way in which we offer our financial support. It is really on the basis of a partnership.
>
> (IMF, 2014)

Lagarde's assessment of conditionality clearly lacked objectivity and a recent analysis of IMF documents conducted by two GUFs (EI, PSI) and ActionAid revealed major constraints and cuts to public sector wage bills which undermine progress with regard to the SDGs. The report concluded that the lack of progress with regard to education and health goals promotes gender inequality and a loss of decent work opportunities in the public sector.

Emergency loans issued during the Covid-19 pandemic have further strengthened the power of the IMF. Despite some shifts in rhetoric from its headquarters, the austerity-based policy reforms that countries agree with the IMF, either as conditions or coercive advice, are unchanged. The recent Global Austerity Alert suggests that 154 countries face austerity in 2021, rising to 159 countries in 2022. Public sector wage bill cuts are flagged as one of the most prevalent austerity measures with negative social outcomes.

(ActionAid, 2021: 9)

The issue of conditionality still plays a significant role in the dialogue and presents a concern for trade unions. In their statement to the spring meetings of the IFIs in April 2022, the Global Unions recommended a reform of conditionality and policy advice of labour (Global Unions, 2022). These recommendations as well as demands to 'turn the page on the failed policies of austerity, deregulation, and market fundamentalism' (Global Unions, 2020: 2) are not new and have been repeated many times. In terms of outcomes, trade unionists have noticed an increase in organisational awareness on the side of the IFIs and to some extent a change in rhetoric and 'tone' at the IMF (Interview ITUC06, 2019; ITUC, 2021b). The ITUC General Secretary noted in this regard that whilst the rhetoric about issues 'is often right', the IMF has continued the conditionality with loan agreements (Interview ITUC08, 2018). An Oxfam study revealed that 13 out of 15 IMF loans negotiated during the second year of the pandemic required new austerity measures, and that 43 out of 55 African countries face public expenditure cuts totalling US$183 billion over the next five years (Oxfam, 2022a). Ortiz and Cummins (2021), who expect austerity to prevail until 2025, suggest alternatives such as the use of progressive taxation and the expansion of social security coverage.

It can be argued that the dialogue has a positive influence on the direction of the IFIs; however, this needs to be consolidated in terms of actions by the IFIs. In order to achieve that, the IMF would need to develop a 'different mindset from the modified neoliberalism that currently sets the parameters of its thinking' and to embrace inequality and social protection 'as matters of principle and not just pragmatically driven sideshows' (UN Human Rights Council, 2018a: 17). This kind of change also requires the support from all the organisational shareholders which constitutes a challenge in itself. Furthermore, a more robust assessment of IMF programmes and their impact on social and welfare protection is fundamental (IMF, 2019h). Over a decade ago a representative of the IEO suggested to evaluate 'by results and not by goals' (Interview IMF02, 2008). This would require a clear definition and implementation of sub-goals and appropriate monitoring:

What is not specified is: What are you trying to achieve? What are the steps that you think will lead you there? And then monitor whether those steps are taken, and they lead to where you want to go. That is what is missing. The most important thing is the result on the ground. A friend of mine always said that 'if you don't know where you want to go, you never get lost'. So you go to a country, you suggest doing 10 good things, and then some of those things are done, others are not done. Those that are done, some have good results, others don't have so good results, and at the same time in the country some good things are happening. You can always say 'well, this is what I achieved'. And if you don't specify what you want to achieve, then you can take credit for all the good that came out.

(Interview IMF02, 2008)

In order to achieve satisfactory outcomes of policy reforms, stakeholders such as trade union and government representatives need to be involved in the planning and monitoring process of reforms. The institutionalised dialogue between the Global Unions and the IFIs is, as many dialogue participants have noticed, without alternative. However, there is room for improvement regarding its structure and overall functioning. Although some of the challenges have already been highlighted, the next sections will consider in more detail some of the drivers and obstacles for the dialogue in practice.

Drivers and obstacles to the dialogue

The last two decades have shown that the dialogue and relationships between stakeholders are never static but always changing. The dialogue depends on organisational representatives and their attitudes and willingness to cooperate and is facilitated by organisational cultures and values. Attitudes, opinions, and perceptions of individual actors influence whether cooperation takes place and the scope and depth of cooperation. An attitude is a predisposition of an individual actor to respond in a particular way to other individual actors and, for example, events such as the high-level meetings and the dialogue in general. In other words, an attitude 'is a predisposition to respond in a favorable way or unfavorable manner with respect to a given attitude object' (Oskamp and Schultz Wesley, 2014: 9). Individual attitudes and opinions are constructed by individual actors and are not behaviour per se, they can change over time as a result and 'in reaction to persuasive messages' (Ibid., 2014: 264). The dialogue depends on a process by which individual actors interpret information provided in joint meetings and mutual perceptions of all those involved, and it is the latter which guides and determines the behaviour of individuals (Wilson and Rees, 2007). Furthermore, perception processes form the cognitive basis of attitudes, and as such they determine the formation of attitudes and opinions as well as changes in this regard over time (Oskamp and Schultz Wesley, 2014). For example, positive perceptions can have a favourable influence on attitudes of individual actors which could then result in a more positive conduct towards the dialogue partners. Both attitudes and perceptions are linked to and influenced by organisational characteristics such as the organisational structure, culture, identity, and learning.

The coordination of the dialogue from the side of the WB and the IMF (decentralised vs. centralised approach) impact on joint communications and the time it takes for trade union representatives to get in touch with the right people. The interviews with representatives from the Global Unions, the ILO, and the IFIs suggest that there is a wide agreement between the different representatives involved that all the different levels of the dialogue are essential and important. However, these favourable opinions are not necessarily reflected in actions which would be necessary for further enhancing the dialogue.

Perceptions of trade union and ILO representatives

For the ITUC, the importance of the dialogue with the IFIs is determined by its perspective of the dialogue as a 'strategic instrument' which is aimed at achieving change with regard to IFI policies and a 'seat at the table'. As mentioned earlier, the Global Unions engage in the dialogue with clear objectives and a clear purpose which are the main drivers for the dialogue and trade union engagement. However, relationships between individuals and consultations at organisational level are shaped by ups and downs which are partly determined by the individual actors themselves, and partly by organisational changes such as the restructuring processes at the WB. From the perspective of trade unionists, the 'old ideology' still has a place in the IFIs thinking (Interview ITUC08, 2018). To the present day, the IFIs promote neoliberal economic policies which arguably impact workers negatively and for that reason reforming the organisations is fundamental from a trade union perspective:

> I do think that the IMF particularly has been instrumental in pushing the neo-liberal model abroad, and a large part of what we in the US struggle with is the fact, the way the global economy is structured, it sort of puts all labour into one global pool, in competition with one another and drives down wages and standards because of the neo-liberal model that the IMF is a big part of championing. . . . So I think we definitely do see a lot of value in working on reforming the IMF and the WB, because those policies are actually directly impacting our workers.
>
> (Interview AFL-CIO, 2017)

The interviews with trade union representatives revealed several factors which are closely related to the achievement of organisational and policy changes within the IFIs, some of which can be actively influenced by the trade unions whilst others cannot. One factor which is considered to be important is *time*. Trade unionists widely acknowledged that policy changes within the IFIs cannot be achieved in the short-term, but that it comes slowly and in connection with economic cycles (Interview IFJ, 2008).

> (. . .) if you ask me, do you think that dialogue is important? Yes, it is important. Is it going to bring changes? Yes, it will bring changes. It will bring changes in the long term.
>
> (Interview EI, 2008)

A former director of the ITUC/Global Unions office expressed the importance of time as follows: 'The very first meeting I attended at the WB was in 1999 and maybe we will get a result in 2017' (Interview ITUC02, 2015). The dialogue process goes through different phases and there are times when progress is made and other times 'when things move more slowly' (Interview ITUC01, 2008). For example, the time of organisational restructuring at the WB was a rather unproductive period for the dialogue as some WB individuals who acted as key interlocutors left the organisation (Interview ITUC02, 2017). At that time, it was 'much easier [*for the trade unions*] to reach specific agreements with the IMF' than it was with the WB (Interview ITUC06, 2019). Since 2017 some promising work has been achieved in the area of green transition and talks have been held with WB staff on climate policies. However, no further progress was achieved with the WB social protection and jobs unit during that time (Interview ITUC06, 2019). Times when only little progress can be achieved require trade unions to be *persistent* and *consistent* in their presence and demands and to deal with setbacks resulting from bilateral communication with IFI staff. According to one PSI representative, this gives the message to IFI representatives – 'look we are here, you've got to talk to us' (Interview PSI, 2008). The TUAC also plays an important role in this context as it provides a consistent high level of economic expertise which helps to raise the international reputation of trade unions (Interview DGB, 2008). Another channel of demonstrating persistence and consistence in trade union demands are the ITUC/Global Union statements to the spring and annual meetings of the IFIs. In the past, some trade unionists suggested that the trade unions should apply a more proactive approach as the 'the finance industry and businesses always take up the initiative and workers follow behind' (Interview IFJ, 2008 *translated from Spanish*). To some extent this has been implemented and trade unions have become more proactive by, for example, calling for a new social contract and rebuilding multilateralism (Global Unions, 2019b; ITUC, 2020b). Yet trade unions also need to apply a focused and realistic approach in order to be successful (Interview BWI, 2009; Interview EI, 2008), and this includes the 'learning of structures' and organisational 'passwords' and to 'move things in paragraphs' (Interview BWI, 2009). It also requires the strengthening of the capacity of national trade union affiliates.

Other factors which are important for the success of the dialogue, and which cannot be influenced by the trade unions, are *organisational leadership* and the *influence of individual actors* at the IFIs (Interview IG Metall, 2008). The WB President and the IMF Managing Director serve renewable terms of five years which means that potential 'reformers' have a cyclical influence and that reforms introduced can be undone by the next leader. In addition, attitudes of organisational leaders, which are influenced by their work experiences and cultural socialisation, impact their openness towards trade unions and organisational reforms. For example, under the Trump presidency in the USA, trade unionists perceived an increasing hesitation of WB representatives to cooperate with trade unions (Interview ITUC02, 2017). This trend continued when David Malpasse became President of the WB in 2019. At the IMF, Managing Director Christine Lagarde made some attempts to follow established policies and directions of her predecessor, but later trade unions perceived that her 'personal openness and desire to collaborate' with trade unions diminished (Interview ITUC02, 2015). This kind of assessment was also shared by some ILO representatives:

> She is extremely correct and very open, but I think her own views are a little bit stiffer than Strauss-Kahn's, he was really prepared to be much more adventurous. But I think there are in a sense more important things about the culture of the IMF than just the personality of the managing director as to what affects these things.
>
> (Interview ILO06, 2016)

The leadership of the IFIs influences the organisational culture and openness towards trade unions to some extent and with that a potential window of opportunity for trade unions to be heard by IFI organisational representatives. In the past, the organisational culture of the IFIs was often less favourable towards staff who took a more supportive approach in relation to trade unions:

> The problem we found in the past, is that the people who were good with us, either they really stagnated in their positions, or they started gaining more power and becoming influential and forgot about us. You don't move forward within the Bank by being friendly with trade unions.
>
> (Interview ITUC02, 2015)

Individuals in leading positions at the IFIs can make a positive contribution to the dialogue or they can 'make things difficult' for trade unions, even though they are not able to stop the communication processes entirely' (Interview ITUC02, 2008). For example, 'true believers' at the WB who prefer to make alterations to existing policies instead of 'starting on a different basis' hinder organisational learning (Interview PSI, 2008). The same applies to individuals who complicate the exchange of information and delay responses to requests from trade unions as happened with a former director of the then SP&L department (Interview ITUC02, 2008). In addition to a 'constructive' attitude of individuals at the IFIs, an understanding of trade union positions facilitates communication. For example, in the opinion of the former ITUC/Global Unions office director, the IMF chief economist Maurice Obstfeld had a 'clear understanding of the instability emanating from weakened bargaining power for workers and the lost labour share of national income in a lot of countries' (Interview ITUC06, 2019). Although the work produced by the IMF research department has only a limited influence within the IMF, the communication of these positions at press conferences does give a positive signal to trade unions. However, decoupling and a silo mentality within the IFIs, often facilitated by the *organisational structure*, makes the dialogue more inefficient. From a trade union perspective, WB country teams and IMF mission teams have a lot of discretion over their decisions and actions, and they are inadequately controlled by management. For IFI staff on the ground this means that they often continue to apply long established and institutionalised organisational processes and ways of thinking which have their roots in the 1980s (Interview ITUC06, 2019).

The dialogue has enabled the trade unions to define areas of joint work with the IFIs, to raise awareness for their concerns, and to achieve a seat at the table. In this context, informal relationships between individuals outside of the institutionalised dialogue structure support the formal communication process (Interview ITUC02, 2008). The trade unions continuously signal a readiness to talk and to further promote communication within the dialogue. This is because from their perspective this is the only way to make progress with regard to reducing inequality and to strengthen collective bargaining and other key labour market institutions. During the technical meetings in 2022, the trade unions expressed their interest in renewing the past in-depth dialogue on labour market institutions with the IMF and on the Bank's publication on jobs and regulations from 2015.[5] However, these efforts cannot neglect the fact that many trade unionists still perceive the neoliberal paradigm as dominant in the IFIs.

Secondments to the World Bank

Over the years there have been several secondments of trade unionists to the WB which shaped individual and collective trade union perceptions about the IFIs. The secondments aim to provide ITUC and GUF representatives with the opportunity to experience the institutional culture of the WB and to improve cooperation between the two organisations. As yet there have been no secondments of WB representatives to the trade unions, which some trade unionists consider as an obstacle regarding the development of a mutual understanding:

> I think just as people from unions going on secondment to the IFIs, they get an
> insight into the thinking and then, basically as well the culture of that particular

organisation. Now, it doesn't necessarily mean that it changes their mind, but it provides for better understanding of where they're coming from. I think that could work very well if you had a flow in the opposite direction.

(Interview ITGLWF, 2009)

This one-way exchange is determined by financial reasons to some extent as the WB pays the salary of the trade union secondees, and it would be difficult for the trade unions to reciprocate for WB secondees. The resulting financial 'dependence' of trade union secondees is considered critically by some trade unionists as it impacts on the implementation of their projects during the secondment.

Between 2003 and 2005, five trade union secondments took place. Trade unionists came from the ICFTU-AFRO, the PSI, the BWI, the WCL, and the ITF. The secondments varied in length (2–11 months) and were spent at different WB departments. At the beginning trade unionists felt that their arguments were not considered seriously, and that some WB staff exhibited hostile attitudes (Interview PSI, 2008; Interview BWI, 2009). According to the BWI representative, staff of the WB's procurement department seemed to be looking for somebody 'who would just fit in nice and quietly' and 'not someone who is going to run around trying to persuade everyone that the inclusion of labour clauses in standard bidding documents was a burning issue' (Interview BWI, 2009). The BWI representative recalled:

> I had someone on me the whole time to try and slow me down. The Director of Procurement at that time . . . he was afraid that the arguments were so persuasive that people were getting carried away and feeling that it might become the Bank policy. We really had to wait until he retired. He was extremely opposed to trade union rights and equal opportunities and non-discrimination. He felt that these had absolutely no place in a construction contract and were entirely inappropriate.
>
> (Interview BWI, 2009)

The preparation for the secondment involved discussions with ILO staff and the preparation of a background document that would justify the need for labour clauses in the Bank's standard procurement documents. The background document also considered processes around construction contracts, capacity building, and the promotion of a dialogue between key stakeholders included contractor associations and ministries of public works and labour. The reluctance of WB staff to the secondment in the first place made it very difficult for the BWI representative to get some attention and feedback on these issues. According to a WB procurement specialist, the secondment had only been accepted because staff of the WB's procurement department had come under pressure from the trade unions. By accepting the secondment, the WB hoped to remove this pressure, but there was no intrinsic desire to consider any policy changes (Interview WB03, 2009). Although the secondment of the BWI representative lasted only a few weeks, it had a major impact on the integration of the ILO CLS in the Banks's standard procurement documents, and it helped to extend the BWI's involvement in the area of procurement within the Bank which continues until today (Interview BWI, 2009).

> We have been able to kind of elbow our way in and make a little niche. This is not a formalised thing; it is entirely a grace and a favour arrangement by the Bank itself. Now we are beginning to be more involved.
>
> (Interview BWI, 2009)

From the BWI perspective, the success of the secondment was related to its tight focus and the technical expertise offered by the BWI. Representatives from other GUFs, however, were not that successful during their secondments. For example, a PSI representative who spent some time at the WB's public transport department felt as if he was treated 'just as an extra office boy to do some photocopying for them' (Interview PSI, 2008).

> (. . .) frequently you were meeting with people [*at the WB*] who were pretty true believers in what they were doing, who were prepared to know that sometimes things didn't work out exactly as they had intended, but still they felt that that was just a matter of tidying the policy up rather than ditching it and starting on a different basis.
>
> (Interview PSI, 2008)

Although the PSI representative complained and the WB President (James Wolfensohn) considered the complaint seriously, it did not result in an improved relationship with staff in that particular department. The complaint led to the establishment of a formal contact point between the PSI and the WB which, however, never worked in practice (Ibid., 2008).

The latest secondment of a trade union representative took place in 2017 and lasted eight months. The ITUC-Africa representative was seconded to the Bank's job group with a focus on informal workers. At the beginning of the secondment, the trade union representative welcomed the opportunity to work at the Bank stating that 'the fact that they are already thinking about informal workers, it's a big step for us' and 'the fact that they allow me to somehow make a contribution, it's another step' (Interview ITUC07, 2017). In the course of the secondment, the cooperation with WB staff was limited and this as well as the overall experience contributed to a change of perception:

> I'm not even sure why they accepted the secondment, they didn't seem to really know what they wanted to do with it; I don't know whether it's just a way in which they think they can perhaps calm down the trade unions in a way and say at least we have had one of yours with us, because even the work

that the people before me, especially the one immediately before me has done, I haven't seen it featured in the Bank's broad discussions around issues on particular importance.

(Interview ITUC07, 2019)

The main outcome of this secondment was a publication about social insurance coverage and informal workers[6] with two WB staff. However, a paper on collective bargaining and informal workers produced by the secondee was not published. Budget constraints hindered the collection of primary data about social insurance coverage in selected countries which the secondee stated was 'really demoralising' (Interview ITUC07, 2019). In order to make future secondments more successful and to expand the influence of trade unions in relation to a specific topic, the secondee suggested that it would be beneficial for the trade unions to send more than one secondee at the same time. Furthermore, the ITUC needs to consider the time frame more carefully and ideally provide financial resources so that financial dependency on the WB can be avoided.

Perceptions of IFI representatives

A few years after the dialogue protocol was signed in 2002, the IFIs considered that the headquarters-level dialogue had moved from an 'ideological debate to a more constructive one' (World Bank, 2006: 1–2). A former WB senior communication officer pointed out that the dialogue with trade unions is 'very important' to the Bank because 'trade unions are a key constituency within civil society' (Interview WB01, 2008). Their large membership base and democratic organisational procedures provide them with considerable legitimacy which is acknowledged by the IFIs. Over the years 'acceptance' developed into 'understanding' of the trade unions and their role, at least to some extent:

I think we accept; we understand the role of trade unions and we understand that they have their positions. I personally think that there is much more common ground then we even think there is today.

(Interview WB01, 2008)

A former Executive Director stated in this context that there has been a general 'openness towards trade unions which is not tactical but serious' (Interview WB05, 2009).

The *organisational legitimacy* of trade unions and the perception of *common ground* are important driving factors for the IFIs to expand their engagement in the dialogue. The Bank's programmes concern workers in different sectors and particularly during crises times, jobs and labour markets play a key role in terms of economic recovery. Positive attitudes of IFI representatives and informal relationships also strengthen the dialogue as the following statement from an IFC representative underlines:

> I think we have a very good dialogue, and I think Peter [*former ITUC/Global Unions office director*] feels he can just give a call and I feel I can just give him a call with anything. . . . So, I think we have built a good dialogue, I think we have a lot of trust on both sides which is really helpful.
>
> (Interview IFC03, 2017)

However, individual attitudes and relationships between organisational representatives do not follow a continuous pattern, but are influenced by organisational changes and the organisational leadership. Like trade union representatives, some WB representatives consider the *leadership* at the IFIs as crucial with regard to the quality of the dialogue and its implementation (Interview WB01, 2017). For example, during the high-level meetings in 2013, the then IMF Managing Director Christine Lagarde confirmed the commitment of the IMF to the 'Jobs and Growth' agenda and stated that the IMF 'is willing to listen, engage in dialogue and change its views' (ITUC, 2013: 5). In 2021, Managing Director Kristalina Georgieva thanked the trade unions for their continuing input through the dialogue (ITUC, 2021b).

In the opinion of a former WB representative, one of the factors which distinguishes the IFIs from the trade unions is the *approach to* and *use of economics* which he ascribes to the fact that the IFIs are mainly run by economists. He perceived the IFIs as quite 'theoretical' in their approach, which is reflected in the studies produced by their research departments. The trade unions were perceived to have 'more of a practical approach', although they also undertake research activities and economic forecasts (Interview WB01, 2008). In practice this means that information and expertise provided by the trade unions is often not awarded the same importance by IFI staff as the information produced within their own organisations. In former times the director of the then WB SP&L department even considered it necessary to offer training to trade unionists in order to provide them with a 'better understanding' of the WB's economic approach (Interview WB02, 2008).

Organisational characteristics, including economic paradigms and approaches, still shape individual perceptions and determine the interpretation of information on both sides. In comparison to the trade unions, the IFIs have a less defined approach towards the dialogue, and the lack of clear organisational objectives means that perceptions and attitudes of individual actors can have a greater influence on communication within the dialogue. In other words, so-called 'reformers' might be more open and supportive towards the dialogue than for example 'hardliners' who do not question long-established organisational principles. Nevertheless, in the opinion of a former WB representative, the dialogue has changed the IFIs over the years:

> I see these organisations definitely moving forward, slower than we would like, but definitely moving forward. And I think the voice of civil society has

had a real impact because 30 years ago, you didn't have safeguards, gender or environment. Today that's all embedded in the Bank's agenda, but they are still organisations run by economists, and you still have very conservative Southern governments who don't like this agenda with the power, so you have to take all of them into consideration.

(Interview WB01, 2017)

The internal complexity of the IFIs, including the diverse perspectives amongst shareholders, requires compromises in decision-making and decisions are often based on the lowest common denominator which also impacts the dialogue. This might explain to some extent why, despite the newly arising global challenges, the push for more robust consultations and an in-depth dialogue comes from the international trade union movement and the ILO and not the IFIs. In order to re-build and strengthen multilateralism in the long term and to develop a new social contract, a more symmetrical power relationship between the IFIs, the Global Unions, and the ILO would need to be established.

Information and knowledge exchange and organisational learning

The efficient and meaningful exchange of information between the dialogue partners plays a significant role for the functioning of the dialogue at all levels. Efficiency is related to the pace and frequency of the information exchange, the scope of information which is exchanged and the regularity of follow-ups on specific issues. The high-level meetings cover a broad range of issues and time pressures often only allow a verbal expression of individual opinions and organisational positions rather than a profound exchange of information. Yet these meetings are important, because they allow the dialogue partners to present their positions and views on specific topics, such as labour market trends and social protection, which then can be discussed in technical meetings in more depth. In the past, technical meetings also led to the establishment of focal points such as the technical meeting about gender issues in 2009, which aimed to investigate and define future opportunities for cooperation in this area. Amongst other things, the meeting included an update on the implementation of the WB's gender action plan and on women's advances in the trade union movement, and it resulted in the creation of a focal point on gender between the ITUC equality team and the WB gender and development team (Observation minutes technical meeting, 2009). To the disappointment of the trade unions the focal point did not lead to further cooperation (Interview ITUC02, 2015).

The underlying idea of a focal point is to promote a quick and efficient transfer of information between a specific WB department and a trade union organisation (ITUC or GUF). In those cases where staff of the involved WB department are committed to having regular contacts with trade unions, meetings and information exchanges are more consistent within the framework of the focal point. Otherwise, the dialogue is only 'sporadic' or does not exist at all (Interview ITUC02,

2008). Generally, the overall functioning and outcomes of focal points, such as in the areas of education and transport, were often limited and disappointing for trade unions. In this context, an ITF consultant considered the ITF to be 'very successful in getting the attention of the World Bank' (Interview ITF, 2008), but he also stated:

> Now we know that the World Bank transport sector chief understands our concerns very well. But is he able to educate the World Bank people about our concerns? Well, that will depend on a whole range of issues. To what extent is it a priority for him to do so? Probably it is not a very big priority. To what extent is he able to do so? Probably he is not able. That's not his background. He is a transport engineer, he is a transport specialist, he is a World Bank official. Is he in a good position to train the World Bank people about our concerns? He is in a better position now than he was before when we met with him for a day, but he is still not able to convey it very clearly. There is a lot of loss from him downwards. There is a lot of loss of understanding of our concerns.
>
> (Interview ITF, 2008)

The statement highlights two things. First, it emphasises the importance of individual perceptions and attitudes of WB staff regarding communication. Second, the organisational structure and intra-organisational power relations in the WB can lead to a 'loss of understanding' of trade union concerns at lower organisational levels which makes it less likely that WB staff will take the initiative.

There are no focal points with the IMF, but there are joint workshops and seminars, such as on jobs and growth, which provide opportunities for an information exchange between the trade unions, the ILO, and the IMF (Interview IMF03, 2017). At the country level, information exchange is highly dependent on the attitudes and engagement of individual IFI representatives. For example, at the IMF, 'some country team leaders are very involved in dialogue' and others 'see it as a box that has to be ticked off' (Interview IMF01, 2008). In comparison to the WB and the IMF, IFC project teams often exchange information with local trade unions and consider their views in project assessments (Interview IFC03, 2017). Throughout the dialogue the trade unions have repeatedly highlighted the importance of a timely exchange of information. From their perspective, early consultations and an involvement in the appraisal and monitoring process of projects would lead to a more meaningful participation and the early discovery of potential labour issues (Observation minutes high-level meetings, 2017).

The communication between individual actors directly influences organisational learning and the institutionalisation of the dialogue whereby organisational learning can be related to the dialogue process itself and to specific issues discussed during the meetings. On the part of the international trade union movement, the ITUC supported by the ILO takes the lead in the dialogue. For the ITUC and the

Global Unions, organisational learning means to develop a better understanding of the ways the IFIs function and the management of organisational differences within the dialogue. In this regard, it can be argued that the ITUC learns *about* the IFIs through the dialogue, even though learning *from* the IFIs may be limited to only 'some instances' (Interview ITUC02, 2008). The democratic structure of the ITUC and the GUFs allows information to be disseminated to all affiliates on an equal basis and to provide them with the opportunity to reflect on the information. This means that learning about the IFIs is not limited to the ITUC and GUF headquarters. However, not all affiliates are likely to consider the disseminated information as useful or relevant for their own work as resources within these organisations are often limited and priority is given to topics which are of concern to their members.

In contrast to the Global Unions, organisational learning at the IFIs is, at least to some extent, influenced by the organisational structure as well as shareholder interests and behaviours:

> (. . .) one thing is the institutional behaviour of these institutions, but that institutional behaviour can be changed if the behaviour of the governments that are members change, and if the behaviour of those governments change, by the virtue of the changes in their societies, the institutions in those societies . . . there are countries where there are strong institutions of civil society organisations and so on that can make their governments be more conscious of what they do.
>
> (Interview ILO08, 2017)

In other words, in order to achieve a process of deep organisational learning at the IFIs, national governments as shareholders need to change their perspectives. In the past, some trade unionists suggested that the high-profile work at the IFI headquarters needs to be replicated at country level with individual governments (Interview ITGLWF, 2009).

Furthermore, the decentralised organisational structure of the WB limits the flow of knowledge and organisational learning across the organisation. One example is the 'jobs group' which is the main contact point for trade unions, and which is no longer in direct contact with country directors after the structural reform (Interview WB06, 2019). Nowadays the 'jobs group' works within the CCSA and acts more as an advisory unit which means knowledge is only dispersed if a country director or sector staff request it. As a result, the jobs group is not any longer leading the discussion about jobs. A former WB representative commented that although during his time at the Bank there was a good collaboration with the ITUC, it failed to 'trickle down' to the country level (Interview WB06, 2019). Another restriction to organisational learning is the lack of monitoring and evaluation of employment outcomes within the different WBG operations which is related to organisational accountability. In recent times, the WB recognised this knowledge gap and launched two initiatives which both follow the 'Supporting Effective Jobs Lending at Scale' (SEJLS) programme developed by the Jobs Multi-Donor Trust Fund (Divanbeigi and Saliola, 2022). One of them is the 'Jobs and Economic Transformation' (JET) pilot which aims to estimate indirect job outcomes in 20 IDA countries. In comparison to the WB, the organisational culture at the IFC is perceived as less conservative and more innovative (Interview WB03, 2009) and more open towards the ideas of trade unions (Interview WB01, 2008). The continuous documentation of knowledge and sharing of experiences enable staff to learn from each other and to make tacit knowledge available across the organisation (Interview IFC03, 2017).

In the case of the IMF the 'Public Affairs' division helps to organise contacts for the trade unions with IMF representatives and departments. The IMF is a centralised organisation, and the Managing Director can 'take essential decisions' which can be 'implemented throughout the organisation quite quickly' (Interview ITUC01, 2008). Some IMF representatives consider the IMF as a 'learning institution' which has learnt its lessons from former crises (Minutes high-level meeting, 2017). For example, nowadays the IMF is less opposed to the issue of capital controls (Interview IMF03, 2017) and providing fiscal space on social protection (Interview WB06, 2019). The IEO plays a key role in assessing the IMF's work and initiating learning processes, although the report from Kaberuka et al. (2018: 1) concluded that the IEO still has too little impact in the IMF. In order to promote organisational accountability and learning more efficiently, it needs to become 'an effective change agent'. This perception is shared by an ILO representative who perceives organisational learning as a 'haphazard process' despite the fact that some IMF staff has become 'more alert and interested' in the ILO (Interview ILO06, 2017). From an IMF perspective, there is awareness about trade union positions, and trade union statements to the spring and annual meetings of the IFIs are disseminated within the organisation and the IMF acknowledges their consistency (Interview IMF03, 2017).

In summary, there are several factors which either promote or hinder organisational learning within the different organisations. Obstacles to learning include the selective or even nonprocessing of information at individual level and an inconsistency regarding the dissemination of knowledge at organisational level. Further challenges are posed by the different organisational paradigms and the language connected with these paradigms, which in the case of the trade unions can be described as a 'language of justice' and in the case of the IFIs as a 'language of shareholder value'.

What comes next? – future prospects and challenges

In the early years, the dialogue mainly served the objective of developing mutual understanding between the dialogue partners which is a precondition for meaningful cooperation. At the beginning trade unionists often felt as if they were not perceived as a source of information and were being treated as 'economically illiterate', in particular when they did not agree with the policies and measures applied by the IFIs (Interview ITUC04, 2009; Interview IG Metall, 2008). A few years later some WB staff were 'quite receptive' to some of the information provided by the trade unions (Interview PSI, 2008), and the dialogue partners had defined some common ground (World Bank, 2009).

The interviews with representatives from the Global Unions, the ILO, and the IFI suggest that there is a wide agreement that the dialogue on all its different levels is essential and important. The trade unions consider the dialogue as a strategic instrument, and it can be argued that this kind of dialogue has the potential to strengthen multilateralism. Over the years mutual understanding has improved and the awareness of the IFIs regarding the importance of the creation of jobs, decent work, and social protection has increased. The international trade union movement has achieved a seat at the table although as one trade union representative stated, it is important to 'go beyond that' and to develop joint policies for going forward (Interview ITGLWF, 2009). Overall, the WB has become more progressive in its rhetoric despite the implementation gap that remains (Interview WB01, 2017), whilst the IMF has put an increasing emphasis on issues such as inequality, gender and women's empowerment, and climate change since the mid-2000s (Interview IMF03, 2017). These organisational developments are also visible in the debates about a 'new social contract' and universal social protection, even though there 'is no consensus' yet regarding the best design and implementation of arrangements (Interview WB06, 2019). The trade unions are aware that a fundamental change of the IFIs can only be delivered by a new global governance system and that the development of such a system takes time; it is an 'evolution' and not a 'revolution' (Interview EI, 2008).

One of the main challenges for the dialogue is the different organisational missions and values. For example, the WB is a development bank and has a long-term focus which distinguishes it from other financial market players. In contrast to the trade unions and the ILO, however, the WB is driven by 'efficiency' and 'financial results', and it depends on lending money for projects (Interview ILO08, 2017). In addition, trade unions representatives feel that there is a divide between the rhetoric of the IFIs and the implementation of verbal commitments:

> I feel that's a pretty common theme with the IFIs and especially the IMF in general, they come up with stuff that's good on paper and then it doesn't get executed. (. . .), there's a lot of stuff coming out of the research department that we would like to see implemented when they are making country recommendations, . . . they've come a long way in terms of research in the last 10 years to debunk a lot of the austerity, like privatise everything, deregulate everything, make cuts to everything, every labour market regulation is terrible, but when it comes to actually making recommendations on a country-level,

then their programme people in the country are still touting the same things they were, it's like the Washington consensus stuff.

(Interview AFL-CIO, 2017)

There is still a big gap between what they say in terms of research, in terms of analysis and what they do on the ground. They still continue recommending to different states cutting public spending, not boosting public spending . . . there is nothing about the need to enforce collective bargaining, for example on the ground to make sure that we can really modify the income distribution in different countries, tackling inequalities.

(Interview ETUC, 2017)

Trade union representatives miss an honest reflection and evaluation of the impact of neo-liberal market reforms by the IFIs. Some of the research studies conducted by the IFIs have marked a change in direction, but intra-organisational decoupling often hinders the implementation of new insights and ideas on the ground. For example, whilst the IMF research department considers the 'world as a whole' and 'international multipliers', the Article IV process is still based on the working assumption that the 'rest of the world is as it is' and that it does not change (Interview ILO06, 2016). Trade union representatives have noted repeatedly that policy research and policy recommendations need to go together, although from the perspective of an IMF representative the criticism of decoupling is not entirely fair as the IMF aims to promote inclusive policies on the ground, such as minimum wages (Interview IMF03, 2017). At the WB, the organisational structure and integrated silo mentality also support decoupling with regard to knowledge development and implementation. From a trade union perspective there are limited collaborative efforts between their main contact point at the WB, the jobs group, and other departments (Interview ITUC06, 2019). Similar to the IMF, WB operational staff on the ground are perceived as very influential when it comes to decision-making as 'these are the ones that are really creating the policy' (Interview ETUC, 2017). The trade unions aim to apply a more proactive approach when dealing with WB country offices (Interview ITUC07, 2019), but their participation in consultations depends to a large extent on the reception of their efforts by country office staff. Another example of decoupling within the WBG is the production of the former Doing Business report which was in stark contrast to other initiatives such as the promotion of decent work through the 'Better Work' programme.

A varying degree of decoupling is part of the organisational nature of the IFIs which has a detrimental impact on the efficiency and impact of the dialogue. But there are other challenges too, for example, the influence of the finance ministers representing governments at the IMF, as well as the 'language' and perspectives around macroeconomics, including fiscal and monetary policies.

The ILO and the IMF do talk quite a lot, but we work to completely different ministries, so if the ministries back home aren't talking to each other, there's only so far with the best will in the world that Lagarde and Ryder can figure out how to do something together. We can do a bit together, but in the end if the ministries are not working, and I have to say most finance ministries look down a very long nose at the labour ministries.

(Interview ILO06, 2017)

In the past, IMF chief economist Olivier Blanchard provided some evidence-based research around collective bargaining and minimum wages which the trade unions and the ILO considered as partial breakthrough, because their own studies have shown that collective bargaining is the 'best mitigator' against inequality (Interview ILO06, 2016; Interview ITUC08, 2018). This could also be relevant with regard to the future of work debate, where the trade unions and the ILO suggest a broadening of the definition of 'macroeconomic policy'. The latter would support the development of new approaches which are required to resolve issues such as the stagnation of wages (Interview ILO06, 2017), and it could also help the IFIs to resist the attempt to 'wrap up old ideas in a new package' (Interview ITUC06, 2019). Despite all the remaining gaps and challenges, the achievements of the dialogue should not be underestimated. There is agreement between all the dialogue stakeholders on the need to join forces in order to tackle poverty and inequality and to achieve a new social contract. However, fundamental organisational change at the IFIs can only be achieved through the involvement of their shareholders which is why trade unions arguably need to promote a dialogue with national governments at the same time.

Notes

1 The PRSP process replaced the SAPs at the early 2000s and requires governments of developing countries to describe the country's macroeconomic, structural, and social policies in order to promote economic growth and reduce poverty rates.
2 The Commission was established by the ILO in 2002 and examined the different dimensions of globalisation and its implications for economic and social progress. The final report was released in February 2004.
3 Source: For example, Core Courses (2019) 'Framing: Social Protection and Jobs' by Margaret Grosh (Senior Advisor WB) https://pubdocs.worldbank.org/en/475911572357498863/SPJCC19-D1-S1-Grosh-Framing.pdf
4 The 'Systems Approach for Better Education Results' (SABER) was launched by the WB in 2011 and aims to produce data on and knowledge on national education policies and institutions which help to evaluate and analyse education systems. It forms part of the WB Education Strategy, 2020.
5 Kuddo, A., Robalino, D.A. and Weber, M. (2015) *Balancing Regulations to Promote Jobs: From Employment Contracts to Unemployment Benefits*, Working Paper. http://documents1.worldbank.org/curated/en/636721468187738877/pdf/101596-REPLACEMENT-WP-PUBLIC-12-9-15-Box394816B-Balancing-regulations-to-promote-jobs-FINAL-web-version.pdf [Accessed 3 March 2020]
6 Winkler, H., Ruppert, E. and Mote, H. (2017) *Expanding Social Insurance Coverage to Informal Workers*, Washington, DC: World Bank.

7 Conclusion

In 2002, the IFIs (WBG and IMF), the ICFTU/Global Unions and the WCL adopted a formal protocol which forms the basis for a regular and structured policy dialogue at the global level. The dialogue was originally initiated by the trade unions with the objective to influence the agenda and decision-making processes at the IFIs and to promote human and workers' rights. The Global Unions aimed to achieve a permanent seat at the table within the IFIs so that the concerns of workers regularly find their way into policy discussion within these organisations. Whilst the Global Unions initiated the dialogue with the explicit objective of trying to influence IFI policies which impact on workers, the IFIs have become involved in the dialogue in order to become more transparent to civil society in general, and more responsive to trade union criticism in particular. This move towards greater transparency has arguably become more important for the IFIs from the 1980s onwards when their legitimacy was increasingly questioned by civil society organisations.

The examined dialogue has not received much attention in the literature yet. Although it has some similarities with social dialogue and lobbying as described earlier, it cannot be classified in one of these categories and requires its own definition. The dialogue can be defined as a form of international policy dialogue which helps to establish and to maintain a long-term relationship and trust between the dialogue stakeholders which form the basis for cooperation. The dialogue takes place at three levels, which are all equally important and relevant for the Global Unions. These levels are the headquarters level, which includes high-level, technical and interim meetings, and the sector and country level. The focus of the book was on the HQ level although the other levels were also included as examples. The book examined the influence of organisational characteristics and individual perceptions and attitudes on the functioning and outcomes of the dialogue and organisational learning.

So far, nongovernmental actors and global trade union organisations in particular have received little systematic attention in the global governance debate. Institutionalist global governance research acknowledges the importance of non-state actors but focuses still predominantly on intergovernmental organisations

DOI: 10.4324/9781315458410-7

and states. According to Scholte (2021) a reorientation with regard to global governance actors is therefore necessary and further organisational forms and their influence at different levels (global-regional-national) need to be analysed. In this context, the book contributes to knowledge as it examined the role, articulation, and steering function of the international trade union movement in the global governance system. In addition, by focusing on the Global Unions as social, political, and industrial relations actors and the promotion of the policy dialogue, the study also contributes to research on international trade unionism as a specialist area of union action which is still underresearched (Hyman and Gumbrell-McCormick, 2020). The study applied an actor-driven focus and attempted to integrate the characteristics of the involved corporate actors (IFIs, Global Unions, and ILO) and their deeper social structures (norms, ideologies, institutionalised practices, etc.) in the analysis of power relations, policy development, and cooperation within the policy dialogue. As the organisational characteristics also influence individual actors which represent the organisations and their attitudes, perceptions and actions, particular attention has been given to those. However, it needs to be acknowledged that individual actors are not passive and powerless in their behaviours, but that they have the capacity to trigger organisational learning and change. In order to capture and explain the role and influence of individual and corporate actors, and to analyse the relationships within and between the organisations which are involved in the policy dialogue, organisation theories have been applied. The examination of organisational structures, values, cultures, knowledge management, and financial and nonfinancial resources helped to illuminate and explain commonalities and potential obstacles between the dialogue stakeholders and to further develop the analytical dimension of the global governance concept.

Yet no other in-depth qualitative research study has been carried out on the type of policy dialogue examined in the book. The data were derived predominantly from 56 expert interviews which were conducted with representatives from the Global Unions and their affiliate organisations as well as with representatives from the World Bank, the IFC, the IMF, and the ILO. Data were collected over a time span of ten years whereby most interviews were conducted between 2008 and 2011 and between 2016 and 2019. The majority of the interviews were carried out with trade union and ILO representatives. Furthermore, the author observed one technical meeting on gender-related issues (2009) and two high-level meetings (2009 and 2017) between the Global Unions and the IFIs in Washington D.C. The data were further complemented by an analysis of documentary materials which included various reports, minutes of meetings and organisational statements.

The growing institutional complexity in global governance means that different corporate actors are involved in the government of specific policy issues. Following the theorisation of global governance complexity as suggested by Eilstrup-Sangiovanni and Westerwinter (2021), it can be argued that the WBG, the IMF, the Global Unions and the ILO form a 'global governance complex' around the issues of jobs and job creation, social protection and poverty reduction. Although the organisations are permanently interconnected through the formalised dialogue mechanism, their heterogeneity expressed in different organisational interests and practices influences the dialogue process and outcomes. The WBG and the IMF are both intergovernmental organisations, whilst the Global Unions are international nongovernmental organisations. The ILO is unique because of its tripartite structure, which includes governments and worker and employer representatives. Similarities between the organisations include the large voluntary membership of collective actors. In the case of the IFIs and the ILO, these are national governments and in the case of the Global Unions national trade union confederations and sector trade unions. Furthermore, all organisations rely on formal decision-making procedures and bureaucratic structures which help them to administer their programmes and activities. The organisational structure of each organisation exhibits power imbalances as some affiliates are more powerful than others. For example, the USA has an influential position within the ILO and the IFIs. Generally, more powerful affiliates are usually based in the industrialised countries, although countries such as China and Saudi-Arabia have become more influential in the IFIs in the last decade.

However, despite some similarities organisational differences prevail and manifest in the type and characteristics of affiliates, organisational missions, decision-making structures, transparency and accountability, collective self-understanding, organisational culture, knowledge creation, ideology, and paradigms, and the amount of available material and nonmaterial resources. The IFIs have substantially more financial resources available than the Global Unions and the ILO, which impacts staffing and the number of projects and research which can be implemented. Furthermore, in contrast to the IFIs which are willing to accept applications for membership from governments of all political colours irrespective of being democratic or otherwise, the respect of democratic principles is a precondition for membership of the Global Unions. The power of the international trade union movement is based on its large membership base and representativity of workers. Decision-making processes within the Global Unions are supported by democratic procedures and procedural fairness, whilst within the IFIs the economic power of a member determines its voting power. At the ILO the principle of tripartism helps to promote the democratic involvement of stakeholders even if it faces many challenges.

Although all organisations offer some space for the enforcement of interests of more influential members, for example through the contribution of financial resources, it can be argued that the scale of influence of affiliates varies between the organisations. At the micro level, individual actors in leading positions at the Global Unions have much less power in comparison to some individual actors in the IFIs. However, one of the most significant organisational differences is the ideology, which in the case of the IFIs was and still is to some extent shaped by the policy recommendations of the Washington Consensus. In comparison, the

Global Unions and the ILO follow a paradigm which is based on global social justice, human and workers' rights and Keynesian macroeconomic theory. Although there may be some subtle variations in outlook amongst the Global Unions, the predominant vision could be described as close to 'democratic socialism' (Abbott, 2011: 166).

At the global level social policy is not a clearly defined policy-field, but rather it can be understood as a cross-organisational responsibility. The establishment of a global social order requires efficient multilateral cooperation and policy coherence. In this context, the policy dialogue between the IFIs and the Global Unions helps to structure interactions and communication between the participating organisations. This cooperation is further facilitated by the joint inter-organisational 'mission' to achieve the UN SDGs and to reduce poverty and inequality by promoting jobs, a just transition and universal social protection. The ITUC organises and coordinates the dialogue with the IFIs on behalf of the Global Unions through the ITUC/Global Unions office in Washington D.C. The latter is financed by the ITUC and the GUFs and is responsible for maintaining regular contact with the IFIs. The GUFs value and support the work of the ITUC, although due to their limited resources the dialogue is not a priority for them. In addition to the policy dialogue in which the ILO participates, the ILO has its own relationships with the IFIs. For example, SPIAC-B, which is co-chaired by the ILO and the WB, is an important venue for conversations and work towards more coherence between organisations and donors in the field of social protection (Interview ITUC06, 2019).

The policy dialogue between the Global Unions and the IFIs has helped to avoid mutual silence and 'speechlessness' between the dialogue stakeholders and to develop a sustainable basis for a constructive exchange of arguments. By the end of the high-level meetings in 2002, the WB vice-president stated that supporting the UN Millennium Development Goals (which were replaced by the SDGs in 2015) and the objectives of job creation and poverty reduction were common grounds for the WB and trade unions (World Bank, 2002). These objectives have since been reaffirmed and other joint objectives such as universal social protection have been added. The analysis suggests that the dialogue helped to increase awareness amongst IFI staff about labour issues and social protection. However, the engagement of IFI staff is still influenced by individual perceptions and attitudes and the predominant organisational ideology. At national level the influence and effectiveness of trade unions also determines the level of cooperation.

Based on the findings, it can be argued that relationships between organisational representatives and the organisations involved in the dialogue are not static but subject to continuous change. These changes are driven by external factors (such as global crises and newly arising issues) and internal factors (such as the organisational leadership, individual attitudes of staff and organisational restructuring processes). At the beginning of the dialogue there were fundamental differences between the Global Unions and the IFIs and many trade unionists perceived the attitudes of IFI representatives as 'hostile'. Some IFI representatives openly considered trade unions as 'market imperfections' (Interview ITUC02, 2008). Nowadays relationships are shaped by mutual respect and on some occasions an in-depth dialogue takes place. In recent years, the relationship between the Global Unions and the IMF has deepened and the dialogue is generally perceived as essential and important by all dialogue stakeholders.

In terms of output, in particular regarding the promotion of the CLS in WB and IFC policy documents, some progress has been achieved over the years. The IFC had a pioneering role in this context and aimed to make sure that its rhetoric and practices were consistent when it introduced the CLS in its Performance Standards (Bakvis, 2005). Following the IFC, the WB included the CLS in the Standard Bidding Documents under 'General Conditions' from 2010 onwards and made the CLS mandatory in investment project financing. Others, at least partial successes, include the suspension of the 'Employing Workers Indicator' in the WB flagship publication 'Doing Business' in 2009. The report which promoted a deregulation agenda and low taxes was terminated in 2021. In recent years, the dialogue has focused more strongly on economic policies for a just transition and universal social protection; however, no specific results have been achieved so far.

Despite the continuity of the dialogue, which can be considered as a success in itself, and the interest of the trade unions to further strengthen the dialogue, many challenges remain. Individual actors which represent the participating organisations still hold different opinions on many issues including amongst other things privatisation, the role of the public sector, minimum wages, collective bargaining, and taxing mechanisms. These differences are mainly related to organisational missions, ideologies, and paradigms. The fact that the IFIs still promote labour market deregulation and neoliberal austerity policies is related to an organisational mindset which is dominated by a neoliberal ideology and policy model. Although the rhetoric of the IFIs has become more inclusive to some extent, its implementation on the ground is often still poor. Loan conditionality and policy advice which encourage governments to implement legal and political reforms based on deregulation and fiscal constraints remain on the agenda and often weaken labour, economic, and social rights. As a result, the erosion of collective bargaining power and the political and economic influence of trade unions, as well as fiscal consolidation measures, increase inequality and lower standards of living. The Global Unions and their affiliates encounter the ideology of the IFIs by pursuing social justice and economic and industrial democracy. Trade unions at all levels consider themselves as 'collective means for workers to defend their human rights against the dehumanising imperatives of profit' (Bernaciak et al., 2014: 23). From a trade union perspective, the provision of public goods by the private sector is not compatible with the basic human right of social protection as enshrined in the UN Universal Declaration of Human Rights and the ILO Philadelphia Declaration.

Over time the cooperation in the area of research between the Global Unions and the IFIs has increased and the IFIs have produced some research studies which evidence the importance of collective bargaining and social dialogue as redistri-bution mechanisms. Furthermore, there were attempts to promote social dia-logue at national level (e.g. ILO–IMF country pilot projects) and new pilot studies on social protection are planned. A challenge for the IFIs is the implementation of research findings at country level, for example by promoting an appropriate legal framework in the case of collective bargaining and social dialogue. From the perspective of trade unions, legal frameworks which allow for genuine col-lective bargaining and trade union rights increase the representativeness and the capacity of social partners and ensure decent work and sustainable development (Interview ETUC, 2017; Interview UNI, 2019). The trade unions argue that there is no evidence that more flexibility for employers promotes sustainable eco-nomic growth and inclusive jobs (Interview ITUC02, 2015). This argument has been supported by a recent study which concluded that 'coordinated bargaining systems are associated with higher employment, a better integration of vulner-able groups and lower wage inequality than fully decentralized systems' (Garnero, 2020: 12–13). The lack of integration of research findings on the ground and the lack of implementation of verbally expressed intentions by the IFIs can be related to shortcomings with regard to their organisational accountability within the dialogue and in general. With regard to the dialogue, apart from the minutes of the meetings there is no document which records specific commitments and a timeframe which could form the basis for the monitoring of progress achieved through the dialogue.

Since its formal establishment in 2002, the dialogue has undergone different cycles. In other words, there are times when trade union representatives are more successful in gaining a response to their demands and other times when they can only try to prevent things from going backwards. A remaining challenge is the provision of information from IFI staff and their departments. In the case of the WB, the decentralised organisational structure makes it sometimes more difficult for trade unions to get the attention from staff which is working on an issue of concern. Trade union representatives have consistently argued that timely con-sultations would be helpful regarding the development of new programmes and conditions attached to IFI loans on issues which concern labour. As yet this is often not the case, and in particular at sectoral and national level consultations are still limited.

Nevertheless, despite its shortcomings and remaining challenges the structured policy dialogue between the Global Unions and the IFIs is unique in terms of its level of formality, structure, and continuity. Although the dialogue cannot level out the asymmetric distribution of power between the dialogue stakeholders, it can be considered as a strategic instrument which ensures continuous commu-nication and information exchange. The dialogue enables the Global Unions to influence the present global logic at least in terms of partly transforming this logic. The achievement of concrete results through the dialogue often takes a long time, also because the dialogue is still dependent on individual attitudes of IFI staff which open up 'space' for the trade unions. It can be concluded that so far only a partial institutionalisation of the dialogue has been achieved. In the future, a more mandatory approach and guidelines within the IFIs which would require staff to consult with trade unions on labour issues could change the dynamic and efficiency of the dialogue and embed the dialogue within these organisations more deeply.

Finally, the findings have shown that there is no alternative to the dialogue, in particular against the background of the current economic and political climate. Economic and social challenges such as the health pandemic, stagnating wages and wage inequality, the informal sector, digitalisation and climate change require cooperation and policy coherence between global governance actors. Initiatives and mechanisms such as SPIAC-B and the 'Global Deal' also aim to coordinate efforts between corporate actors, but they are not comparable to the dialogue between the Global Unions and the IFIs in terms of its structure and formalisation. However, from the perspective of trade unions the 'Global Deal' multi-stakeholder initiative, which was initiated by the Swedish Prime Minister in 2016 and developed in cooperation with the ILO and the OECD, could be another steppingstone towards a more people centred multilateralism and more equal societies. The latter aims to address challenges in the global labour market by sharing experiences and good practices about social dialogue between governments, trade unions, and businesses.

With regard to the examined policy dialogue, the trade unions have expressed their interest in strengthening the dialogue with the IFIs and to develop a more progressive vision for the global economy which helps to overcome the neoliberal narrative of flexibilisation and deregulation. The trade unions consider themselves as 'troublemakers' and 'contract makers' at the same time and there is agreement between the dialogue partners that a 'new social contract' is required in order to tackle economic and social inequality and to ensure rights and security for workers. In this context, the trade unions demand a universal labour guarantee for all workers and to put people back at the centre of the economy. A new social contract also needs to go along with a reform of the current multilateral system, a stronger international cooperation, and new rules for multinational corporations. However, despite the importance of the policy dialogue, fundamental change of the IFIs can only be achieved through their own affiliates and in particular those governments with the largest shares. Therefore, for the trade unions it is pivotal that they form alliances with other nongovernmental organisations and that they continue to build political pressure on governments at national and international level, in addition to further promoting the policy dialogue with the IFIs.

References

Abbott, K.W. (2011) 'Theorising International Trade Unionism', *Global Labour Journal*, 2, 3: 160–179.

Abbott, K.W. and Snidal, D. (2010) *Strengthening International Regulation Through Transnational New Governance: Overcoming the Orchestration Deficit*, TranState Working Papers, No. 127, Bremen: University Sonderforschungsbereich 579 Staatlichkeit im Wandel [online]. Available at: http://econstor.eu/bitstream/10419/41589/1/635597918.pdf [Accessed 7 July 2017]

Abouharb, M.R. and Cingranelli, D. (2007) *Human Rights and Structural Adjustment*, Cambridge, New York, Melbourne, Madrid, Cape Town, Singapore, Sao Paulo and New Delhi: Cambridge University Press.

ActionAid (2021) *The Public Versus Austerity: Why Public Sector Wage Bill Constraints Must End* [online]. Available at: https://actionaid.org/sites/default/files/publications/The_public_vs_austerity.pdf [Accessed 6 February 2022]

Adams, R. and Goldenberg, S. (2007) 'After Bitter Battle, Wolfowitz Resigns From World Bank', *Guardian*, 18 May [online]. Available at: https://www.theguardian.com/business/2007/may/18/imf.economics1 [Accessed 5 May 2016]

Adler, A. and Varoufakis, Y. (2019) 'The World Bank and IMF Are in Crisis: It's Time to Push a Radical New Vision', *The Guardian* [online]. Available at: https://www.theguardian.com/commentisfree/2019/jan/31/world-bank-imf-bretton-woods-banking-keynes [Accessed 8 April 2019]

Ahrne, G. and Brunsson, N. (2005) 'Organizations and Meta-Organizations', *Scandinavian Journal of Management*, 21, 4: 429–449.

Alavi, M. and Leidner, D.E. (2001) 'Review: Knowledge Management and Knowledge Management Systems: Conceptual Foundations and Research Issues', *MIS Quarterly*, 25, 1: 107–136.

Albert, M. (2005) 'Politik der Weltgesellschaft und Politik der Globalisierung: Überlegungen zur Emergenz von Weltstaatlichkeit', in *Zeitschrift für Soziologie, Sonderheft 'Weltgesellschaft'*, Stuttgart: Lucius & Lucius: 223–238.

Albert, S. and Whetten, D.A. (1985) 'Organizational Identity', *Research in Organizational Behavior*, 7: 263–295.

Alston, P. (2004) 'Core Labour Standards and the Transformation of the International Labour Rights Regime', *European Journal of International Law*, 15, 3: 457–521.

Alston, P. and Heenan, J. (2004) 'Shrinking the International Labour Code: An Unintended Consequence of the 1998 ILO Declaration on Fundamental Principles and Rights at Work?', *New York University Journal of International Law and Politics*, 36, 2–3: 221–264.

Andersson, L. and Pan Fagerlin, W. (2011) *Barriers to Organizational Learning: A Case Study of a Change Project*, Conference Paper, Conference for Organizational Learning, Knowledge and Capabilities, Hull, 12–14 April.

Apodaca, C. (2017) 'Expanding Responsibilities: The Consequences of World Bank and IMF Policies on Child Welfare', in Brysk, A. and Stohl, M. eds. *Expanding Human Rights: 21st Century Norms and Governance*, Cheltenham, Northampton and Washington, DC: Edward Elgar: 215–234.

Argote, L., McEvily, B. and Reagans, R. (2003) 'Managing Knowledge in Organizations: An Integrative Framework and Review of Emerging Themes', *Management Science*, 49, 4: 571–582.

Argote, L. and Miron-Spektor, E. (2011) 'Organizational Learning: From Experience to Knowledge', *Organization Science*, 22, 5: 1123–1137.

Baccaro, L. and Mele, V. (2012) 'Pathology or Path Dependency? The ILO and the Challenge of New Governance', *ILR Review*, 65, 2: 195–224.

Bacchetta, M. and Jansen, M. (2011) *Making Globalization Socially Sustainable*, Geneva: ILO.

Bakvis, P. (2005) 'Wolfensohn to Wolfowitz: What Does the Change at the Top of the World Bank Mean for Labour?', *Transfer: European Review of Labour and Research*, 11, 4: 633–638.

Bakvis, P. (2009a) 'The World Bank's Doing Business Report: A Last Fling for the Washington, DC Consensus?', *Transfer: European Review of Labour and Research*, 15, 3–4: 419–438.

Bakvis, P. (2009b) 'World Bank Orders Suspension of *Doing Business* Labour Market Deregulation Indicator', *Transfer: European Review of Labour and Research*, 15, 2: 319–322.

Bakvis, P. (2014a) *Major Weaknesses in World Bank's Draft Labour Standards Safeguard*, ITUC/Global Unions Washington Office, 22 July [online]. Available at: https://www.ituc-csi.org/IMG/pdf/ess2-wb_ituc-critique_0914.pdf [Accessed 8 August 2015]

Bakvis, P. (2014b) 'The World Bank Needs to Take Labour Market Policy Out of the Hands of "Doing Business"', *Equal Times*, 29 October [online]. Available at: https://www.equaltimes.org/the-world-bank-needs-to-take?lang=en#.VFDNCxZkzm4 [Accessed 18 June 2019]

Bakvis, P. and McCoy, M. (2008) *Core Labour Standards and International Organizations: What Inroads Has Labour Made?*, Friedrich Ebert Stiftung, Briefing Papers, No. 6, Bonn: FES.

Barder, O. (2019) 'Time, Gentlemen, Please – Next President of the World Bank', *Inter Press Service* [online]. Available at: http://www.ipsnews.net/2019/02/time-gentlemen-please-next-president-world-bank/ [Accessed 2 June 2019]

Barley, S.R. and Tolbert, P.S. (1997) 'Institutionalization and Structuration: Studying the Links Between Action and Institution', *Organization Studies*, 18, 1: 93–117.

Barnard, C.I. (1968) *The Functions of the Executive*, Cambridge and London: Harvard University Press.

Barnett, M. and Finnemore, M. (1999) 'The Politics, Power, and Pathologies of International Organizations', *International Organization*, 53, 4: 699–732.

Barnett, M. and Finnemore, M. (2004) *Rules for the World: International Organizations in Global Politics*, Ithaca and London: Cornell University Press.

Barnett, W.P. and Carroll, G.R. (1995) 'Modeling Internal Organizational Change', *Annual Review of Sociology*, 21, 1: 217–236.

Barrett, S. (2014) 'Global Public Goods and International Development', in Evans, J.W. and Davies, R. eds. *To Global to Fail: The World Bank at the Intersection of National and Global Public Policy in 2025*, Washington, DC: World Bank: 38–77.

Barton, R. and Fairbrother, P. (2009) 'The Local Is Now Global: Building a Union Coalition in the International Transports and Logistics Sector', *Industrial Relations*, 64, 4: 685–703.

Baumgartner, F.R., Berry, J.M., Hojnacji, M., Kimball, D.C. and Leech, B.L. (2009) *Lobbying and Policy Change: Who Wins, Who Loses, and Why*, Chicago: The University of Chicago Press.

Baunach, L. (2019) 'The New World Bank Presidency and the Crisis of Multilaterlism', *Equal Times* [online]. Available at: https://www.equaltimes.org/the-new-world-bank-presidency-and?lang=en#.XNBv8Y5Kjct [Accessed 10 June 2019]

Baunach, L. (2020) 'Close the Fiscal Stimulus Gap to Prevent a Lost Decade for Workers and Development', *Global Labour Column* [online]. Available at: https://globallabour column.org/2020/12/21/close-the-fiscal-stimulus-gap-to-prevent-a-lost-decade-for-workers-and-development/ [Accessed 16 January 2021]

Baunach, L., Astor, E. and Kidd, S. (2019) 'The World Bank's New White Paper Falls Short on Its Objective of "Protecting All"', *Development Pathways*, 22 October [online]. Available at: https://www.developmentpathways.co.uk/blog/the-world-banks-new-white-paper-falls-short-on-its-objective-of-protecting-all/ [Accessed 20 January 2020]

Bazbauers, A.R. (2014) 'The Wolfensohn, Wolfowitz, and Zoellick Presidencies: Revitalising the Neoliberal Agenda of the World Bank', *Forum for Development Studies*, 41, 1: 91–114.

Becker, M., John, S. and Schirm, S.A. (2007) *Globalisierung und Global Governance*, Paderborn: Wilhelm Fink.

Beckert, J. (2010) 'Institutional Isomorphism Revisited: Convergence and Divergence in Institutional Change', *Sociological Theory*, 28, 2: 150–166.

Benanav, A. (2019) 'The Origins of Informality: The ILO at the Limit of the Concept of Unemployment', *Journal of Global History*, 14, 1: 107–125.

Bernaciak, M., Gumbrell-McCormick, R. and Hyman, R. (2014) *Trade Unions in Europe – Innovative Responses to Hard Times*, Berlin: FES.

BetterAid (2011) *Making Development Cooperation Architecture Just: Governance Principles and Pillars. Discussion Note From the BetterAid Platform: Final Version* [online]. Available at: https://www.betteraid.org/sites/newbetteraid/files/Making%20development%20coop eration%20just.pdf [Accessed 7 August 2017]

Bieler, A. (2012) 'Workers of the World, Unite? Globalisation and the Quest for Transnational Solidarity', *Globalizations*, 9, 3: 365–378.

Birdsall, N. (2007) 'The World Bank: Toward a Global Club', in Bradford Jr., C.I. and Linn, J.F. eds. *Global Governance Reform*, Washington, DC: Brooking Institutions Press: 50–59.

Blanchard, O., Jaumotte, F. and Loungani, P. (2013) 'Labour Market Policies and IMF Advice in Advanced Economies During the Great Recession', *IMF Research Department*, 29 March [online]. Available at: https://www.imf.org/external/pubs/ft/sdn/2013/sdn1302.pdf [Accessed 7 February 2021]

Blanton, R.G., Blanton, S.L. and Peksen, D. (2015) 'The Impact of IMF and World Bank Programs on Labor Rights', *Political Research Quarterly*, 68, 2: 324–336.

Blau, P.M. and Schoenherr, R.A. (1971) *The Structure of Organizations*, New York and London: Basic Books.

Boorman, J. (2007) 'IMF Reform: Congruence With Global Governance Reform', in Bradford, C.I. and Linn, J.F. eds. *Global Governance Reform: Breaking the Stalemate*, Washington, DC: Brooking Institutions Press: 15–31.

Boswell, P. (2008) *Changes to the FIDIC Construction Contract General Conditions*, 1st ed. [online]. Available at: https://fidic.org/sites/default/files/cons_mdb_changes_8apr08.pdf [Accessed 19 February 2020]

Botero, J.C., Djankov, S., La Porta, R., Lopes-De-Silanes, F. and Shleifer, A. (2004) 'The Regulation of Labor', *The Quarterly Journal of Economics*, 119, 4: 1339–1382.

Bourque, R. (2008) 'International Framework Agreements and the Future of Collective Bargaining in Multinational Companies', *Just Labour: A Canadian Journal of Work and Society*, Spring, 12: 30–47.

Bradford, C.I. and Linn, J.F. (2007) 'Introduction and Overview', in Bradford, C.I. and Linn, J.F. eds. *Global Governance Reform: Breaking the Stalemate*, Washington, DC: Brooking Institutions Press: 1–11.

Brand, U. (2007) 'Zwischen Normativität, Analyse und Kritik. Die jüngere Diskussion um Global Governance', *Journal für Entwicklungspolitik*, XXIII, 1: 26–50.

Brand, U. and Scherrer, C. (2005) 'Contested Global Governance: Konkurrierende Formen und Inhalte Globaler Regulierung', in Behrens, M. ed. *Globalisierung als politische Herausforderung. Global Governance zwischen Utopie und Realität*, Wiesbaden: VS-Verlag: 115–129.

Braun, R. and Gearhart, J. (2004) 'Who Should Code Your Conduct? Trade Unions and NGO Differences in the Fight for Workers' Rights', *Development in Practice*, 14, 1–2: 183–196.

Bretton Woods Project (2003) *IFC "Doubts" Labour Fears in Haiti, Approves Loan* [online]. Available at: https://www.brettonwoodsproject.org/2003/11/art-27499/ [Accessed 17 June 2021]

Bretton Woods Project (2013) *World Bank Group Strategy: Who Benefits?* [online]. Available at: https://www.brettonwoodsproject.org/2013/10/world-bank-group-strategy-benefits/ [Accessed 17 November 2016]

Bretton Woods Project (2015) *World Bank Global Practices and Cross-Cutting Solution Areas* [online]. Available at: https://www.brettonwoodsproject.org/2015/09/world-bank-global-practices-and-cross-cutting-solution-areas/ [Accessed 20 November 2016]

Bretton Woods Project (2019a) *What Are the Main Criticisms of the World Bank and the IMF?* [online]. Available at: https://www.brettonwoodsproject.org/wp-content/uploads/2019/06/Common-Criticisms-FINAL.pdf [Accessed 2 August 2019]

Bretton Woods Project (2019b) *The IMF and PPPs: A Master Class in Double Speak* [online]. Available at: https://www.brettonwoodsproject.org/2019/04/the-imf-and-ppps-a-master-class-in-double-speak/ [Accessed 22 February 2022]

Bretton Woods Project (2019c) *US Supreme Court Rules Against World Bank's Claim of Absolute Immunity* [online]. Available at: https://www.brettonwoodsproject.org/2019/04/us-supreme-court-rules-against-world-banks-claim-of-absolute-immunity/ [Accessed 14 March 2022]

Bretton Woods Project (2020a) *IMF and World Bank Decision-Making and Governance* [online]. Available at: https://www.brettonwoodsproject.org/2020/04/imf-and-world-bank-decision-making-and-governance-2/ [Accessed 18 July 2020]

Bretton Woods Project (2020b) *Senior-Level Staff Changes at World Bank and IMF, Bretton Woods Observer*, Spring [online]. Available at: https://www.brettonwoodsproject.org/wp-content/uploads/2020/03/Spring-2020-Observer-web.pdf [Accessed 19 July 2020]

Bretton Woods Project (2020c) *The World Bank, Covid-19 and Public Education: Two Steps Forward One Step Back* [online]. Available at: https://www.brettonwoodsproject.org/2020/07/the-world-bank-covid-19-and-public-education-two-steps-forward-one-step-back/ [Accessed 20 January 2022]

Brickson, S.L. (2005) 'Organizational Identity Orientation: Forging a Link Between Organizational Identity and Organizations Relations With Stakeholders', *Administrative Science Quarterly*, 50, 4: 576–609.

Brinkmann, S. and Kvale, S. (2018) *Doing Interviews*, London: Sage.

Bronfenbrenner, K. (ed.) (2007) *Global Unions: Challenging Transnational Capital Through Cross-Border Campaigns*, Ithaca: Cornell University Press.

Brown, A.D. and Starkey, K. (2000) 'Organizational Identity and Learning: A Psychodynamic Perspective', *The Academy of Management Review*, 25, 1: 102–120.

Brühl, T. and Rittberger, V. (2001) 'From International to Global Governance: Actors, Collective Decision-Making, and the United Nations in the World of the Twenty-First Century', in Rittberger, V. ed. *Global Governance and the United Nations System*, Tokyo, New York and Paris: United Nations University Press: 1–47.

Brunt, C. and McCourt, W. (2012) 'Walk the Talk? Reconciling the "Two Participations" in International Development', *Journal of International Development*, 24, 5: 585–601.

Bunderson, J.S. and Reagans, R.E. (2011) 'Power, Status, and Learning in Organizations', *Organization Science*, 22, 5: 1182–1194.

Burchielli, R. (2006) 'The Purpose of Trade Union Values: An Analysis of the ACTU Statement of Values', *Journal of Business Ethics*, 68, 2: 133–142.

Burgmann, V. (2016) *Globalization and Labour in the Twenty-First Century*, London and New York: Routledge.

BWI (2017) *Statutes*, Congress, Durban, 30 November–1 December [online]. Available at: https://www.bwint.org/web/content/cms.media/1812/datas/EN_BWI_Statutes_FINAL.pdf [Accessed 4 February 2018]

BWI (2018) *Dirty Loan: When the IFC Knowingly Breached Its Own Labour Standards at SFI* [online]. Available at: https://www.bwint.org/web/content/cms.media/1252/datas/SFI%20IFC%20Report%20update.pdf [Accessed 15 June 2020]

CAO (2018) *CAO Investigation of IFC Environmental and Social Performance in Relation to: Bilt Paper B.V. Malaysia (Bilt-02), Compliance Investigation*, 13 April [online]. Available at: http://www.cao-ombudsman.org/cases/document-links/documents/BiltInvestigationReportApril132018.pdf [Accessed 16 June 2020]

CAO (2019a) *Annual Report 2019* [online]. Available at: https://cao-ar19.org/CAO-Annual-Report-2019.pdf [Accessed 4 April 2020]

CAO (2019b) *CAO Update*, Issue 17, November [online]. Available at: http://www.cao-ombudsman.org/newsroom/documents/CAOQ1NewsletterFY2020_000.pdf [Accessed 4 April 2020]

Carbone, M. (2007) 'Supporting or Resisting Global Public Goods? The Policy Dimension of a Contested Concept', *Global Governance*, 13, 2: 179–198.

Carbonnier, G. and Gironde, C. (2019) 'The ILO @ 100: In Search of Renewed Relevance', in Gironde, C. and Carbonnier, G. eds. *The ILO @ 100: Addressing the Past and Future of Work and Social Protection*, Leiden and Boston: Brill: 3–18.

Carew, A., Dreyfus, M., Goethem, G. and Gumbrell-McCormick, R. (2000) *The International Confederation of Free Trade Unions*, Bern: Peter Lang.

Chan, A. and Ross, R.J.S. (2003) 'Racing to the Bottom: International Trade Without a Social Clause', *Third World Quarterly*, 24, 6: 1011–1028.

Charnovitz, S. (2015) 'Reinventing the ILO', *International Labour Review*, 154, 1: 91–96.

Charrett, D. (2010) *FIDIC Conditions of Contract for Construction, Multilateral Development Banks (MDB) Harmonised Edition, Presented at the FIDIC Contracts Users Conference, Beijing*, June [online]. Available at: https://fidic.org/sites/default/files/charrett_beijing_2010.pdf [Accessed 19 February 2020]

Child, J. and Heavens, S.J. (2001) 'The Social Constitution of Organizations and Its Implications for Organizational Learning', in Dierkes, M., Antal Berthoin, A., Child, J. and Nonaka, I. eds. *Handbook of Organizational Learning and Knowledge*, New York: Oxford University Press: 308–326.

Chin, M. (2021) 'What Are Global Public Goods?', *Finance & Development*, June [online]. Available at: https://www.imf.org/Publications/fandd/issues/2021/12/Global-Public-Goods-Chin-basics [Accessed 28 September 2022]

Chorev, N. and Babb, S. (2009) 'The Crisis of Neoliberalism and the Future of International Institutions: A Comparison of the IMF and the WTO', *Theory and Society*, 38, 5: 459–484.

Civil Society Forum (2015) *Declaration From the Addis Ababa Civil Society Forum on Financing for Development*, 12 July [online]. Available at: https://csoforffd.files.wordpress.com/2015/07/addis-ababa-cso-ffd-forum-declaration-12-july-2015.pdf [Accessed 4 September 2019]

Clarke, V. and Braun, V. (2017) 'Thematic Analysis', *The Journal of Positive Psychology*, 12, 3: 297–298.

Coen, D. and Pegram, T. (2018) 'Towards a Third Generation of Global Governance Scholarship', *Global Policy*, 9, 1: 107–113.

Coleman, J.S. (1990) *Foundations of Social Theory*, Cambridge: Harvard University Press.

Compa, L. (2004) 'Trade Unions, NGOs, and Corporate Code of Conducts', *Development in Practice*, 14, 1–2: 210–215.

Contu, A. and Willmott, H. (2003) 'Re-Embedding Situatedness: The Importance of Power Relations in Learning Theory', *Organization Science*, 14, 3: 283–296.

Cooper, L. (2006) 'The Trade Union as a "Learning Organisation"? A Case Study of Informal Learning in a Collective, Social-Action Organisational Context', *Journal of Education*, 39, 1: 27–46.

Copelovitch, M.S. (2010) *The International Monetary Fund in the Global Economy: Banks, Bonds, and Bailouts*, Cambridge: Cambridge University Press.

Cotton, E. and Gumbrell-McCormick, R. (2012) 'Global Unions as Imperfect Multilateral Organizations: An International Relations Perspective', *Economic and Industrial Democracy*, 33, 4: 707–728.

Cox, R. and Jacobson, H.K. (1997) 'The Framework for Inquiry', in Diehl, P.F. ed. *The Politics of Global Governance: International Organizations in an Interdependent World*, Boulder, CO: Lynne Rienner Publishers: 75–90.

Crossan, M.M., Lane, H.W. and White, R.E. (1999) 'An Organizational Learning Framework: From Intuition to Institution', *The Academy of Management Review*, 24, 3: 522–537.

Croucher, R. and Cotton, E. (2009) *Global Unions, Global Business: Global Union Federations and International Business*, London: Middlesex University Press.

Cyert, R.M. and March, J.G. (1992) *A Behavioural Theory of the Firm*, Cambridge and Oxford: Blackwell.

Daar, N. (2019) *World Bank President Jim Kim Resigns: What's His Legacy and What Happens Next?*, Washington, DC: Oxfam [online]. Available at: https://oxfamblogs.org/fp2p/world-bank-president-jim-kim-resigns-whats-his-legacy-and-what-happens-next/ [Accessed 8 June 2019]

Darrow, M. (2003) *Between Light and Shadow: The World Bank, the International Monetary Fund and International Human Rights Law*, Oxford: Hart-Publishing.

Deitelhoff, N. and Daase, C. (2021) 'Rule and Resistance in Global Governance', *International Theory*, 13: 122–130.

Deranty, J.-P. and Macmillan, C. (2012) 'The ILO's Decent Work Initiative: Suggestions for an Extension of the Notion of "Decent Work"', *Journal of Social Philosophy*, 43, 4: 386–405.

De Schutter, O. (2020) *Call for Reactions: Proposal for a Global Fund for Social Protection* [online]. Available at: https://www.ohchr.org/EN/Issues/Poverty/Pages/global-fund-social-protection.aspx [Accessed 23 March 2021]

Development Committee (2010) *Joint Ministerial Committee of the Boards of Governors of the Bank and the Fund on the Transfer of Real Resources to Developing Countries*, 25 April [online]. Available at: https://www.devcommittee.org/sites/dc/files/download/Communiques/FinalCommunique-E-042510.pdf [Accessed 11 September 2022]

Development Committee (2012) *World Bank Group Innovations in Leveraging the Private Sector for Development: A Discussion Note* [online]. Available at: http://siteresources.worldbank.org/DEVCOMMINT/Documentation/23170401/DC2012-0002(E)LeveragingPrivateSector.pdf [Accessed 3 March 2020]

Development Committee (2021) *Joint Ministerial Committee of the Boards of Governors of the Bank and the Fund on the Transfer of Real Resources to Developing Countries* [online]. Available at: https://www.devcommittee.org/sites/dc/files/download/Communiques/2021-04/Communique%28E%29%20final%20version%204.9.pdf[Accessed 17 September 2022]

DiMaggio, P.J. and Powell, W.W. (1983) 'The Iron Cage Revisited: Institutional Isomorphism and Collective Rationality in Organizational Fields', *American Sociological Review*, 48, 2: 147–160.

Dingwerth, K. and Pattberg, P. (2006) 'Was It Global Governance?', *Leviathan*, 34, 3: 377–399.

Dingwerth, K., Schmidtke, H. and Weise, T. (2020) 'The Rise of Democratic Legitimation: Why International Organizations Speak the Language of Democracy', *European Journal of International Relations*, 26, 3: 714–741.

Divanbeigi, R. and Saliola, F. (2022) *Mobilizing Development Lending to Create More and Better Jobs* [online]. Available at: https://blogs.worldbank.org/jobs/mobilizing-development-lending-create-more-and-better-jobs [Accessed 20 July 2022]

Döringer, S. (2021) 'The Problem-Centred Expert Interview. Combining Qualitative Interviewing Approaches for Investigating Implicit Expert Knowledge', *International Journal of Social Research Methodology*, 24, 3: 265–278.

Dosi, G., Faillo, M. and Marengo, L. (2008) 'Organizational Capabilities, Patterns of Knowledge Accumulation and Governance. Structures in Business Firms: An Introduction', *Organization Studies*, 20, 8–9: 1165–1185.

Dreher, A., Lang, V.F. and Richert, K. (2019) 'The Political Economy of International Finance Corporation Lending', *Journal of Development Economics*, 140: 242–254.

Easterly, W. (2005) 'What Did Structural Adjustment Adjust? The Association of Policies and Growth With Repeated IMF and World Bank Adjustment Loans', *Journal of Development Economics*, 76, 1: 1–22.

Ebert, F.C. and Novitz, T. (2020) 'Introduction: International Institutions, Public Governance and Future Regulation of Work', *International Organizations Law Review*, 17: 1–9.

Edwards, S. (2019a) 'David Malpasse Unchallenged to Be Next World Bank President', *Devex* [online]. Available at: https://www.devex.com/news/david-malpass-unchal lenged-to-be-next-world-bank-president-94500 [Accessed 2 June 2019]

Edwards, S. (2019b) 'As Jim Kim Steps Down, a Tumultuous World Bank Presidency Comes to an End', *Devex* [online]. Available at: https://www.devex.com/news/as-jim-kim-steps-down-a-tumultuous-world-bank-presidency-comes-to-an-end-94247 [Accessed 5 June 2019]

Egels-Zandén, N. and Hyllman, P. (2011) 'Differences in Organizing Between Unions and NGOs: Conflict and Cooperation Among Swedish Unions and NGOs', *Journal of Business Ethics*, 101, 2: 249–261.

EI (2011) *Policy Paper on Education: Building the Future Through Quality Education* [online]. Available at: https://www.ei-ie.org/en/item/21581:policy-paper-on-education-build ing-the-future-through-quality-education [Accessed 4 October 2021]

EI (2016) *Bridge vs Reality: A Study of Bridge International Academies' for-Profit Schooling in Kenya* [online]. Available at: https://download.ei-ie.org/Docs/WebDepot/Bridge%20 vs%20Reality_GR%20Report.pdf [Accessed 16 December 2021]

EI (2018) *Open Letter to the World Bank on Draft 2019 World Development Report*, Brussels: Head Office, 19 September.

EI (2019) *Constitution of Education International* [online]. Available at: https://www.ei-ie. org/en/item/23028:constitution-of-education-international [Accessed 28 April 2020]

Eilstrup-Sangiovanni, M. and Westerwinter, O. (2021) 'The Global Governance Complexity Cube: Varieties of Institutional Complexity in Global Governance', *The Review of International Organizations*, 17: 233–262.

Eldridge, J.E.T. and Crombie, A.D. (2013) *A Sociology of Organisations*, New York: Routledge.

Elliott, L. (2020) 'Dozens of Poorer Nations Seek IMF Help Amid Coronavirus Crisis', *The Guardian* [online]. Available at: https://www.theguardian.com/world/2020/mar/27/ dozens-poorer-nations-seek-imf-help-coronavirus-crisis [Accessed 24 July 2020]

ETUI (2020) *Greece: IMF Blocks Return of Sectoral Bargaining and Social Dialogue* [online]. Available at: https://www.etui.org/covid-social-impact/greece/greece-imf-blocks-return-of-sectoral-bargaining-and-social-dialogue [Accessed 25 March 2021]

Eurodad (2006) *World Bank and IMF Conditionality: A Development Injustice* [online]. Available at: https://eurodad.org/files/pdf/454-world-bank-and-imf-conditionality-a-devel opment-injustice.pdf [Accessed 3 April 2016]

Eurodad (2019) *Flawed Conditions: The Impact of the World Bank's Conditionality on Developing Countries* [online]. Available at: https://eurodad.org/files/pdf/1547058-flawed-conditions-the-impact-of-the-world-bank-s-conditionality-on-developing-countries. pdf [Accessed 4 June 2019]

Evju, S. (2013) 'Labour Is Not a Commodity: Reappraising the Origins of the Maxim', *European Labour Law Journal*, 4, 3: 222–229.

Fairbrother, P. and Hammer, N. (2005) 'Global Unions: Past Efforts and Future Prospect', *Industrial Relations*, 60, 3: 405–431.

Falk, R. and Unmüßig, B. (2011) 'Wie Christine Lagarde den Fonds reformieren sollte: Die Herausforderungen vor der neuen IWF-Chefin', *Informationsbrief Weltwirtschaft & Entwicklung* [online]. Available at: http://www.weltwirtschaft-und-entwicklung.org/wearchiv/53168697a70a67901/042ae69f170fcd012.php [Accessed 5 September 2017]

Farquhar, A., Evans, P. and Tawadey, K. (1989) 'Lessons From Practice in Managing Organizational Change', in Evans, P., Doz, Y. and Laurent, A. eds. *Human Resource Management in International Firms: Change, Globalization, Innovation*, Houndmills, Basingstoke, Hampshire and London: Palgrave Macmillan: 33–55.

Felsch, A. (2010) *Organisationsdynamik: Zur Konstitution organisationaler Handlungssysteme als kollektive Akteure*, Wiesbaden: Verlag für Sozialwissenschaften.

FIDIC (2005) *Conditions of Contract for Construction: For Building and Engineering Works Designed by the Employer. Multilateral Development Bank Harmonised Edition*, May [online]. Available at: https://fidic.org/sites/default/files/cons_mdb_gc_v1_unprotected.pdf [Accessed 20 February 2019]

FIDIC (2014) *Statutes and By-Laws: International Federation of Consulting Engineers* [online]. Available at: http://fidic.org/sites/default/files/FIDIC%20Statutes_2014_0.pdf [Accessed 10 December 2014]

FIDIC (2019) *What the FIDIC-World Bank Contracts Agreement Means for Members* [online]. Available at: http://fidic.org/sites/default/files/FIDIC%20Statutes_2014_0.pdf [Accessed 10 February 2020]

Finkelstein, L.S. (1995) 'What Is Global Governance?', *Global Governance*, 1, 3: 367–372.

Flick, U. (2018a) *An Introduction to Qualitative Research*, 6th ed., Los Angeles, London, New Delhi, Singapore and Washington, DC: Sage.

Flick, U. (2018b) *Managing Quality in Qualitative Research*, 2nd ed., London: Sage.

Ford, M. and Gillan, M. (2015) 'The Global Union Federations in International Industrial Relations: A Critical Review', *Journal of Industrial Relations*, 57, 3: 456–475.

Foreman, P. and Whetten, D.A. (2002) 'Members' Identification With Multiple-Identity Organizations', *Organization Science*, 13, 6: 618–635.

Fox-Hodess, K. (2017) '(Re-)Locating the Local and National in the Global: Multi-Scalar Political Alignment in Transnational European Dockworker Union Campaigns', *British Journal of Industrial Relations*, 55, 3: 626–647.

Fox-Hodess, K. (2022) 'The Iron Law of Oligarchy and North-South Relations in Global Union Organizations: A Case Study of the International Dockworkers Council's Expansion in the Global South', *Labor History*, Ahead of Print, 1–20.

Frey, D.F. and MacNaughton, G. (2016) 'A Human Rights Lens on Full Employment and Decent Work in the 2030 Sustainable Development Agenda', *Journal of Workplace Rights*, April–June, 1–13.

Friedberg, E. (1994) *Ordnung und Macht: Dynamiken organisierten Handelns*, Frankfurt am Main and New York: Campus.

Gallin, D. (2000) 'Trade Unions and NGOs: A Necessary Partnership for Social Development, Civil Society and Social Movements Programme Paper Number 1', *United Nations Research Institute for Social Development* [online]. Available at: http://www.unrisd.org/80256B3C005BCCF9/httpNetITFramePDF?ReadForm&parentunid=5678DFBA8A99EEB780256B5E004C3737&parentdoctype=paper&netitpath=80256B3C005

BCCF9/(httpAuxPages)/5678DFBA8A99EEB780256B5E004C3737/$file/gallin.pdf [Accessed 3 June 2016]

Gallin, D. (2002) 'Labour as Global Social Force. Past Divisions and New Tasks', in Harrod, J. and O'Brien, R. eds. *Global Unions? Theories and Strategies of Organized Labour in the Global Political Economy*, London, New York: Routledge: 235–250.

Garnero, A. (2020) 'The Impact of Collective Bargaining on Employment and Wage Inequality: Evidence From a New Taxonomy of Bargaining Systems', *European Journal of Industrial Relations*, Ahead of Print, 1–18.

Gavetti, G., Levinthal, D. and Ocasio, W. (2007) 'Neo-Carnegie: The Carnegie School's Past, Present, and Reconstructing for the Future', *Organization Science*, 18, 3: 523–536.

Georgieva, K. (2020a) 'Reduce Inequality to Create Opportunity', *IMFBlog*, 7 January [online]. Available at: https://blogs.imf.org/2020/01/07/reduce-inequality-to-create-opportunity/?utm_medium=email&utm_source=govdelivery [Accessed 20 July 2020]

Georgieva, K. (2020b) 'Beyond the Crisis', *Finance & Development*, June [online]. Available at: https://www.imf.org/Publications/fandd/issues/2020/06/turning-crisis-into-opportunity-kristalina-georgieva [Accessed 20 March 2022]

Ghigliani, P. (2005) 'International Trade Unionism in a Globalizing World: A Case Study of New Labour Internationalism', *Economic and Industrial Democracy*, 26, 3: 359–382.

Global Unions (2006) *Agreement Between the Global Union Federations, the International Trade Union Confederation and the Trade Union Advisory Committee re: Council of Global Unions* [online]. Available at: https://www.ituc-csi.org/IMG/pdf/No_03_Annexe_-_Council_of_Global_Unions-2.pdf?noframes=1 [Accessed 8 July 2016]

Global Unions (2009) *Getting the World to Work: Global Union Strategies for Recovery*, Belgium: Druk.

Global Unions (2014) *Need for IFIs to Follow Pro-Employment and Anti-Inequality Rhetoric With Action*, Statement by Global Unions to the 2014 Spring Meetings of the IMF and World Bank, Washington, DC, 11–13 April [online]. Available at: http://www.ituc-csi.org/IMG/pdf/statement_ifi_en.pdf [Accessed 2 February 2021]

Global Unions (2018) *Toward Future of Work That Drives Sustainable Economic Growth*, Statement by Global Unions to the 2018 Annual Meetings of the IMF and World Bank, Bali, 12–14 October [online]. Available at: https://www.ituc-csi.org/IMG/pdf/statement.imfwb.1018.pdf [Accessed 10 February 2019]

Global Unions (2019a) *Reform the International Financial Institutions to Promote Sustainable Economic Growth, Full Employment and Decent Work*, Statement by Global Unions to the Annual Meetings of the IMF and World Bank, Washington, DC, 18–20 October [online]. Available at: https://www.ituc-csi.org/IMG/pdf/global_unions_statement_imfwb_10-2019.pdf [Accessed 16 July 2020]

Global Unions (2019b) *The International Financial Institutions Should Contribute to a New Social Contract*, Statement by Global Unions to the 2019 Spring Meetings of the IMF and World Bank, Washington, DC, 12–14 April [online]. Available at: https://www.ituc-csi.org/IMF-World-Bank-reform-fair-multilateralism [Accessed 16 July 2020]

Global Unions (2020) *Support Recovery Through Public Investment for Quality Jobs, Not More Harmful Austerity*, Statement by Global Unions to the Annual Meetings of the IMF and World Bank, Washington, DC, October [online]. Available at: https://www.ituc-csi.org/IMG/pdf/global_unions_statement_imf-wbg_10-2020_en.pdf [Accessed 2 February 2022]

Global Unions (2021) *Just Recovery and Transition: IFIs Must Act to End the Pandemic and Achieve a Sustainable Future*, Statement by Global Unions to the Annual Meetings of the IMF and World Bank, October [online]. Available at: ituc-csi.org/just-recovery-and-transition-en?msdynttrid=H-SrbhSAsf6BNwefbsKXSpc5qTME3QFlvIe-wzsDpOk [Accessed 25 January 2022]

Global Unions (2022) *Decent Work, Collective Bargaining, and Universal Social Protection: The IMF and World Bank at a Crossroads*, Statement by Global Unions to the Spring Meetings of the IMF and World Bank, April [online]. Available at: https://www.ituc-csi.org/IMG/pdf/en_global_unions_statement_imf-wbg_4-2022.pdf [Accessed 5 May 2022]

Gordon, M.E. (2000) 'The International Confederation of Free Trade Unions: Bread, Freedom and Peace', in Turner, L. and Gordon, M.E. eds. *Transnational Cooperation Among Labor Unions*, Ithaca: Cornell University Press: 81–101.

Gottfurcht, H. (1962) *Die internationale Gewerkschaftsbewegung im Weltgeschehen. Geschichte, Probleme, Aufgaben*, Köln: Bund-Verlag.

Greven, T. and Scherrer, C. (2005) *Globalisierung gestalten: Weltökonomie und soziale Standards*, Bonn: Bundeszentrale für Politische Bildung.

Gumbrell-McCormick, R. (2006) 'From the Old Trade Union Internationals to the New', *LabourStart* [online]. Available at: http://www.labourstart.org/docs/en/000382.html [Accessed 4 November 2017]

Gumbrell-McCormick, R. (2008) 'International Actors and International Regulation', in Blyton, P., Bacon, N., Fiorito, J. and Heery, E. eds. *Handbook of Industrial Relations*, London: Sage: 325–345.

Gumbrell-McCormick, R. (2013a) 'The International Labour Movement. Structures and Dynamics', in Fairbrother, P., Hennebert, M.-A. and Lévesque, C. eds. *Transnational Trade Unionism, Building Union Power*, New York and London: Routledge: 183–202.

Gumbrell-McCormick, R. (2013b) 'The International Trade Union Confederation: From Two (or More) Identities to One', *British Journal of Industrial Relations*, 51, 2: 240–263.

Gumbrell-McCormick, R. and Hyman, R. (2019) 'Democracy in Trade Unions, Democracy Through Trade Unions?, *Economic and Industrial Democracy*, 40, 1: 91–110.

Gunaydin, H. (2018) 'Who Can Reform the Labor Market? IMF Conditionality, Partisanship, and Labor Unions', *International Interactions*, 44, 5: 888–918.

Hafner-Burton, E.M. and Montgomery, A.H. (2006) 'Power Positions: International Organizations, Social Networks, and Conflict', *The Journal of Conflict Resolution*, 50, 1: 3–27.

Hale, A. (2004) 'Beyond the Barriers: New Forms of Labour Internationalism', *Development in Practice*, 14, 1–2: 158–162.

Hammer, N. (2005) 'International Framework Agreements: Global Industrial Relations Between Rights and Bargaining', *Transfer*, 11, 4: 511–530.

Harrod, J. and O'Brien, R. (2002) 'Organized Labour and the Global Political Economy', in Harrod, J. and O'Brien, R. eds. *Global Unions? Theory and Strategies of Organized Labour in the Global Political Economy*, London: Routledge: 3–28.

Haus, M. (2010) 'Governance-Theorien und Governance-Probleme: Diesseits und jenseits des Steuerungsparadigmas', *Politische Vierteljahresschrift*, 51, 3: 457–479.

Heijden, A.H.C. van der (1992) *Selective Attention in Vision*, London: Routledge.

Held, D. (2006) 'Democratic Accountability and Political Effectiveness from a Cosmopolitan Perspective', in Schuppert, G.F. ed. *Global Governance and the Role of Non-State Actors*, Baden-Baden: Nomos: 9–30.

Held, D. (2007) *Soziale Demokratie im globalen Zeitalter*, Frankfurt/Main: Suhrkamp.

Hennebert, M.-A. and Bourque, R. (2011) 'The International Trade Union Confederation (ITUC): Insights From the Second World Congress', *Global Labour Journal*, 2, 2: 154–159.

Hepple, B. (2005) *Labour Laws and Global Trade*, Oxford: Hart Publishing.

Holgate, J. (2015) 'An International Study of Trade Union Involvement in Community Organizing: Same Model, Different Outcomes', *British Journal of Industrial Relations*, 53, 3: 460–483.

Holzmann, R., Sipos, S. and the Social Protection Team (2009) 'Social Protection and Labor at the World Bank: An Overview', in Holzmann, R. ed. *Social Protection and Labor at the World Bank, 2000 – 2008*, Washington, DC: World Bank: 1–10.

Howard, A. (2007) 'The Future of Global Unions: Is Solidarity Still Forever?', *Dissent*, 54, 4: 62–70.

Huber, G.P. (1991) 'Organizational Learning: The Contributing Processes and the Literatures', *Organization Science*, 2, 1: 88–115.

Huber, J.F. (2008) 'Global Governance – Lösungsweg oder Utopie? Strategien, Kritik und Ausblick', in Gruber, P.C. ed. *Nachhaltige Entwicklung und Global Governance. Verantwortung: Macht. Politik*, Opladen and Farmington Hills: Barbara Budrich: 55–69.

Hyman, R. (2005) 'Shifting Dynamics in International Trade Unionism: Agitation, Organisation, Bureaucracy, Diplomacy', *Labor History*, 46, 2: 137–154.

Hyman, R. (2007) 'How Can Trade Unions Act Strategically?', *Transfer: European Review of Labour and Research*, 13, 2: 193–210.

Hyman, R. and Gumbrell-McCormick, R. (2020) '(How) Can International Trade Union Organisations Be Democratic?', *Transfer*, 26, 3: 253–272.

IBRD (2012) *Articles of Agreement (As Amended Effective 27 June 2012)*, Washington, DC: World Bank [online]. Available at: http://pubdocs.worldbank.org/en/722361541184234501/IBRDArticlesOfAgreement-English.pdf [Accessed 13 January 2016]

IEG (2008) *Doing Business: An Independent Evaluation, Taking the Measure of the World Bank – IFC Doing Business Indicators* [online]. Available at: https://openknowledge.worldbank.org/bitstream/handle/10986/6467/449950PUB0Box310evaluation01PUBLIC1.pdf?sequence=1&isAllowed=y [Accessed 15 June 2020]

IEG (2011) *Self-Evaluation of the Independent Evaluation Group* [online]. Available at: http://documents.worldbank.org/curated/en/891571468339531956/pdf/812600PUB0IEG000Box379835B00PUBLIC0.pdf [Accessed 16 October 2015]

IEG (2015) *Work Program and Budget (FY16) and Indicative Plan (FY17–18)* [online]. Available at: https://www.ecgnet.org/sites/default/files/IEG%202016%20Work%20Program%20and%20Budget.pdf [Accessed 18 November 2018]

IEG (2019) *IEG Work Program and Budget (FY20) and Indicative Plan (FY21–22)* [online]. Available at: https://documents1.worldbank.org/curated/en/329871561057187414/pdf/Independent-Evaluation-Group-IEG-Work-Program-and-Budget-FY20-and-Indicative-Plan-FY21-22.pdf [Accessed 15 October 2019]

IEG (2021) *FY22 Workprogram & Budget, FY23–23 Indicative Plan* [online]. Available at: https://ieg.worldbankgroup.org/sites/default/files/Data/reports/iegworkprogramfy22-24.pdf [Accessed 25 May 2022]

IEG (2022) *An Evaluation of International Finance Corporation Investments in K-12 Private Schools* [online]. Available at: https://ieg.worldbankgroup.org/sites/default/files/Data/Evaluation/files/IFCSupport_K12PrivateEducation.pdf [Accessed 14 July 2022]

IEO (2013) *The Role of the IMF as Trusted Advisor* [online]. Available at: https://www.oecd. org/derec/imf/RITA%20IMF_2013Main_Report.pdf [Accessed 18 July 2020]

IEO (2015) *Self-Evaluation at the IMF – An IEO Assessment* [online]. Available at: https:// ieo.imf.org/en/our-work/Evaluations/Completed/2015-1001-self-evaluation-at-the-imf-an-ieo-assessment [Accessed 23 July 2020]

IEO (2017) *The IMF and Social Protection* [online]. Available at: https://ieo.imf.org/en/ our-work/evaluation-reports/Completed/2017-0724-the-imf-and-social-protection [Accessed 26 January 2021]

IEO (2018a) *Governance of the IMF, Evaluation Update 2018* [online]. Available at: https:// ieo.imf.org/en/our-work/Evaluations/Updates/governance-of-the-imf [Accessed 24 July 2020]

IEO (2018b) *Structural Conditionality in IMD-Supported Programs – Evaluation Update 2018* [online]. Available at: https://ieo.imf.org/en/our-work/Evaluations/Updates/Struc tural-Conditionality-in-IMF-Supported-Programs-Eval [Accessed 24 July 2020]

IEO (2020) *IMF Collaboration With the World Bank on Macro-Structural Issues, Evaluation Report 2020* [online]. Available at: https://ieo.imf.org/en/our-work/Evaluations/Completed/ 2020-1124-imf-collaboration-with-the-world-bank [Accessed 10 May 2022]

IFC (2012a) *The Business Case for Sustainability*, Washington, DC: IFC, World Bank Group.

IFC (2012b) *Policy on Environmental and Social Sustainability* [online]. Available at: https:// www.ifc.org/wps/wcm/connect/topics_ext_content/ifc_external_corporate_site/ sustainability-at-ifc/publications/publications_policy_sustainability-2012 [Accessed 9 February 2016]

IFC (2012c) *Performance Standards on Environmental and Social Sustainability* [online]. Available at: https://www.ifc.org/wps/wcm/connect/topics_ext_content/ifc_external_cor porate_site/sustainability-at-ifc/publications/publications_handbook_pps [Accessed 20 February 2016]

IFC (2014) *Annual Report 2014, Big Challenges: Big Solutions*, Washington, DC: IFC.

IFC (2015) *IFC and Private Equity: Development Impact, Financial Returns* [online]. Available at: http://documents.worldbank.org/curated/en/567291468189571990/IFC-and-private-equity-development-impact-financial-returns [Accessed 16 January 2019]

IFC (2016) *IFC The First Six Decades: Leading the Way in Private Sector Development*, 2nd ed., Washington, DC: IFC World Bank Group.

IFC (2017) *Annual Report 2017, Creating Markets* [online]. Available at: https://www. ifc.org/wps/wcm/connect/aa14d660-c31a-449a-88ea-dcc443c29910/IFC-AR17-Full-Report-Vol-1-v2.pdf?MOD=AJPERES&CVID=lYRjuCw [Accessed 15 January 2019]

IFC (2019a) *Annual Report 2019, Investing for Impact* [online]. Available at: https://www.ifc. org/wps/wcm/connect/4ffd985d-c160-4b5b-8fbe-3ad2d642bbad/IFC-AR19-Full-Report.pdf?MOD=AJPERES&CVID=mV2uYFU [Accessed 16 March 2020]

IFC (2019b) *Investing for Impact: Financial 2019* [online]. Available at: https://www. ifc.org/wps/wcm/connect/d57ed06d-ceb1-4648-9995-ff4602e6d609/IFC-AR19-Volume-2-Financials.pdf?MOD=AJPERES&CVID=mThcJzD [Accessed 16 March 2020]

IFC (2020a) *Articles of Agreement (As Amended through 16 April 2020)* [online]. Available at: https://www.ifc.org/wps/wcm/connect/corp_ext_content/ifc_external_corporate_ site/about+ifc_new/ifc+governance/articles [Accessed 7 June 2020]

IFC (2020b) 'IFC Increases COVID-19 Support to $8 Billion to Sustain Private Sector Companies and Livelyhoods in Developing Countries', *Press Release* [online]. Available at: https://ifcextapps.ifc.org/ifcext/pressroom/ifcpressroom.nsf/0/CCCB1EAC6F61E3 2C8525852E0068124B?OpenDocument [Accessed 2 July 2020]

ILO (1997) *ILO Constitution* [online]. Available at: https://www.ilo.org/dyn/normlex/ en/f?p=1000:62:0::NO:62:P62_LIST_ENTRIE_ID:2453907:NO [Accessed 6 September 2019]

ILO (1998) *ILO Declaration on Fundamental Principles and Rights at Work and Its Follow-Up* [online]. Available at: https://www.ilo.org/wcmsp5/groups/public/---ed_norm/--- declaration/documents/publication/wcms_467653.pdf [Accessed 20 March 2023]

ILO (2002) *The International Labour Organization's Fundamental Conventions* [online]. Available at: http://www.ilo.org/wcmsp5/groups/public/-ed_norm/-declaration/documents/ publication/wcms_095895.pdf [Accessed 7 July 2016]

ILO (2004) 'A Fair Globalization: Creating Opportunities for All', *World Commission on the Social Dimension of Globalization* [online]. Available at: https://www.ilo.org/public/ english/wcsdg/docs/report.pdf [Accessed 5 July 2021]

ILO (2008) *ILO Declaration on Social Justice for a Fair Globalization*, Adopted by the International Labour Conference at its Ninety-Seventh Session, Geneva, 10 June 2008 [online]. Available at: https://www.ilo.org/global/about-the-ilo/mission-and-objectives/WCMS_ 099766/lang-en/index.htm [Accessed 16 October 2022]

ILO (2010) *World of Work: The Magazine of the ILO, No. 70*, December 2010 [online]. Available at: https://www.ilo.org/wcmsp5/groups/public/-dgreports/-dcomm/docu ments/publication/wcms_150107.pdf [Accessed 6 September 2019]

ILO (2012) *World of Work Report 2012: Better Jobs for a Better Economy* [online]. Available at: https://www.ilo.org/global/research/global-reports/world-of-work/WCMS_179453/ lang-en/index.htm [Accessed 17 September 2021]

ILO (2013a) *Reform of the International Labour Organization's Headquarters Organizational Structure* [online]. Available at: https://www.ilo.org/wcmsp5/groups/public/- dgreports/-dcomm/documents/organizationaldescription/wcms_204939.pdf [Accessed 19 September 2020]

ILO (2013b) *Towards the ILO Centenary: Realities, Renewal and Tripartite Commitment* [online]. Available at: https://www.ilo.org/wcmsp5/groups/public/-ed_norm/-relconf/ documents/meetingdocument/wcms_213836.pdf [Accessed 6 October 2020]

ILO (2013c) *Social Dialogue: Recurrent Discussion Under the ILO Declaration on Social Justice for a Fair Globalization*, Geneva: ILO.

ILO (2016a) *Resolution on Advancing Social Justice through Decent Work, Evaluation of the Impact of the ILO Declaration on Social Justice for a Fair Globalization and Conclusion for Future Action*, Adopted by the General Conference at its 105th Session, 2016 [online]. Available at: https://www.ilo.org/wcmsp5/groups/public/-ed_norm/-relconf/docu ments/meetingdocument/wcms_497583.pdf [Accessed 16 October 2020]

ILO (2016b) *Public-Private Partnerships for Decent Work: An Alliance for the Future* [online]. Available at: https://www.ilo.org/wcmsp5/groups/public/-dgreports/-exrel/documents/ publication/wcms_239399.pdf [Accessed 3 March 2021]

ILO (2018) *Third-Party Monitoring of Measures Against Child Labour and Forced Labour During the 2017 Cotton Harvest in Uzbekistan* [online]. Available at: https://www.ilo.org/

wcmsp5/groups/public/-ed_norm/-ipec/documents/publication/wcms_617830.pdf [Accessed 12 February 2021]

ILO (2019a) *Financial Report and Audited Consolidated Financial Statements for the Year Ended,* Geneva: ILO, 31 December.

ILO (2019b) *Compendium of Rules Applicable to the Governing Body of the International Labour Office,* Geneva: ILO.

ILO (2019c) *ILO Centenary Declaration for the Future of Work,* Adopted by the Conference at Its One Hundred and Eight Session, Geneva, 21 June [online]. Available at: https://www.ilo.org/wcmsp5/groups/public/@ed_norm/@relconf/documents/meetingdocument/wcms_711674.pdf [Accessed 23 October 2020]

ILO (2019d) 'The Global Labour Income Share and Distribution, Data Production and Analysis Unit', *ILO Department of Statistics* [online]. Available at: https://www.ilo.org/ilostat-files/Documents/Labour%20income%20share%20and%20distribution.pdf [Accessed 4 February 2021]

ILO (2020a) *Covid-19 May Push Millions More Children Into Child Labour – ILO and UNICEF,* 12 June [online]. Available at: https://www.ilo.org/global/about-the-ilo/newsroom/news/WCMS_747583/lang-en/index.htm [Accessed 3 October 2020]

ILO (2020b) *Restore Progress Towards Attaining the Sustainable Development Goals,* Annual Meetings of the World Bank and the IMF, 15 October [online]. Available at: https://www.ilo.org/global/about-the-ilo/newsroom/statements-and-speeches/WCMS_758222/lang-en/index.htm [Accessed 2 February 2021]

ILO (2020c) *Third-Party Monitoring of Child Labour and Forced Labour During the 2019 Cotton Harvest in Uzbekistan* [online]. Available at: https://www.ilo.org/wcmsp5/groups/public/-ed_norm/-ipec/documents/publication/wcms_735873.pdf [Accessed 12 February 2021]

ILO (2021a) *Tripartite Round Table on Pension Trends and Reforms* [online]. Available at: https://www.ilo.org/wcmsp5/groups/public/@ed_protect/@soc_sec/documents/publication/wcms_789672.pdf [Accessed 18 September 2021]

ILO (2021b) *World Social Protection Report, 2020–22* [online]. Available at: https://www.ilo.org/global/publications/books/WCMS_817572/lang-en/index.htm [Accessed 22 January 2022]

ILO (2021c) *ILO Organizational Structure* [online]. Available at: https://www.ilo.org/global/about-the-ilo/how-the-ilo-works/organigramme/lang--en/index.htm [Accessed 8 February 2022]

ILO and WBG (2015) *Joint Statement by World Bank Group President Jim Yong Kim and ILO Director General Guy Ryder* [online]. Available at: https://www.ilo.org/wcmsp5/groups/public/-dgreports/-dcomm/documents/statement/wcms_378989.pdf [Accessed 30 September 2022]

ILO and World Bank (2012) *Joint Synthesis Report International Labour Organisation and World Bank, Inventory of Policy Responses to the Financial and Economic Crisis* [online]. Available at: https://openknowledge.worldbank.org/bitstream/handle/10986/16610/758240WP0ILO0W00Box371996B00PUBLIC0.pdf?sequence=1 [Accessed 20 September 2021]

IMF (2010) *Press Release: Oslo Conference Calls for Commitment to Recovery Focused on Jobs,* Press Release No 10/339, 13 September [online]. Available at: https://www.imf.org/en/News/Articles/2015/09/14/01/49/pr10339 [Accessed 4 February 2021]

IMF (2014) *Transcript of the International Monetary and Financial Committee (IMFC) Press Briefing*, Washington, DC, Saturday, 12 April [online]. Available at: https://www.imf.org/external/np/tr/2014/tr041214b.htm [Accessed 2 February 2022]

IMF (2015) *Guidance Note for Surveillance Under Article IV Consultation*, Policy Paper [online]. Available at: https://www.imf.org/en/Publications/Policy-Papers/Issues/2016/12/31/Guidance-Note-for-Surveillance-Under-Article-IV-Consultations-PP4949 [Accessed 17 July 2020]

IMF (2016) *Implementation Plan in Response to the Board-Endorsed Recommendations for the IEO Evaluation Report on Self-Evaluation at the IMF* [online]. Available at: https://www.imf.org/external/np/pp/eng/2016/061716.pdf [Accessed 23 July 2020]

IMF (2017) *The IMF and Civil Society Organizations* [online]. Available at: https://www.imf.org/en/search#q=civil%20society&sort=relevancy [Accessed 5 November 2018]

IMF (2018) *2018 Review of the Fund's Capacity Development Strategy – Overview Paper*, Policy Paper [online]. Available at: https://www.imf.org/en/Publications/Policy-Papers/Issues/2018/11/20/2018-review-of-the-funds-capacity-development-strategy [Accessed 17 July 2020]

IMF (2019a) *The IMF at a Glance: Factsheet* [online]. Available at: https://www.imf.org/en/About/Factsheets/IMF-at-a-Glance [Accessed 9 July 2020]

IMF (2019b) *IMF Policies and Practices on Capacity Development* [online]. Available at: https://www.imf.org/en/Publications/Policy-Papers/Issues/2019/11/14/IMF-Policies-and-Practices-on-Capacity-Development-48811 [Accessed 10 July 2020]

IMF (2019c) *A Guide to Committees, Groups, and Clubs* [online]. Available at: https://www.imf.org/en/About/Factsheets/A-Guide-to-Committees-Groups-and-Clubs#IC [Accessed 11 July 2020]

IMF (2019d) *IMF Annual Report – Our Connected World* [online]. Available at: https://www.imf.org/external/pubs/ft/ar/2019/eng/assets/pdf/imf-annual-report-2019.pdf [Accessed 15 July 2020]

IMF (2019e) *A Strategy for IMF Engagement on Social Spending*, Policy Paper [online]. Available at: https://www.imf.org/en/Publications/Policy-Papers/Issues/2019/06/10/A-Strategy-for-IMF-Engagement-on-Social-Spending-46975 [Accessed 19 July 2020]

IMF (2019f) *World Economic Outlook – Global Manufacturing Downturn, Rising Trade Barriers*, October 2019 [online]. Available at: https://www.imf.org/en/Publications/WEO/Issues/2019/10/01/world-economic-outlook-october-2019 [Accessed 22 July 2020]

IMF (2019g) *A Strategy for IMF Engagement on Social Spending – Background Papers*, IMF Policy Paper No. 19/017 [online]. Available at: https://www.imf.org/en/Publications/Policy-Papers/Issues/2019/06/10/A-Strategy-for-IMF-Engagement-on-Social-Spending-Background-Papers-46976 [Accessed 8 February 2021]

IMF (2019h) *2018 Review of Program Design and Conditionality*, IMF Policy Paper No. 19/012 [online]. Available at: https://www.imf.org/en/Publications/Policy-Papers/Issues/2019/05/20/2018-Review-of-Program-Design-and-Conditionality-46910 [Accessed 8 February 2021]

IMF (2020a) *Articles of Agreement* [online]. Available at: https://www.imf.org/external/pubs/ft/aa/pdf/aa.pdf [Accessed 6 July 2020]

IMF (2020b) *The IMF and the World Bank: Factsheet* [online]. Available at: https://www.imf.org/en/About/Factsheets/Sheets/2016/07/27/15/31/IMF-World-Bank [Accessed 6 July 2020]

IMF (2020c) *IMF Capacity Development: Factsheet* [online]. Available at: https://www.imf.org/en/About/Factsheets/imf-capacity-development [Accessed 6 July 2020]

IMF (2020d) *Communique of the Forty First Meeting of the IMFC* [online]. Available at: https://www.imf.org/en/News/Articles/2020/04/16/communique-of-the-forty-first-meeting-of-the-imfc [Accessed 11 July 2020]

IMF (2020e) *Fifteenth and Sixteenth General Review of Quotas – Report of the Executive Board to the Board of Governors*, Policy Paper No. 20/007 [online]. Available at: https://www.imf.org/en/Publications/Policy-Papers/Issues/2020/02/13/Fifteenth-and-Sixteenth-General-Reviews-of-Quotas-Report-of-the-Executive-Board-to-the-Board-49049 [Accessed 18 July 2020]

IMF (2021) *Supplement to the Guidance Note for Surveillance Under Article IV Consultations* [online]. Available at: https://www.imf.org/en/Publications/Policy-Papers/Issues/2021/02/08/Supplement-to-the-Guidance-Note-for-Surveillance-Under-Article-IV-Consultations-50067 [Accessed 24 May 2022]

Independent Panel (2013) *Independent Panel Review of the Doing Business Report* [online]. Available at: http://pubdocs.worldbank.org/en/237121516384849082/doing-business-review-panel-report-June-2013.pdf [Accessed 26 June 2019]

ITF (2018) *Constitution International Transport Workers' Federation (ITF),* October [online]. Available at: https://www.itfglobal.org/sites/default/files/node/page/files/Consitution_2018.pdf [Accessed 18 April 2019]

ITUC (2006) *Programme of the ITUC,* Adopted by the Founding Congress of the ITUC Vienna, 1–3 November [online]. Available at: http://www.ituc-csi.org/IMG/pdf/Programme_of_the_ITUC.pdf [Accessed 10 March 2015]

ITUC (2008) *Challenging the IFIs: Practical Information and Strategies for Trade Union Engagement With International Financial Institutions* [online]. Available at: https://www.ituc-csi.org/IMG/pdf/Challenging_IFI_EN-PDF.pdf [Accessed 1 June 2020]

ITUC (2010a) *Internationally Recognised Core Labour Standards in the United States of America,* Report for the WTO General Council Review of the Trade Policies of the United States of America [online]. Available at: http://www.ituc-csi.org/IMG/pdf/final_US_CLS_2010.pdf [Accessed 7 November 2016]

ITUC (2010b) *Constitution and Standing Orders,* As amended by the 2nd World Congress, Vancouver, Canada, June [online]. Available at: http://www.ituc-csi.org/IMG/pdf/Const-ENG_2WC.pdf [Accessed 10 March 2017]

ITUC (2012) *World Bank's Doing Business 2013: Unfounded Claims About Deregulation* [online]. Available at: https://www.ituc-csi.org/world-bank-s-doing-business-2013 [Accessed 25 October 2018]

ITUC (2013) *Joint Report on Meetings Between the International Trade Union Movement (ITUC/ Global Unions) and the IMF and World Bank,* Washington DC, 12–15 February [Received by ITUC/Global Unions office 29 July 2014] [online]. Available at: https://www.imf.org/external/np/omd/2006/eng/121106.pdf

ITUC (2014) *ITUC Global Rights Index. The World's Worst Countries for Workers* [online]. Available at: https://www.ituc-csi.org/IMG/pdf/survey_ra_2014_eng.pdf [Accessed 14 May 2017]

ITUC (2015) *Framework for Dialogue Between the International Trade Union Confederation (ITUC), International Monetary Fund (IMF) and World Bank 12 February 2013,* Annex: Joint Report on Meeting between the International Labor Movement and Bretton

Woods Institutions, 27 February [online]. Available at: https://www.ituc-csi.org/frame work-for-dialogue-between-the [Accessed 8 April 2021]

ITUC (2018a) *Global Poll: Governments' Failure to Address Low Wages and Insecure Jobs Threatens Trust in Politics and Democracy* [online]. Available at: https://www.ituc-csi.org/ITUC-Global-Poll-2018?lang=en [Accessed 3 December 2018]

ITUC (2018b) *ITUC Global Rights Index* [online]. Available at: https://www.ituc-csi.org/IMG/pdf/ituc-global-rights-index-2018-en-final-2.pdf [Accessed 20 April 2019]

ITUC (2018c) *Constitution and Standing Orders*, As amended by the 4th World Congress, Copenhagen, Denmark, December [online]. Available at: https://www.ituc-csi.org/IMG/pdf/ituc_constitution_2019_en.pdf [Accessed 11 May 2019]

ITUC (2018d) *World Bank Should Scrap Ideologically-Driven Business Regulation Ratings* [online]. Available at: https://www.ituc-csi.org/world-bank-should-scrap [Accessed 23 June 2020]

ITUC (2018e) *Global Conference on Financing Social Protection*, Final Conference Report, Brussels, 17–18 September [online]. Available at: https://www.ituc-csi.org/IMG/pdf/conference_report_global_conference_on_financing_social_protection.pdf [Accessed 20 July 2020]

ITUC (2018f) *ITUC Contribution to Public Consultation on Designing an IMF Strategic Framework on Social Spending* [online]. Available at: https://www.ituc-csi.org/IMG/pdf/ituc_contribution_to_public_consultation_imf_strategic_framework_on_soci._.pdf [Accessed 8 February 2021]

ITUC (2019a) *ITUC Financial Reports for 2018* [online]. Available at: https://www.ituc-csi.org/IMG/pdf/21gc_e_16_d_-_ituc_financial_reports_2018.pdf [Accessed 20 December 2019]

ITUC (2019b) *The IMF Should Support the Financing of Universal Social Protection, Health and Education* [online]. Available at: https://www.ituc-csi.org/the-imf-should-support-the [Accessed 22 July 2020]

ITUC (2020a) *Market Fundamentalism and the World Bank Group: From Structural Adjustment Programmes to Maximizing Finance for Development and Beyond* [online]. Available at: https://www.ituc-csi.org/IMG/pdf/market_fundamentalism_and_the_world_bank_group.pdf [Accessed 8 July 2020]

ITUC (2020b) *Reform Multilateralism to Achieve Sustainable Recovery and Decent Work* [online]. Available at: https://www.ituc-csi.org/reform-multilateralism-to-achieve [Accessed 22 January 2021]

ITUC (2020c) *ITUC Contribution to the Call for Reactions on the Forthcoming UNHCR Report on a Global Fund for Social Protection* [online]. Available at: https://www.ohchr.org/Documents/Issues/Poverty/global-fund-social-protection/ITUC.pdf [Accessed 23 March 2021]

ITUC (2021a) 'ITUC Global Rights Index: The World's Worst Countries for Workers', *Executive Summary* [online]. Available at: https://www.ituc-csi.org/2021-global-rights-index [Accessed 19 January 2022]

ITUC (2021b) *Joint Report on Meetings Between the International Trade Union Movement (ITUC/Global Unions) and the IMF and World Bank*, 22–25 October [Received by ITUC/Global Unions office May 2022] [online]. Available at: https://www.imf.org/external/np/omd/2004/eng/100704.pdf

ITUC (2022a) *Initial ITUC Contribution to the World Bank's Social Protection and Jobs Compass* [online]. Available at: https://www.ituc-csi.org/IMG/pdf/initial_ituc_input_on_world_bank_spj_compass.pdf [Accessed 15 April 2022]

ITUC (2022b) *International Trade Union Confederation Submission on the Business Enabling Environment Pre-Concept Note* [online]. Available at: https://www.ituc-csi.org/IMG/pdf/ituc_submission_bee_pre-concept_note_3-2022.pdf [Accessed 5 May 2022]

ITUC (2022c) *Joint Report on Technical Meetings Between the International Trade Union Movement (ITUC/Global Unions), the IMF and World Bank*, Virtual, 28 February [Received by ITUC/Global Unions office May 2022] [online]. Available at: https://www.imf.org/external/np/omd/2004/eng/100704.pdf

IUF (2022) *Guinea: Sheraton Grand Conakry Closes After Workers Submit Strike Notice*, 16 June [online]. Available at: https://www.iuf.org/news/guinea-sheraton-grand-conakry-closes-after-workers-submit-strike-notice/ [Accessed 10 July 2022]

Jakovleski, V., Jerbi, S. and Biersteker, T. (2019) 'The ILO's Role in Global Governance: Limits and Potential', in Gironde, C. and Carbonnier, G. eds. *The ILO @ 100: Addressing the Past and Future of Work and Social Protection*, Leiden and Boston: Brill: 82–108.

Jaumotte, F. and Buitron Osorio, C. (2015) 'Inequality and Labour Market Institutions', *IMF Research Department*, July [online]. Available at: https://www.imf.org/external/pubs/ft/sdn/2015/sdn1514.pdf [Accessed 7 February 2021]

John, S. (2002) *The Persuaders: When Lobbyists Matter*, Basingstoke and New York: Palgrave Macmillan.

Johnson, E. and Prakash, A. (2007) 'NGO Research Program: A Collective Action Perspective', *Policy Sciences*, 40, 3: 221–240.

Kaberuka, D., Jiun, C.D. and Meyersson, P. (2018) *Time for a Reboot at a Critical Time for Multilateralism – The Third External Evaluation of the IEO*, Washington, DC: IMF.

Karns, M.P. and Mingst, K.A. (2004) *International Organizations: The Politics and Processes of Global Governance*, Boulder, CO and London: Lynne Rienner Publishers.

Kellerson, H. (1998) 'The ILO Declaration of 1998 on Fundamental Principles and Rights: A Challenge for the Future', *International Labour Review*, 137, 2: 223–227.

Kennard, M. (2012) 'Haiti and the Shock Doctrine', *OpenDemocracy* [online]. Available at: https://www.opendemocracy.net/en/haiti-and-shock-doctrine/ [Accessed 18 June 2021]

Keohane, R.O. (2021) 'The Global Politics Paradigm: Guide to the Future or Only the Recent Past?', *International Theory*, 13: 112–121.

Kim, J.Y. (2013) *World Bank Group President Jim Yong Kim's Speech at George Washington University – The World Bank Group Strategy: A Path to End Poverty*, Pre-Annual Meetings Speech, 1 October [online]. Available at: http://www.worldbank.org/en/news/speech/2013/10/01/world-bank-group-president-jim-yong-kim-speech-at-george-washington-university [Accessed 12 November 2016]

King, B.G., Felin, T. and Whetten, D.A. (2010) 'Finding the Organization in Organizational Theory: A Meta-Theory of the Organization as a Social Actor', *Organization Science*, 21, 1: 290–305.

Koch-Baumgarten, S. (2006) 'Globale Gewerkschaften und Industrielle Beziehungen in der Global Governance', *Industrielle Beziehungen*, 13, 3: 205–222.

Koch-Baumgarten, S. (2011) 'Gewerkschaften und Global Governance: Grenzen und Möglichkeiten einer grenzüberschreitenden Regulierung von Erwerbsarbeit', *Internationale Politik und Gesellschaft*, 2: 51–67.

Koenig-Archibugi, M. (2003) 'Mapping Global Governance', in Held, D. and McGrew, A. eds. *Power, Authority and Global Governance*, Cambridge: Polity Press: 46–69.

Köhler, H.-D. and González Begega, S. (2010) 'The European Works Council as a Multidimensional Contested Terrain', *Employee Relations*, 32, 6: 590–605.

Korpi, W. (1985) 'Developments in the Theory of Power and Exchange Power Resources Approach vs. Action and Conflict: On Causal and Intentional Explanations in the Study of Power', *Sociological Theory*, 3, 2: 31–45.

Kott, S. (2019) 'ILO: Social Justice in a Global World? A History in Tension', in Gironde, C. and Carbonnier, G. eds. *The ILO @ 100: Addressing the Past and Future of Work and Social Protection*, Leiden and Boston: Brill: 21–39.

La Hovary, C. (2015) 'A Challenging Menage a Trois? Tripartism in the International Labour Organization', *International Organizations Law Review*, 12, 1: 204–236.

Lambert, R. and Webster, E. (2017) 'The China Price: The All-China Federation of Trade Unions and the Repressed Question of International Labour Standards', *Globalizations*, 14, 2: 313–326.

Lawrence, B. (2008) 'Power, Institutions and Organizations', in Greenwood, R., Oliver, C., Suddaby, R. and Sahlin, K. eds. *The Sage Handbook of Organizational Institutionalism*, Los Angeles, London, New Delhi and Singapore: Sage: 170–197.

Lévesque, C., Hennebert, M.-A., Murray, G. and Bourque, R. (2018) 'Corporate Social Responsibility and Worker Rights: Institutionalizing Social Dialogue Through International Framework Agreements', *Journal of Business Ethics*, 153, 1: 215–230.

Lévesque, C. and Murray, G. (2002) 'Local Versus Global: Activating Global Union Power in the Global Economy', *Labor Studies Journal*, 27, 3: 39–65.

Lindner, F. and Wald, A. (2011) 'Success Factors of Knowledge Management in Temporary Organizations', *International Journal of Project Management*, 29, 7: 877–888.

Long, D. and Woolley, F. (2009) 'Global Public Goods: Critique of a UN Discourse', *Global Governance*, 15, 1: 107–122.

Louis, M. (2019) 'Who Decides?: Representation and Decision-Making at the International Labour Organization', in Gironde, C. and Carbonnier, G. eds. *The ILO @ 100: Addressing the Past and Future of Work and Social Protection*, Leiden and Boston: Brill: 40–58.

Lucas, C. and Kline, T. (2008) 'Understanding the Influence of Organizational Culture and Group Dynamics on Organizational Change and Learning', *The Learning Organization*, 15, 3: 277–287.

Malpass, D. (2018) 'Statement of Under Secretary David Malpass Before the U.S. House Financial Services Subcommittee on Monetary Policy and Trade', *U.S. Department of Treasury, Testimonies*, 12 December [online]. Available at: https://home.treasury.gov/news/press-releases/sm572 [Accessed 13 November 2019]

Malpass, D. (2019a) *Address by David Malpass*, Speech to the Plenary Session of the Annual Meetings of the Board of Governors, 18 October [online]. Available at: http://documents.worldbank.org/curated/en/371631572381483285/pdf/Address-by-David-Malpass-President-of-the-World-Bank-Group-at-the-2019-Annual-Meetings.pdf [Accessed 13 November 2019]

Malpass, D. (2019b) *Letter to Secretary of the Treasury – Doing Business Report* [online]. Available at: https://financialservices.house.gov/uploadedfiles/malpass_ltr_mnuchin_12162019_dblr.pdf [Accessed 4 July 2020]

March, J.G. and Olsen, J.P. (1975) 'Organizational Learning Under Ambiguity', *European Journal of Policy Review*, 3, 2: 147–171.

March, J.G. and Simon, H.A. (1961) *Organizations*, New York: Wiley.

March, J.G. and Simon, H.A. (1976) *Organisation und Individuum: Menschliches Verhalten in Organisationen*, Wiesbaden: Gabler.

Marginson, P. (2016) 'Governing Work and Employment Relations in an Internalized Economy: The Institutional Challenge', *ILR Review*, 69, 5: 1033–1055.

MarketLine (2019) *Company Profile International Finance Corporation*, London: MarketLine, 30 August.

Martinez-Diaz, L. (2008) *Executive Boards in International Organizations: Lessons for Strengthening IMF Governance*, Background Paper IEO [online]. Available at: http://poli cydialogue.org/files/events/Martinez-Diaz_strengthening_IMF_gov.pdf [Accessed 2 September 2019]

Maupain, F. (2005) 'Revitalization Not Retreat: The Real Potential of the 1998 ILO Declaration for the Universal Protection of Workers' Rights', *The European Journal of International Law*, 16, 3: 439–465.

Maupain, F. (2009) 'New Foundation or New Facade? The ILO and the 2008 Declaration on Social Justice for a Fair Globalization', *The European Journal of International Law*, 20, 3: 823–852.

Maupain, F. (2013) *The Future of the International Labour Organisation in the Global Economy*, Oxford: Hart Publishing.

Mayntz, R. (2004) 'Governance im Modernen Staat', in Benz, A. ed. *Governance-Regieren in komplexen Regelsystemen*, Wiesbaden: VS Verlag: 65–76.

Mayntz, R. (2008) 'Embedded Theorizing. Perspectives on Globalization and Global Governance', in Bröchler, S. and Lauth, H.-J. eds. *Politikwissenschaftliche Perspektiven*, Wiesbaden: VS Verlag: 93–116.

Mayntz, R. (2009) *Über Governance: Institutionen und Prozesse politischer Regelung*, Schriften aus dem Max-Planck-Institut für Gesellschaftsforschung Köln, Band 62, Frankfurt and New York: Campus.

McCallum, J.K. (2013) 'The Campaign Against G4S: Globalizing Governance Struggles', in McCallum, J.K. ed. *Global Unions, Local Power*, New York: Cornell University Press: 74–98.

McCormack, G. (2018) 'Why "Doing Business" With the World Bank May Be Bad for You', *European Business Organization Law Review*, 19, 3: 649–676.

MDTF (2010) *Multi Donor Trust Fund Labor Markets, Jobs Creation, and Economic Growth: Scaling Up Research, Capacity Building, and Action on the Ground – Updates of Activities, Work Plan, and Budget* [online]. Available at: http://siteresources.worldbank.org/INTLM/Resources/390041-1212776476091/5078455-1267646113835/REPORT-JANUARY18_2010.pdf [Accessed 8 January 2015]

Meardi, G. and Marginson, P. (2014) 'Global Labour Governance: Potential and Limits of an Emerging Perspective', *Work, Employment and Society*, 28, 4: 651–662.

Meek, V.L. (1993) 'Organizational Culture: Origins and Weaknesses', in Salaman, G. ed. *Human Resource Strategies*, 2nd ed., London, Newbury Park and New Delhi: Sage: 192–212.

Messner, D. (2005) 'Global Governance: Globalisierung im 21. Jahrhundert gestalten', in Behrens, M. ed. *Globalisierung als politische Herausforderung: Global Governance zwischen Utopie und Realität*, Wiesbaden: VS-Verlag: 27–54.

Meyer, J.W., Drori, S.G. and Hwang, H. (2006) 'World Society and the Proliferation of Formal Organization', in Drori, S.G., Meyer, J.W. and Hwang, H. eds. *Globalization and Organization: World Society and Organizational Change*, Oxford: Oxford University Press: 25–49.

Meyer, J.W. and Rowan, B. (1977) 'Institutionalized Organizations: Formal Structure as Myth and Ceremony', *American Journal of Sociology*, 83, 2: 340–363.

Mintzberg, H. (1983) *Power in and Around Organizations*, Englewood Cliffs: Prentice-Hall.

Morgan, G. (1997) *Images of Organization*, Thousand Oaks, London and New Delhi: Sage.

Mountford, A. (2008) *The Formal Governance Structure of the International Monetary Fund*, Washington, DC: IEO Background Paper.

Müller, T., Platzer, H.-W. and Rüb, S. (2004) *Globale Arbeitsbeziehungen in globalen Konzernen? Zur Transnationalisierung betrieblicher und gewerkschaftlicher Politik*, Wiesbaden: VS-Verlag.

Müller, T., Platzer, H.-W. and Rüb, S. (2006) 'Weltbetriebsräte und globale Netzwerke – Instrumente internationaler Solidarität?', *WSI-Mitteilungen*, 1: 5–9.

Müller, T., Platzer, H.-W. and Rüb, S. (2010) *Global Union Federations and the Challenges of Globalisation* [online]. Available at: https://library.fes.de/pdf-files/id/ipa/07437.pdf [Accessed 16 June 2016]

Munck, R.P. (2010) 'Globalization and the Labour Movement: Challenges and Responses', *Global Labour Journal*, 1, 2: 218–232.

Murphy, H. (2014) 'The World Bank and Core Labour Standards: Between Flexibility and Regulation', *Review of International Political Economy*, 21, 2: 399–431.

Myant, M. and Piasna, A. (2017) 'Introduction', in Piasna, A. and Myant, M. eds. *Myth of Employment Deregulation: How It Neither Creates Jobs Nor Reduces Labour Market Segmentation*, Brussels: ETUI: 7–21.

Nelson, P. (2006) 'The Varied and Conditional Integration of NGOs in the Aid System: NGOs and the World Bank', *Journal of International Development*, 18, 5: 701–713.

Nonaka, I. and von Krogh, G. (2009) 'Tacit Knowledge and Knowledge Conversion: Controversy and Advancement in Organizational Knowledge Creation Theory', *Organization Science*, 20, 3: 635–652.

Nonaka, I., von Krogh, G. and Voelpel, S. (2006) 'Organizational Knowledge Creation Theory: Evolutionary Paths and Future Advances', *Organization Studies*, 27, 8: 1179–1208.

Nuscheler, F. (2002) 'Global Governance', in Ferdowsi, M.A. ed. *Internationale Politik im 21. Jahrhundert*, München: Wilhelm Fink Verlag: 71–86.

O'Brien, R. (2000) 'Workers and World Order: The Tentative Transformation of the International Union Movement', *Review of International Studies*, 26, 4: 533–555.

O'Brien, R., Goetz, A.M., Scholte, J.A. and Williams, M. (2000) *Contesting Global Governance: Multilateral Economic Institutions and Global Social Movements*, Cambridge: Cambridge University Press.

O'Brien, R. and Williams, M. (2016) *Global Political Economy: Evolution and Dynamics*, 5th ed., London and New York: Palgrave Macmillan.

Ocampo, J.A., Griesgraber, J.M., Martin, M. and Coplin, N. (2017) *Are the Multilateral Organizations Fighting Inequality?*, Berlin: Friedrich-Ebert Stiftung.

OECD (2011a) *Multilateral Aid 2010* [online]. Available at: https://read.oecd-ilibrary.org/development/multilateral-aid-2010_9789264046993-en#page5 [Accessed 10 September 2022]

OECD (2011b) *Divided We Stand: Why Inequality Keeps Rising* [online]. Available at: https://www.oecd.org/els/soc/dividedwestandwhyinequalitykeepsrising.htm [Accessed 17 September 2021]

OECD (2015) *Multilateral Aid 2015: Better Partnerships for a Post-2015 World*, Paris: OECD Publishing.

OECD (2017) *OECD Work on Employment, Social Protection and International Migration*, Paris: OECD Publishing.

OECD (2018) *Good Jobs for all in a Changing World of Work*, The OECD Jobs Strategy [online]. Available at: https://www.oecd.org/employment/jobs-strategy/good-jobs-for-all-in-a-changing-world-of-work-9789264308817-en.htm [Accessed 19 March 2023]

OECD (2019a) *Recommendation of the Council on Artificial Intelligence* [online]. Available at: https://www.fsmb.org/siteassets/artificial-intelligence/pdfs/oecd-recommendation-on-ai-en.pdf [Accessed 17 November 2021]

OECD (2019b) *The Future of Work, OECD Employment Outlook* [online]. Available at: https://www.oecd-ilibrary.org/employment/oecd-employment-outlook-2019_9ee00155-en [Accessed 20 February 2020]

OECD (2022) *Stocktaking Exercise on the OECD Guidelines for Multinational Enterprises, Consultations March 2021–April 2022, Submissions Received from TUAC* [online]. Available at: https://mneguidelines.oecd.org/stocktaking-exercise-oecd-guidelines-mnes-public-consultation-tuac-submissions.pdf [Accessed 19 May 2022]

Oestreich, J.E. (2007) *Power and Principle: Human Rights Programming in International Organizations*, Washington, DC: Georgetown University Press.

Offe, C. (1985) *Disorganized Capitalism: Contemporary Transformations of Work and Politics*, Cambridge: Polity Press.

Ortiz, I. and Cummins, M. (2019) *Austerity: The New Normal – A Renewed Washington Consensus 2010–24*, Working Paper, Initiative for Policy Dialogue, International Trade Union Confederation, Public Services International, Eurodad, Bretton Woods Project [online]. Available at: http://policydialogue.org/files/publications/papers/Austerity-the-New-Normal-Ortiz-Cummins-6-Oct-2019.pdf [Accessed 29 July 2020]

Ortiz, I. and Cummins, M. (2021) *Global Austerity Alert: Looming Budget Cuts in 2021–2025 and Alternative Pathways*, Working Paper, Initiative for Policy Dialogue, Global Social Justice, International Trade Union Confederation, Public Services International, Arab Watch Coalition, Bretton Woods Project, Third World Network [online]. Available at: https://policydialogue.org/files/publications/papers/Global-Austerity-Alert-Ortiz-Cummins-2021-final.pdf [Accessed 14 April 2021]

Oskamp, S. and Schultz Wesley, P. (2014) *Attitudes and Opinions*, 3rd ed., New York and London: Psychology Press.

Oswald, R. (2009) 'It's About Power . . .', in Global Unions ed. *Getting the World to Work: Global Union Strategies for Recovery*, Belgium: Hoeilaart: 12–13.

Oxfam (2022a) *IMF Must Abandon Demands for Austerity as Cost-of-Living Crisis Drives Up Hunger and Poverty Worldwide* [online]. Available at: https://www.oxfam.org/en/press-releases/imf-must-abandon-demands-austerity-cost-living-crisis-drives-hunger-and-poverty [Accessed 25 April 2022]

Oxfam (2022b) *First Crisis, Then Catastrophe*, Oxfam Media Briefing, 12 April [online]. Available at: https://oi-files-d8-prod.s3.eu-west-2.amazonaws.com/s3fs-public/2022-04/Oxfam%20briefing%20-%20First%20Crisis%20Then%20Catastrophe_0.pdf [Accessed 2 September 2022]

Peck, A. (2012) *World Bank Lending Facilities* [online]. Available at: https://www.brettonwoodsproject.org/2012/10/art-571192/ [Accessed 15 January 2016]

Peet, R. (2009) *Unholy Trinity: The IMF, World Bank and WTO*, London and New York: Zed Books.

Perulli, A. (2018) *The Declaration of Philadelphia*, Working Paper No. 143, Geneva: Centre for the Study of European Labour Law "Massimo D'Antona".

Phillips, D.A. (2009) *Reforming the World Bank: Twenty Years of Trial – and Error*, Cambridge, New York, Melbourne, Madrid, Cape Town, Singapore and Sao Paulo: Cambridge University Press.

Piketty, T. (2015) *The Economics of Inequality*, Cambridge and London: Harvard University Press.

Piketty, T. (2017) *Capital in the Twenty-First Century*, Cambridge and London: Harvard University Press.

Platzer, H.-W. and Müller, T. (2009) *Die globalen und europäischen Gewerkschaftsverbände. Handbuch und Analysen zur transnationalen Gewerkschaftspolitik*, Cambridge: HBS Edition Sigma.

Poole, M. (1981) *Theories of Trade Unionism: A Sociology of Industrial Relations*, London, Boston and Henley: Routledge & Kegan Paul.

Portugal, M. (2005) 'Improving IMF Governance and Increasing the Influence of Developing Countries in IMF Decision-Making', in Buira, A. ed. *Reforming the Governance of the IMF and the World Bank*, London and New York: Anthem Press: 75–106.

Provost, C. (2014) 'A World Bank of Trouble?', *The Guardian* [online]. Available at: http://www.theguardian.com/global-development-professionals-network/2014/dec/04/a-world-bank-of-trouble?CMP=share_btn_fb [Accessed 20 December 2014]

Provost, C. (2017) 'Farmers Sue World Bank Lending Arm Over Alleged Violence in Honduras', *The Guardian* [online]. Available at: https://www.theguardian.com/global-development/2017/mar/08/farmers-sue-world-bank-lending-arm-ifc-over-alleged-violence-in-honduras [Accessed 14 March 2022]

PSI (2018) *Unions Assert the Need for a Binding Treaty to Hold TNCs and IFIs Accountable* [online]. Available at: https://publicservices.international/resources/news/unions-assert-the-need-for-a-binding-treaty-to-hold-tncs-and-ifis-accountable-?id=8054& lang=en [Accessed 2 July 2020]

Reinhart, C.M. and Trebesch, C. (2016) 'The International Monetary Fund: 70 Years of Reinvention', *Journal of Economic Perspectives*, 30, 1: 3–28.

Reinsberg, B., Stubbs, T., Kentikelenis, A. and King, L. (2019) 'The Political Economy of Labor Market Deregulation During IMF Interventions', *International Interactions*, 45, 3: 532–559.

Rice, A. (2016) 'How the World Bank's Biggest Critic Became Its President', *The Guardian* [online]. Available at: https://www.theguardian.com/news/2016/aug/11/world-bank-jim-yong-kim [Accessed 17 November 2016]

Rich, B. (2002) 'The World Bank Under James Wolfensohn', in Pincus, J.R. and Winters, J.A. eds. *Reinventing the World Bank*, Ithaca, NY: Cornell University Press: 26–52.

Rickard, S.J. and Caraway, T.L. (2019) 'International Demands for Austerity: Examining the Impact of the IMF on the Public Sector', *The Review of International Organizations*, 14: 35–57.

Rittberger, V. (2008) *Global Governance: From 'Exclusive' Executive Multilateralism to Inclusive, Multipartite Institutions*, Tübinger Arbeitspapiere zur internationalen Politik und Friedensforschung, No. 52 [online]. Available at: http://tobias-lib.uni-tuebingen.de/volltexte/2008/3672/pdf/tap52.pdf [Accessed 12 November 2017]

Rittberger, V., Zangl, B. and Kruck, A. (2012) *International Organization*, New York and Basingstoke: Palgrave Macmillan.

Ritzer, G. and Dean, P. (2019) *Globalization: The Essentials*, Oxford: Wiley Blackwell.

Robalino, D.A., Mahmood, F., Tokle, S.E., Gonzalez, A., Madhvani, S., Parikh, V.B. and Yan, E. (2017) *Jobs Umbrella Multidonor Trust Fund Annual Report 2017*, Washington, DC [online]. Available at: http://documents.worldbank.org/curated/en/697831508239477911/Jobs-umbrella-multidonor-trust-fund-annual-report-2017 [Accessed 20 December 2017]

Rodgers, G., Lee, E., Swepston, L. and Van Daele, J. (2009) *The International Labour Organization and the Quest for Social Justice, 1919–2009*, Geneva: ILO.

Rombouts, S.J. (2019) 'The International Diffusion of Fundamental Labour Standards: Contemporary Content, Scope, Supervision and Proliferation of Core Workers' Rights Under Public, Private, Binding and Voluntary Regulatory Regimes', *Columbia Human Rights Law Review*, 50, 3: 78–175.

Rombouts, S.J. and Zekic, N. (2020) 'Decent and Sustainable Work for the Future? The ILO Future of Work Centenary Initiative, the UN 2030 Agenda for Sustainable Development, and the Evolution of the Meaning of Work', *UCLA Journal of International Law and Foreign Affairs*, 24, 2: 317–358.

Rowley, J. and Gibbs, P. (2008) 'From Learning Organization to Practically Wise Organization', *The Learning Organization*, 15, 5: 356–372.

Royle, T. (2010) 'The ILO's Shift to Promotional Principles and the 'Privatization' of Labour Rights: An Analysis of Labour Standards, Voluntary Self-Regulation and Social Clauses', *The International Journal of Comparative Labour Law and Industrial Relations*, 26, 3: 249–271.

Royle, T. and Rueckert, Y. (2020) 'McStrike! Framing, (Political) Opportunity and the Development of a Collective Identity: McDonald's and the UK Fast-Food Rights Campaign', *Work, Employment and Society*, Ahead of Print, 1–20.

Ryder, G. (2019) *Opening Remarks by Guy Ryder*, ILO Director-General, at the 108th Session of the International Labour Conference, Geneva, 10 June [online]. Available at: https://www.ilo.org/global/about-the-ilo/how-the-ilo-works/ilo-director-general/statements-and-speeches/WCMS_710069/lang-en/index.htm [Accessed 18 September 2020]

Sarkar, P. (2020) 'Does Labor Regulation Reduce Total and Youth Employment?', *Structural Change and Economic Dynamics*, 52: 374–381.

Schein, E.H. (1989) 'Organizational Culture: What It Is and How to Change It', in Evans, P., Doz, Y. and Laurent, A. eds. *Human Resource Management in International Firms: Change, Globalization, Innovation*, Houndmills, Basingstoke, Hampshire and London: Palgrave Macmillan: 56–82.

Schein, E.H. (1993) 'Coming to a New Awareness of Organizational Culture', in Salaman, G. ed. *Human Resource Strategies*, 2nd ed., London, Newbury Park and New Delhi: Sage: 237–253.

Scherrer, C. and Brand, U. (2011) 'Global Governance: Konkurrierende Formen und Inhalte Globaler Regulierung', *Friedrich-Ebert-Stiftung* [online]. Available at: http://library.fes.de/pdf-files/akademie/online/50334-2011.pdf [Accessed 3 March 2016]

Schneider, B., Brief, A.P. and Guzzo, R.A. (1996) 'Creating a Climate and Culture for Sustainable Organizational Change', *Organizational Dynamics*, 24, 4: 7–19.

Scholte, J.A. (2021) 'Beyond Institutionalism: Toward a Transformed Global Governance Theory', *International Theory*, 13: 179–191.

Schwartz, M.J. and Rist, R.C. (2016) *The International Monetary Fund and the Learning Organization: The Role of Independent Evaluation*, Washington, DC: IEO.

Scott, W.R. (1998) *Organizations. Rational, Natural and Open Systems*, Upper Saddle River, NJ: Prentice Hall.

Scott, W.R. (2001) *Institutions and Organizations*, London and New Delhi: Sage.

Scott, W.R. and Davis, G.F. (2007) *Organizations and Organizing: Rational, Natural, and Open System Perspectives*, Upper Saddle River, NJ: Pearson Prentice Hall.

Senge, K. (2006) 'Zum Begriff der Institution im Neo-Institutionalismus', in Senge, K. and Hellmann, K.-U. eds. *Einführung in den Neo-Insitutionalismus*, Wiesbaden: VS Verlag: 35–47.

Sengenberger, W. (2005) *Globalization and Social Progress: The Role and Impact of International Labour Standards*, Bonn: Friedrich-Ebert-Stiftung.

Shirley, M.M. (1992) 'The What, Why, and How of Privatization: A World Bank Perspective', *Fordham Law Review*, 60, 6: 23–36.

Silva, V. (2021) 'The ILO and the Future of Work: The Politics of Global Labour Policy', *Global Social Policy*, March, 1–18.

Sommer, M. (2011) 'Wo steht die internationale Gewerkschaftsbewegung heute?', *Internationale Politik und Gesellschaft*, 2: 11–21.

Standing, G. (2008) 'The ILO: An Agency for Globalization?', *Development and Change*, 39, 3: 355–384.

Stelzl, B. (2006) *Internationale Gewerkschaftsarbeit in Zeiten der Globalisierung*, Berlin: Friedrich-Ebert Stiftung.

Stephens, P. (2014) 'IFC "Refocusing" Through Internal Reorganization', *Devex* [online]. https://www.devex.com/news/ifc-refocusing-through-internal-reorganization-83325 [Accessed 21 July 2019]

Stieglitz, J.E. (2002) *Globalization and Its Discontents*, London: Penguin.

Stieglitz, J.E. (2010) *The Stieglitz Report: Reforming the International Monetary and Financial Systems in the Wake of the Global Crisis*, New York and London: The New Press.

Stirling, J. (2010) 'Global Unions: Chasing the Dream or Building the Reality?', *Capital & Class*, 34, 1: 107–114.

Strand, J.R. and Retzl, K.J. (2016) 'Did Recent Voice Reforms Improve Good Governance Within the World Bank?', *Development and Change*, 47, 3: 415–445.

Sullivan, L.E. (2009) *The Sage Glossary of the Social and Behavioural Sciences*, Thousand Oaks: Sage.

Supiot, A. (2020) 'The Tasks Ahead of the ILO at Its Centenary', *International Labour Review*, 159, 1: 117–136.

Thomas, H. and Turnbull, P. (2018) 'From Horizontal to Vertical Labour Governance: The International Labour Organization (ILO) and Decent Work in Global Supply Chains', *Human Relations*, 71, 4: 536–559.

Thompson, P. and McHugh, D. (2009) *Work Organisations: A Critical Approach*, 4th ed., Hampshire and New York: Palgrave Macmillan.

Thornton, P.H. and Ocasio, W. (2008) 'Institutional Logics', in Greenwood, R., Oliver, C., Suddaby, R. and Sahlin, K. eds. *The Sage Handbook of Organizational Institutionalism*, Los Angeles, London, New Delhi and Singapore: Sage: 99–129.

Torfason, M.T. and Ingram, P. (2010) 'The Global Rise of Democracy: A Network Account', *American Sociological Review*, 75, 3: 355–376.

Tosi, H.L. (2009) 'James March and Herbert Simon, Organizations', in Tosi, H.L. ed. *Theories of Organization*, Los Angeles, London, New Delhi, Singapore and Washington, DC: Sage: 93–102.

Traub-Merz, R. and Eckl, J. (2007) 'International Trade Union Movement: Mergers and Contradictions', *FES International Trade Union Cooperation* [online]. Available at: http://library.fes.de/pdf-files/iez/04589.pdf [Accessed 18 September 2011]

TUAC (2005) *Workers' Voice in Corporate Governance – A Trade Union Perspective*, Global Unions Discussion Paper [online]. Available at: https://old.tuac.org/statemen/communiq/0512cgpaper.pdf [Accessed 22 July 2015]

TUDCN (2018) *Aligning Blended Finance to Development Effectiveness: Where We Are at*, Research Pape [online]. Available at: https://www.ituc-csi.org/IMG/pdf/aligning_blended_finance_to_development_-_web_-_en.pdf

Turner, L. (2004) 'Why Revitalize? Labour's Urgent Mission in a Contested Global Economy', in Frege, C. and Kelly, J. eds., *Varieties of Unionism: Strategies for Union Revitalization in a Globalizing Economy*, Oxford and New York: Oxford University Press.

Tussie, D. and Riggirozzi, M.P. (2001) 'Pressing Ahead With New Procedures for Old Machinery: Global Governance and Civil Society', in Rittberger, V. ed. *Global Governance and the United Nations System*, Tokyo, New York and Paris: United Nations University Press: 158–180.

Twomey, P. (2007) 'Human Rights-Based Approaches to Development: Towards Accountability', in Baderin, M.A. and McCorquodale, R. eds. *Economic, Social and Cultural Rights in Action*, New York: Oxford University Press: 45–69.

UN (2015) *Outcome Document of the Third International Conference on Financing for Development: Addis Ababa Action Agenda* [online]. Available at: https://www.un.org/ga/search/view_doc.asp?symbol=A/CONF.227/L.1 [Accessed 4 September 2019]

UNDP (1999) *Global Public Goods: International Cooperation in the 21st Century* [online]. Available at: http://www.act.nato.int/images/stories/events/2010/gc/ws_gen_gpg_intlcoop.pdf [Accessed 10 October 2018].

UN Human Rights Council (2018a) *Report of the Special Rapporteur on Extreme Poverty and Human Rights*, A/HRC/38/33, 8 May [online]. Available at: https://undocs.org/A/HRC/38/33 [Accessed 28 January 2021]

UN Human Rights Council (2018b) *Report of the Special Rapporteur on Extreme Poverty and Human Rights*, A/73/396, 26 September [online]. Available at: https://undocs.org/A/73/396 [Accessed 20 September 2021]

Valticos, N. (1998) 'International Labour Standards and Human Rights: Approaching the Year 2000', *International Labour Review*, 137, 2: 135–147.

Vestergaard, J. (2011a) *Voice Reform in the World Bank*, DIIS Report, Copenhagen: Danish Institute of International Studies.

Vestergaard, J. (2011b) *The G20 and Beyond: Towards Effective Global Economic Governance*, DIIS Report, Copenhagen: Danish Institute of International Studies.

Vestergaard, J. and Wade, R.H. (2013) 'Protecting Power: How Western States Retain the Dominant Voice in the World Bank's Governance', *World Development*, 46: 153–164.

Vodopivec, M., Fares, J. and Justesen, M. (2009) 'Labor Markets in World Bank Lending and Analytical Work, 2000 – 2007', in Holzmann, R. ed. *Social Protection and Labor at the World Bank, 2000 – 2008*, Washington, DC: World Bank: 45–72.

Waddington, J. (2010) *European Works Councils: Transnational Industrial Relations Institutions in the Making*, London: Routledge.

Waters, M. (1995) *Globalization*, London: Routledge.

Weisbrot, M. and Jorgensen, H. (2013) *Macroeconomic Policy Advice and the Article IV Consultations: Comparative Overview of the European Union Member States*, ILO Research Paper No. 7 [online]. Available at: https://www.ilo.org/wcmsp5/groups/public/-dgreports/-inst/documents/publication/wcms_218547.pdf [Accessed 7 July 2020]

Weiss, T.G. (2013) *Global Governance: Why, What, Whither*, Cambridge and Malden: Polity Press.

Weiss, T.G. and Wilkinson, R. (2014) 'Rethinking Global Governance? Complexity, Authority, Power Change', *International Studies Quarterly*, 58, 1: 207–215.

Whetten, D.A. (2006) 'Albert and Whetten Revisited: Strengthening the Concept of Organizational Identity', *Journal of Management Inquiry*, 15, 3: 219–234.

Whetten, D.A. and Mackey, A. (2002) 'A Social Actor Conception of Organizational Identity and Its Implications for the Study of Organizational Reputation', *Business & Society*, 41, 4: 393–414.

Williamson, O.E. (1995) *From Chester Barnard to the Present and Beyond*, New York and Oxford: Oxford University Press.

Wilson, E. and Rees, C. (2007) 'Perception, Stereotyping, and Attribution', in Mills, A.J., Helm Mills, J.C., Forshaw, C. and Bratton, J. eds. *Organizational Behaviour in a Global Context*, Toronto: Broadview Press: 123–147.

Wolfensohn, J. (1997) *The Challenge of Inclusion 1997 Annual Meetings Address*, Hong Kong SAR, China, 23 September [online]. Available at: http://documents.worldbank.org/curated/en/454151468000900806/pdf/99936-WP-Box393210B-PUBLIC-1997-09-23-The-Challenge-of-Inclusion-1997-Annual-Meetings-Address.pdf [Accessed 12 November 2017]

Woods, N. (2003) 'Global Governance and the Role of Institutions', in Held, D. and McGrev, A. eds. *Governing Globalization: Power, Authority and Global Governance*, Cambridge: Polity Press: 25–45.

Woods, N. (2006) *The Globalizers: The IMF, the World Bank, and Their Borrowers*, Ithaca and London: Cornell University Press.

Woods, N. and Lombardi, D. (2006) 'Uneven Patterns of Governance: How Developing Countries Are Represented in the IMF', *Review of International Political Economy*, 13, 3: 480–515.

Wooten, M. and Hoffman, A.J. (2017) 'Organizational Fields: Past, Present and Future', in Greenwood, R., Oliver, C., Lawrence, T.B. and Meyer, R.E. eds. *The Sage Handbook of Organizational Institutionalism*, Los Angeles, London, New Delhi, Singapore, Washington, DC and Melbourne: Sage: 55–74.

World Bank (2000) *ICFTU/World Bank/IMF Meetings Joint Report*, Washington, DC, 23–25 October [online]. Available at: http://go.worldbank.org/WTUVC6C1H0 [Accessed 7 July 2008, no longer publicly available]

World Bank (2001a) *Social Protection Sector Strategy*, January [online]. Available at: http://documents.worldbank.org/curated/en/299921468765558913/pdf/multi-page.pdf [Accessed 5 April 2019]

World Bank (2001b) *Assessment of the Strategic Compact* [online]. Available at: http://documents.worldbank.org/curated/en/225561468780000463/pdf/265180Scode0901of0Strategic0Compact.pdf [Accessed 5 April 2019]

World Bank (2001c) *Joint Report From World Bank/IMF Meeting With the World Confederation of Labour*, Washington, DC, March [online]. Available at: http://go.worldbank.org/WTUVC6C1H0 [Accessed 7 July 2008, no longer publicly available]

World Bank (2002) *Joint Report on Meetings Between the International Trade Union Movement (Global Unions and WCL) and the IMF and World Bank*, Washington, DC, 21–23 October [online]. Available at: http://documents.worldbank.org/curated/en/88161 1468328171671/Joint-report-on-meetings-between-the-international-trade-union-movement-Global-Unions-and-WCL-and-the-IMF-and-World-Bank-21-23-October-2002-Washington [Accessed 6 April 2021].

World Bank (2003a) *Joint Report Interim Meeting Between the World Bank and IMF and the International Trade Union Movement*, 5 November [online]. Available at: https://documents1.worldbank.org/curated/en/310571468158710698/pdf/42002optmzd0TU1t1 Nov51200301PUBLIC1.pdf [Accessed 13 September 2021]

World Bank (2003b) *Report on World Bank – Trade Union Meeting on Pension Reform*, 21–22 May [online]. Available at: https://documents1.worldbank.org/curated/en/509451468160189779/pdf/41876optmzd0WB1ort0May200301PUBLIC1.pdf [Accessed 13 September 2021]

World Bank (2004) *Joint Report on Meetings Between the International Trade Union Movement (Global Unions and WCL) and the IMF and World Bank*, Washington DC 7–8 October [online]. Available at: https://documents1.worldbank.org/curated/en/531581468155363983/pdf/42004ptmzd0WBTU0MeetingOct701PUBLIC1.pdf [Accessed 5 June 2021]

World Bank (2005) *Engaging Civil Society in World Bank Training Programs: Results of an Assessment Study* [online]. Available at: http://documents.worldbank.org/curated/en/115751468316166282/Engaging-civil-society-in-World-Bank-training-programs-results-of-an-assessment-study [Accessed 10 Marc 2020]

World Bank (2006) *Joint Report on Meetings Between the International Trade Union Movement and the IMF and World Bank*, Washington, DC, 11–13 December [online]. Available at: https://documents1.worldbank.org/curated/en/520371468178449309/pdf/42005opt mzd0WB1ing0Dec200601PUBLIC1.pdf [Accessed 16 June 2021]

World Bank (2007) *Joint Background Paper: Review of Five Years of Structured Dialogue Between the International Trade Union Movement and the International Financial Institutions*, December [online]. Available at: http://documents.worldbank.org/curated/en/898191468137699466/Joint-background-paper-review-of-five-years-of-structured-dialogue-between-the-international-trade-union-movement-and-the-international-financial-institutions [Accessed 6 April 2021]

World Bank (2009) *Joint Report on Meetings Between the International Trade Union Movement (ITUC/Global Unions) and the IMF and World Bank*, Washington, DC, 14–16 January [online]. Available at: https://documents1.worldbank.org/curated/en/283 691468153858532/pdf/516070WP0GU1IF10Box342046B01PUBLIC1.pdf [Accessed 5 June 2021]

World Bank (2010a) *Doing Business: Reforming Through Difficult Times, Comparing Regulation in 183 Economies* [online]. Available at: https://www.doingbusiness.org/content/dam/doingBusiness/media/Annual-Reports/English/DB10-FullReport.pdf [Accessed 20 June August 2020]

World Bank (2010b) *Joint Report on Trade Union – IMF – World Bank Meeting on Pension Reform*, Washington, DC, 8–9 March [online]. Available at: https://documents1.

worldbank.org/curated/en/578891468151495203/pdf/584630WP0Box351rade0Unio n01PUBLIC1L.pdf [Accessed 20 September 2021]

World Bank (2011a): *A Guide to the World Bank*, 3rd ed. [online]. Available at: http:// documents.worldbank.org/curated/en/406871468139488518/pdf/638430PUB0Exto0 0Box0361527B0PUBLIC0.pdf [Accessed 5 May 2019]

World Bank (2011b) *Guidelines. Procurement of Goods, Works, and Non-Consulting Services Under IBRD Loans and IDA Credits & Grants by World Bank Borrowers*, January [online]. Available at: https://documents1.worldbank.org/curated/en/634571468152711050/ pdf/586680BR0procu0IC0dislosed010170110.pdf [Accessed 2 May 2020]

World Bank (2011c) *The State of World Bank Knowledge Services: Knowledge for Development 2011* [online]. Available at: http://documents.worldbank.org/curated/en/3539 31468337483106/pdf/651950Revised0box361556B00PUBLIC005.pdf [Accessed 8 March 2016]

World Bank (2012a) *Resilience, Equity, and Opportunity: The World Bank's Social Protection and Labor Strategy 2012–2022*, Washington, DC [online]. Available at: http://documents.world bank.org/curated/en/443791468157506768/Resilience-equity-and-opportunity-the-World-Banks-social-protection-and-labor-strategy-2012-2022 [Accessed 4 April 2018]

World Bank (2012b) *World Development Report 2013: Jobs* [online]. Available at: https:// openknowledge.worldbank.org/handle/10986/11843 [Accessed 8 April 2013]

World Bank (2012c) *Annual Report 2012: Volume 1. Main Report* [online]. Available at: https://openknowledge.worldbank.org/handle/10986/11844 [Accessed 8 April 2019]

World Bank (2013a) *The World Bank Group Strategy: Overview*, Washington, DC [online]. Available at: http://documents.worldbank.org/curated/en/602031468161653927/ Overview [Accessed 8 April 2020]

World Bank (2013b) *Doing Business 2013: Smarter Regulations for Small and Medium-Size Enterprises. Comparing Business Regulations for Domestic Firms in 185 Economies*, Washington, DC [online]. Available at: https://www.doingbusiness.org/content/dam/doing Business/media/Annual-Reports/English/DB13-full-report.pdf [Accessed 11 November 2019]

World Bank (2014) *IFC Road Map, FY 2015–17: Implementing the World Bank Group Strategy* [online]. Available at: http://documents.worldbank.org/curated/en/8269 31468161664106/IFC-road-map-FY2015-17-implementing-the-World-Bank-Group-strategy [Accessed 3 October 2017]

World Bank (2015) *Balancing Regulations to Promote Jobs* [online]. Available at: http://docu ments1.worldbank.org/curated/en/636721468187738877/pdf/101596-REPLACE-MENT-WP-PUBLIC-12-9-15-Box394816B-Balancing-regulations-to-promote-jobs-FINAL-web-version.pdf [Accessed 3 March 2020]

World Bank (2016) *Annual Report 2016* [online]. Available at: http://documents.world-bank.org/curated/en/763601475489253430/World-Bank-annual-report-2016 [Accessed 10 December 2017]

World Bank (2017a) *The World Bank Environmental and Social Framework* [online]. Available at: http://pubdocs.worldbank.org/en/837721522762050108/Environmental-and-Social-Framework.pdf [Accessed 20 April 2018]

World Bank (2017b) *Doing Business: Equal Opportunity for All, Comparing Business Regulation for Domestic Firms in 190 Economies* [online]. Available at: https://www.doingbusiness.

org/content/dam/doingBusiness/media/Annual-Reports/English/DB17-Report.pdf [Accessed 20 June 2020]

World Bank (2018a) *The World Bank Procurement Regulations for IPF Borrower – Procurement in Investment Project Financing – Goods, Work, Non-Consulting and Consulting Services,* July 2016, Revised November 2017 and August 2018 [online]. Available at: http://pubdocs.worldbank.org/en/178331533065871195/Procurement-Regulations.pdf [Accessed 10 December 2019]

World Bank (2018b) *A Beginner's guide for Borrowers, Procurement Under World Bank Investment Project Financing* [online]. Available at: http://pubdocs.worldbank.org/en/684421525277630551/Beginners-Guide-to-IPF-Procurement-for-borrowers.pdf [Accessed 10 December 2019]

World Bank (2018c) *Ethics and Business Conduct, Annual Report 2018* [online]. Available at: http://documents.worldbank.org/curated/en/172361546547469758/Ethics-and-Business-Conduct-Embedding-Ethics-Throughout-the-World-Bank-Group-Annual-Report-2018.pdf [Accessed 5 March 2019]

World Bank (2018d) *Maximizing Finance for Development (MFD)* [online]. Available at: http://documents1.worldbank.org/curated/en/168331522826993264/pdf/124888-REVISED-BRI-PUBLIC-Maximizing-Finance.pdf [Accessed 16 June 2020]

World Bank (2018e) *World Development Report: Learning to Realize Education's Promise,* Washington, DC [online]. Available at: https://www.worldbank.org/en/publication/wdr2018 [Accessed 4 February 2022]

World Bank (2019a) *World Development Report 2019: The Changing Nature of Work* [online]. Available at: http://documents.worldbank.org/curated/en/816281518818814423/pdf/2019-WDR-Report.pdf [Accessed 10 January 2020]

World Bank (2019b) *Protecting All: Risk Sharing for a Diverse and Diversifying World of Work* [online]. Available at: http://documents.worldbank.org/curated/en/997741568048792164/pdf/Protecting-All-Risk-Sharing-for-a-Diverse-and-Diversifying-World-of-Work.pdf [Accessed 10 January 2020]

World Bank (2019c) *Ethics and Business Conduct, Annual Report 2019* [online]. Available at: http://pubdocs.worldbank.org/en/496191573656292441/EBC-FY19-Annual-Report-FINAL-for-distribution.pdf [Accessed 11 December 2019]

World Bank (2019d) *Annual Report 2019 Ending Poverty, Investing in Opportunity* [online]. Available at: https://www.worldbank.org/en/about/annual-report#anchor-annual [Accessed 3 March 2020]

World Bank (2020a) *Additions to IDA Resources: Nineteenth Replenishment – Ten Years to 2030: Growth, People, Resilience,* Washington, DC [online]. Available at: http://documents.worldbank.org/curated/en/459531582153485508/pdf/Additions-to-IDA-Resources-Nineteenth-Replenishment-Ten-Years-to-2030-Growth-People-Resilience.pdf [Accessed 2 March 2020]

World Bank (2020b) *Doing Business 2020: Comparing Business Regulation in 190 Economies,* Washington, DC [online]. Available at: https://openknowledge.worldbank.org/bitstream/handle/10986/32436/9781464814402.pdf [Accessed 23 June 2020]

World Bank (2020c) *The World Bank Environmental and Social Framework (ESF) – Implementation Update,* September [online]. Available at: https://thedocs.worldbank.org/en/doc/982711602165538091-0290022020/original/ESFImplementationUpdateOctober2020.pdf [Accessed 14 July 2021]

World Bank (2020d) *The Covid-19 Pandemic: Shocks to Education and Policy Responses* [online]. Available at: https://openknowledge.worldbank.org/bitstream/handle/10986/33696/148198.pdf?sequence=4&isAllowed=y [Accessed 10 January 2022]

World Bank (2020e) *The World Bank Organizational Chart* [online]. Available at: https://thedocs.worldbank.org/en/doc/404071412346998230-0090022021/The-World-Bank-Organizational-Chart-English [Accessed 28 November 2020]

World Bank (2021a) *Standard Procurement Document. Request for Bids Works (After Prequalification)*, January [online]. Available at: https://www.worldbank.org/en/projects-operations/products-and-services/brief/procurement-policies-and-guidance#standarddocuments [Accessed 14 July 2021]

World Bank (2021b) *Ending Learning Poverty and Building Skills: Investing in Education From Early Childhood to Lifelong Learning*, September [online]. Available at: https://issuu.com/afaquir-worldbankgroup/docs/wb_educationbrochure_apr.15.21_final?cid=edu_tt_education_en_ext [Accessed 27 January 2022]

World Bank (2022) *Pre-Concept Note Business Enabling Environment (BEE)*, 4 February [online]. Available at: https://www.worldbank.org/content/dam/doingBusiness/pdf/BEE-Pre-Concept-Note-Feb-8-2022.pdf [Accessed 5 May 2022]

Wouters, J. and Odermatt, J. (2014) 'Comparing the "Four Pillars" of Global Economic Governance: A Critical Analysis of the Institutional Design of the FSB, IMF, World Bank, and WTO', *Journal of International Economic Law*, 17, 1: 49–76.

Zajak, S. (2017) *Transnational Activism, Global Labor Governance, and China*, New York: Palgrave Macmillan.

Zoellick, R.B. (2008) *Modernizing Multilateralism and Markets*, Annual Meeting, Board of Governors of the World Bank Group Remarks of Robert B. Zoellick, 13 October [online]. Available at: https://www.imf.org/external/am/2008/speeches/pr03e.pdf [Accessed 12 November 2017]

Zucker, L.G. (1977) 'The Role of Institutionalization in Cultural Persistence', *American Sociological Review*, 42, 5: 726–743.

Zürn, M. (1998) *Regieren jenseits des Nationalstaates: Globalisierung und Denationalisierung als Chance*, Frankfurt am Main: Suhrkamp.

Zürn, M. (2018) *A Theory of Global Governance: Authority, Legitimacy and Contestation*, Oxford: Oxford University Press.

The 1818 Society (2012) *The Key Challenges Facing the World Bank President – An Independent Diagnostic* [online]. Available at: https://siteresources.worldbank.org/1818SOCIETY/Resources/World_Bank_Diagnostic_Exercise.pdf [Accessed 17 November 2016]

The 1818 Society (2019) '1818 Society News and Announcements, October 24: Discussion With President David Malpass', *The 1818 Society Quarterly* [online]. Available at: https://www.wbgalumni.org/1818/wp-content/uploads/2019/12/2020_01-Winter-2019-Quarterly.pdf [Accessed 15 February 2020]

Index

Note: Page numbers in *italics* indicate a figure and page numbers in **bold** indicate a table on the corresponding page.